REFLECTIONS FROM THE BOOKSHELF

SOCIOLOGICAL CONCEPTS IN LITERATURE

By Toby A. Ten Eyck
Michigan State University

cognella®
academic publishing

Bassim Hamadeh, CEO and Publisher
Michael Simpson, Vice President of Acquisitions
Jamie Giganti, Managing Editor
Jess Busch, Graphic Design Supervisor
Becky Smith, Acquisitions Editor
Monika Dziamka, Project Editor
Natalie Lakosil, Licensing Manager
Mandy Licata, Interior Designer

First published in the United States of America in 2014 by Cognella, Inc.

Printed in the United States of America

ISBN: 978-1-62131-833-0 (pbk)/ 978-1-62131-834-7 (br)

www.cognella.com   800-200-3908

CONTENTS

CHAPTER FIVE - WORK

CHAPTER SIX - DEATH AND DYING

CHAPTER SEVEN - RACE

CHAPTER EIGHT - GENDER

CHAPTER NINE - CLASS

DEDICATION

To my parents, George and Nan Ten Eyck, the best teachers I ever had.

ACKNOWLEDGMENTS

There are many people who made this book possible, but had nothing to do with the actual writing. Among them are Dr. Richard Machalek at the University of Wyoming, who taught the one and only undergraduate sociology course I ever took. His enthusiasm for the subject was contagious, and I continue to think of his approach to sociology and learning every time I enter a classroom. Dr. Kelly Hancock, my major professor at Portland State University, said that reading one of my early attempts at being sociological "was like falling down a flight of stairs." After years of writing 30-second radio commercials and trying to do the same in graduate school, it was the kind of direction and motivation that I needed. While I was at Louisiana State University, Dr. Forrest A. Deseran pushed me to always be better, and for that I am eternally grateful. Gary Babcock, a friend for over 40 years (and who was always the better pupil), read the first chapter and said that I was onto something interesting. These are the individuals who gave me the strength to create this book and stick with it.

I am also grateful for my colleagues at Michigan State University. Jason Palmer provided invaluable insights for the chapter on work (Chapter 5). Laurel Hilliker, who is now at Park University, took time to look over and give suggestions for the chapter on death and dying (Chapter 6). Jualynne Dodson read a very early draft of the first chapter and provided comments. Stephanie Nawyn provided references for Chapter 8 (gender). Dan Menchik was kind enough to bring Christopher Edling and Jens Rydgren's edited book *Sociological Insights of Great Thinkers* to my attention to show that I was not the only one to think that literature could teach us a great deal about sociology. Others have been patient with my ideas and provided verbal feedback when I drifted. I am lucky to have access to their friendships and intellectual capabilities. There are countless graduate students who asked if I would sit on their guidance and dissertation committees, all of which offered me the opportunities to learn about such topics as body modifications (Derek Roberts), science and risk (Dilshani Sarathchandra), death and dying (Laurel Hilliker), immigration (Gabriela Saenz), the Middle East (Abdullah Al-Rebh), queering sexualities (Solly Mo), and disabled bodies (Kim Underwood). Their work and ideas, along with those of many other students, continue to push me to learn more about the topics and subjects within our discipline.

I must also thank Monika Dziamka, Sarah Wheeler, and the editorial and production teams at Cognella. Other publishing companies were uninterested in a book aimed at introductory courses that looked different from the typical introductory book. This book would still be nothing more than an idea without their willingness to take a chance.

Finally, I would like to thank Sheri Ten Eyck for her patience throughout this process, and being willing to do the shopping and chores when I was in the process of pounding away at the computer. She, as well as Talone and Sauvonn, two dogs with an ADHD label—"A Distracted Herding Dog"—also knew when it was time to get me out of my chair so I could get some much needed rejuvenation in the fresh air. Thank you for your love, kindness, understanding, and, for the latter two, proving to me that chasing balls and Frisbees can be pure joy.

PREFACE

never took an undergraduate sociology course during my first stint at Portland State University, which is where I started college in 1982. It was not until after I had dropped out of both Portland State and Lane Community College (with a year-and-a-half stint at Sea World of San Diego in-between) and was working as a radio broadcaster in Laramie, WY, that I enrolled for a sociology course at the University of Wyoming. All of my previous failing came rushing back to me when I walked into that large lecture room on the first day of the spring semester of 1989. Having been out of college for two years did little to ease my fears. In fact, the time away made the feeling worse. In an attempt to ease the tension I told myself that none of it mattered, as I was planning on majoring in social work. I had been doing such a great job with my own life that I thought it was time to help others with their concerns. Introduction to Sociology was just another requirement to get out of the way. A 2.0 (C) was all I needed.

Within the first week I was hooked. The required textbook was steeped in the writings of Karl Marx, a person I had grown up thinking was the Antichrist because of his links to the Soviet Union, which was starting to fall apart, and communism. That my maternal grandfather was an immigrant from Russia made no difference in my knowing that the USSR was pure evil. That is what I was constantly being told by the media, an industry that had signed my paychecks since 1986. If I was being paid by them, they must be telling the truth.

What captured my attention and imagination was the fact that Marx wrote about the poor and underserved in society, not the taking over of the world with nuclear bombs. He understood the plight of workers who were exploited and treated poorly by the people who made a profit from their hard labor. While radio broadcasting is as far away from hard labor as almost any job, I quickly recognized the connections. Those of us in the studios who created and played commercials bought by local, regional, national, and international businesses saw a very small portion of the profits in our paychecks. We were reimbursed with a few free meals and ski trips, but that did little to close the gap between ourselves and the stations' managers and owners. They always seemed to have more money and things than those of us who spent our time at the station taking calls from angry listeners because we would not play their favorite songs or announced that it was going to rain on Saturday when they had planned a picnic or fishing trip. Marx's radical thoughts on how to bring about more equality made sense to me.

At the end of that semester, Sheri and I left for Seattle, WA, so that she could fill a veterinarian technician position at her father's animal hospital. I had planned on majoring in sociology at the University of Washington (UW), but lacked the required foreign language credits needed for admissions. I began taking Spanish at Green River Community College (Auburn, WA) to meet those requirements, and was introduced to college radio through KGRG, the student station at GRCC. I decided to take a few more classes so as to lower the costs I was expecting to accrue at UW, and met an astronomy instructor who had graduated from a branch of Southern Illinois University—Carbondale (SIUC) located at McChord Air Force Base in Tacoma, WA. He told me the SIUC program was a one-year program (with a few academic and work experience stipulations), and that it would be a quick way to get a bachelors degree. I took his advice, enrolled in their Vocational Education program, and graduated in May 1992 with no more sociology courses on my transcript.

By this time I had decided to pursue an advanced degree, so I asked for and was given a subscription to the *American Journal of Sociology* (*AJS*) beginning in 1991 by my in-laws. It was my hope that I might learn something in those pages that would help me learn about the field before entering graduate school. Instead of being inspired, the articles were difficult to follow with all the quantitative modeling and theoretical jargon, and thoughts on being able to get through graduate school began turning dark, though I had already enrolled for a Masters at Portland State University. As I began summer courses in 1992, I came across William H. Sewell, Jr.'s "A Theory of Structure: Duality, agency and transformation" in the July 1992 issue of *AJS*. The article begins with the line, "'Structure' is one of the most important and most elusive terms in the vocabulary of current social science." That was easy enough to understand, and I began thinking that this was someone who spoke my language. I understood very little of the rest of the article, though it seemed that Sewell was discussing how sociologists often introduce the notion of structure to their students but that these same students have a hard time seeing these rumored structures when they leave the classroom. To them the world is chaotic and mostly uninteresting, and the only structures they need to worry about are the ones they put in place themselves.

It took me another six years to advance to the point of being able to write a dissertation and be handed a PhD from the Department of Sociology at Louisiana State University (I earned a Masters at Portland State University in 1994 and the PhD in 1998), but that article has continued to motivate me to find ways to show students, as well as friends and family members who have the patience to listen, how structures are part of everything we do, and scholars such as Karl Marx are not to be feared. This is often difficult to do in the US as we are told that we are free to pursue whatever dreams we can create in our hearts and minds, and anyone who argues that such thinking is problematic and only benefits a few people who are already rich is called an anti-freedom, communist pig. I would agree that being able to pursue our dreams is the best possible situation in which to live, but we have a long way to go before we get there.

As I have continued to think about sociology as an academic discipline as well as a tool for navigating everyday experiences, I have come to the conclusion that one of the main barriers to gaining an understanding of how structures impact us is that sociology is often delegated to sociology departments, courses, and textbooks, all of which are ignored or dismissed by the general public that finds more answers to life's problems in self-help books, daytime talk shows, and reality television. Sociology, and remember this is the discipline that pays my room and board, is often practiced in such a way that does little in helping those without advanced training to gain insights into the myriad of social structures that surround us. Instead, we spend our time developing ever more abstract theories and complicated quantitative models so that we can show these to our colleagues at regional, national, and international conferences, as well as get published so that we are granted tenure and never have to worry about finding another job.

Sociology is complex and takes time to learn to the point that someone will pay you for what is in your head, but most people navigate the social structures that are of interest to sociologists without imploding, leaving one to wonder why the discipline exists in its current state. Do ethnic and racial minorities need to fill out surveys to realize they face an uphill battle in school and the workplace? Do women need to be given a complex model that involves bootstrapping and Monte Carlo techniques to understand that they are often treated as second class citizens and expected to work an unpaid double shift at home after working all day at a job where they are more likely than their male colleagues to encounter glass ceilings when trying to climb the corporate ladder? Do gays and lesbians need to comprehend theories of how their sexuality places them at a disadvantage when it comes to developing social networks in a heteronormative society? The list could go on and on. So why do we need sociology if we already know these inequalities exist? Because at its best, sociology provides the tools needed to understand *and* challenge the power structures that are in place that maintain inequalities. Instead of simply experiencing injustices and inequality, sociology can show individuals, groups, and organizations the ways to move toward a more egalitarian society. At its worse, the discipline becomes another tool for the powerful, as they are provided insights into the structures that maintain their advantages. There is also a large middle ground where many sociologists practice their craft. This involves constructing theories and measurements of social structures seasoned with a touch of apathy towards how these tools might be used by others. The processes that turn our work into good or evil is not part of the job.

While I do enjoy developing theories and ways of measuring the social world, I also find it exciting to apply what I know to experiences outside the academy. Everyday experiences such as talking to the customer service person at a department store, a mechanic at the garage, or reading a book feed into the sociological imagination, a concept you will learn more about shortly. To help you have the same experiences, I have borrowed heavily from novels that point to the same social structures that interest sociologists. This approach is expected to help you see how social structures are everywhere, which will go a long way in making your own experiences more interesting and insightful. It can also give you the tools needed to bring about societal changes that will benefit those who are unduly exploited by current social systems. This is not an easy process, and rarely works when only one person tries to take on city hall. The trick is finding others who have the same passions.

I know that most readers are not, and never will be, sociology majors, and for this reason I have tried to stay away from bolding or italicizing words that can bog down the reading because you are constantly reaching for a highlighting marker. There is, however, one distinction of terms that needs to be made. The words "institutions" and "organizations" are often used interchangeably in everyday speech. Sociologists approach these from a different perspective. An institution is a set of rules that encompass many organizations. The roles of father, mother, children, and so forth constitute the family institution, while your own family is an organization within that institution. If you say you are from a single parent household, I will have an idea of how your mother or father acts in their role as the parent because of the family institution and what is supposed to happen within any given family organization. Religion is another institution. It provides a moral compass (e.g., help others in need, live a peaceful life, praise a deity, etc.). The specific church, synagogue, mosque, or temple that you might visit is an organization within that larger institution. Your religious organization may have a greater focus on certain aspects of sacred scripture than the religious organization attended by your neighbor, so while you attend different religious organization, both organizations are within the same institution.

The following chapters are mainly about institutions, so they are about broad organizing patterns that are followed to varying degrees within organizations. If this is confusing, or you think that your approach to life is very different from everyone else, just the fact that you are reading this book in a classroom points to the ubiquitous nature of institutions. Most of us would rather be doing or reading something else, but more than likely you have been told that you need to read this book as part of a class within an organization that is situated within the institution of higher education. This organization and its ties to a specific institution will help you land a good job, or so you are told. Most of our days are spent within such nested clusters of organizations within institutions, as well as within the intersections of institutions. Even the simple act of walking down the street involves an understanding of the institutions of appropriate social behavior and transportation, though you may find that things are done somewhat differently in your hometown than it is in the city where you attend college. These cities can be thought of as organizations within the institution of urbanization that encompass other institutions and organizations.

You may already be wondering how anyone can make heads or tails of these ideas. They seem so commonsensical yet confusing for no good reason. It takes time and patience to understand that sociologists try to make sense of the things we take for granted. A good test of this is to forget everything you know about yourself. You are no longer a member of a certain gender or sex cluster, racial group, have no sexual orientation, no age, and so forth. Try communicating with your neighbors from this standpoint, and you will quickly learn how structures such as these impact our interactions. Being more aware of your surroundings will make you realize how complex, yet exciting, our social world is.

Finally, some of the novels that are used for this book were written and published before there were computers with spell check programs. Some of the readings may come off as strange, especially if you have been educated to use only proper contemporary English. Be open to these new experiences, much like a person who has never read a text message and sees the following on their new phone: "c u 4 din." That is not proper English, and some of us wonder why a person cannot simply take a few more seconds to write, "See you for dinner." As with the discipline of sociology, be patient with some of the readings. Now, sit back, and enjoy the sociology of Don Quixote tilting windmills, Captain Ahab giving chase to Moby Dick, and many other characters trying to navigate the same structures in fiction that we face every day.

REFERENCES

Sewell, William H., Jr. 1992. "A Theory of Structure: Duality, agency, and transformation." *American Journal of Sociology* 98(1):1–29.

1 AGENCY AND STRUCTURE

INTRODUCTION AND *DON QUIXOTE*

"Theory" can be a scary word, scary enough that you want to stop reading and go play a video game or grab a cookie and soda from the cafeteria to drown your sorrows. Theories, however, are how we make it through life. You use a theory when you cross a street—"when the street is clear, it is safe to cross"—or make the decision to grab a cookie and soda—"a cafeteria has food." A theory is an explanation for why a relationship does or does not exist, and it should be testable. Saying that a dog barks is not a theory, but that a dog barks *because it is territorial* is theoretical, as it explains why the dog is barking, and this can be tested. The word "theory" will not be used very often in the pages that follow, but you should know that much of what is written comes from sociological theories and that these can be useful—and tested—in your own life.

Have you ever wondered how society is possible? Where did it come from? Did two early humans come together and start interacting? Once a relationship is started, how does it grow to become a tribe, a town, a global city, a nation—and how do these types of social groupings change? Why do some people do better than others? When we think of all the social injustices in the world—poverty, torture, oppression—why do we see so few uprisings with people fighting for change? How are we supposed to make sense of the actions of one small group, let alone the billions of social relationships that make up our contemporary global village, especially if you are an outsider looking in? Why do we even need someone poking about in our business? We have made it this far, so why all the bother?

1

These are just some of the questions that keep sociologists up at night, and are the impetus for writing sociological articles and books, including this one. Unlike the textbooks that use the writings of Karl Marx, Max Weber, Emile Durkheim, Pierre Bourdieu, Judith Butler, Michel Foucault, and other scholars to make sense of these questions, I will lean heavily on the works of authors such as Miguel de Cervantes, Charles Dickens, Kurt Vonnegut, Jules Verne, Tom Wolfe, and Allen Ginsberg. As with the founders of the sociological discipline, writers of fiction also try to make sense of why people do certain things. All of us are trying to distinguish actions grounded in social structures, such as following speed limits even though you are late for a date, because if you get a ticket your parents will take away your driving privileges, and those that are inspired by agency such as driving recklessly on a crowded highway for a thrill. Some sociologists would go so far as to say that even thrills are grounded in social structures as others have to tell us what is and is not thrilling. This kind of thinking can lead to arguments that all actions are predetermined, which would make sociology both boring and unnecessary.

Don Quixote epitomized this very dilemma when he approached a field of windmills. He saw the windmills as threatening giants, though his decision on what to do next may not have been entirely his own.

… they caught sight of thirty or forty windmills standing on the plain, and as soon as Don Quixote saw them he said to his squire:

"Fortune is directing our affairs even better than we could have wished: for you can see over there, good friend Sancho Panza, a place where stand thirty or more monstrous giants with whom I intend to fight a battle and whose lives I intend to take; and with the booty we shall begin to prosper. For this is a just war, and it is a great service to God to wipe such a wicked breed from off the face of the earth."

"What giants?" said Sancho Panza.

"Those giants that you can see over there," replied his master, "with long arms: there are giants with arms almost six miles long."

"Look you here," Sancho retorted, "those over there aren't giants, they're windmills, and what look to you like arms are sails—when the wind turns them they make the millstones go round."

"It is perfectly clear," replied Don Quixote, "that you are a raw novice in this matter of adventures. They are giants; and if you are frightened, you can take yourself away and say your prayers while I engage them in fierce and arduous combat."

And so saying he set spurs to his steed Rocinante, not paying any attention to his squire Sancho Panza, who was shouting that what he was charging were definitely windmills not giants. But Don Quixote was so convinced that they were giants that he neither heard his squire Sancho's shouts nor saw what stood in front of him, even though he was by now upon them; instead he cried:

"Flee not, O vile and cowardly creatures, for it is but one solitary knight who attacks you" (Cervantes, *Don Quixote*: 63–64).

Tilting at windmills has become synonymous with trying to do tasks that are impossible, and that idea, taken from the above passage from Cervantes, has given rise to numerous books, plays, movies, and even paintings by artists as famous as Picasso. The actions of Don Quixote and Sancho Panza can also be helpful in understanding how sociologists think about the world.

When a sociologist says "structure," he is often talking about those things outside of us that control our actions. This can be something as formal, yet mundane, as a speed limit. Most cars have the capacity to go faster than 25 mph in a school zone, yet we keep our cars at that speed because we are told to do so and because we do not want to put any young children at risk. A social structure can also be as informal as thinking that if you say you hate dogs, you may be ostracized by your friends, who all come from families with dogs, so you keep your mouth shut when everyone else decides to watch the Westminster Dog Show during lunch. If you live in the United States, your right to free speech and saying that you hate dogs is protected under the Constitution, but your friends also have the right to decide they no longer like you if you utter those words. Structures can also be found at the global level, such as peace treaties between nations so you will not be asked to join the military, and as strange as forgoing the playing of a harmonica during a movie at a theater.

Agency, on the other hand, is the idea that we can and do make choices regarding our actions. You can decide to brush your teeth tonight with your opposite hand. If you are reading this while attending college, you probably made the decision concerning which clothes you wore today, and you may have decided to drive 100 mph through a school zone because you were late to class—just to prove me wrong. All of these were choices that you made, regardless of the structures that are in place, and are supposed to make you choose otherwise. Therefore, you have all the agency you can handle, and there is no need for sociology.

There is, however, another way to think about these actions. You did decide on what clothes to wear, but they probably came from a rack at the store, and you had no say concerning what would be offered on those racks. You may have driven 100 mph through a school zone, but you might have wished to have gone 600 mph, but production cars do not have that capacity. Better yet, time travel would have solved everything, yet the laws of physics do not allow such foolishness. In the end, you did make choices, but were they your own choices, or someone else's? Sociologists would argue that no matter how much you want to believe that you have control over your life, there are structures in place that direct your actions. Don Quixote learned that the hard way by being unhorsed.

THE POWER AND DEPTH OF STRUCTURE

Given our current understanding of windmills—none that we know of has turned into an actual giant—most of us would probably have acted like Sancho Panza if one of our friends decided to fight windmills with a lance. Sancho was an illiterate peasant, but he knew a windmill when he saw one and thought that anyone who said differently was a bit mixed up. He had seen these things before, understood how they worked, and probably heard others talking about windmills. His mind was set on what a windmill stood for. In Sancho's mind, there was a narrative that went along with windmills. These were large objects that posed little threat to anyone, except those foolish enough to joust against them.

Don Quixote, on the other hand, came to those windmills from a different vantage point. Unlike Sancho, Quixote was literate and had been reading about knights and their quests for greatness and beautiful damsels. For someone steeped in such stories, those windmills fit with an idea of a specific situation—that of a knight in search of a quest—and that was what Quixote acted upon. To Sancho and the rest of us, the guy was nuts, but Quixote would have let himself down if he had turned and ridden away from the windmills. He was acting in a way that was appropriate for the script he was following. He had to attack and defeat something to become a great and noble knight. That was the structure within which Quixote lived.

There is yet another layer of sociological complexity that should also be taken into account. Let us assume that both Quixote and Sancho determined that the windmills were indeed giants, and that Sancho had cheered Quixote on as he attacked the windmills. That two people came to the same conclusion would have done nothing in terms of changing the fact that the windmills would withstand Quixote's lance. He would have fought like mad with those windmills, and Sancho's cheering would have made no difference to the outcome. A certain structure was in place that could not be overcome with a lance and overzealous cheering. Quixote and Sancho may have become upset with the windmills' unwillingness to cede defeat and set them on fire, but this too would be structural to some extent, as our heroes would need to be familiar with the properties of fire to decide that was the best course of action. Knowledge of the natural world is as much a structure as Quixote thinking he needed to fight giants and the windmills not budging when he tilted at them.

There are many situations like this in real life. You would probably prefer your college tuition to be less expensive, and many of your classmates would most likely agree with you. If you were able to gather everyone together and took the protest to the office of the registrar, people in that office might say you were right, but that the situation was out of their hands. Your group could complain to instructors, staff, janitors, and even the president of the college. It would do little good in most circumstances. There are too many windmills that would have to be knocked down, such as salaries, the costs of constructing classroom buildings, conducting research, and so forth, before any changes could be made. These structures rarely buckle under the kind of pressure you and your classmates can bring to bear. There is little reason to think that setting fire to those buildings and research labs would make any difference either, as there are structures in place to punish people who deliberately set fire to private and public properties, whether those are classrooms or windmills.

Much like Cervantes, Karl Marx saw the difficulties of thinking that agency at the individual level could bring about change to large social structures. He did, however, think that there were two things that could bring about change—dialectical forces and lots of people deciding they did not like their shared fate. According to Marx, the history of the world could be understood by knowing who owned the means of production in any given society. The best hunters and gatherers were able to have their way in early human tribes. This power and status moved to the warriors and priests who controlled farming groups as humans took up horticultural practices. Likely some of the best hunters became some of the best warriors, so power shifted very little within the group, though it became more concentrated and formal. As these groups tried to expand their wealth through wars and trade, a merchant class developed, which controlled the movement of goods, leading to capitalism and the modern global market. Each historical epoch—hunting and gathering, horticulture, agriculture, feudalism, and capitalism—takes centuries to develop, and each is plagued by its own inconsistencies. Hunting and gathering is an easy life if food is abundant and disease and enemies are nowhere to be found, but droughts, diseases, and marauding bands of pillagers can make it rough. Consequently, humans found ways to maintain food stocks by growing crops and raising animals in confined spaces. This leads to conglomerations of people who help with some of the problems, but suddenly the spread of disease can be even worse; wars become larger and more intense. This, in turn, results in the growth of a political body that is expected to lord over the commoners and keep outside troubles at bay through war or divine intervention, much of which is paid for by the peasants' labor. This, then, leads to concerns about having enough wealth to maintain an aristocracy; thus, tradesmen are encouraged to seek riches elsewhere to bring back to the king, and soon we have capitalism. Capitalism, according to Marx, also suffers from its own inconsistencies: Mainly that as money is controlled by fewer and fewer people (the so-called one percent), others who are not part of the economic upper echelons will rise up and take over the role of government. This will lead to communism and socialism, as those who overthrow capitalism will understand the need for money, food, water, housing, medical care, etc., to be more evenly distributed.

Marx, writing at a time when there was a great deal of abject poverty in England that he witnessed firsthand, thought that Germany, England, or the United States would be the prime location for such a Communist uprising. While numerous Communist groups were founded in these countries at the beginning of the 20th century, it was Russia that experienced the first large-scale Communist revolution as the Bolsheviks attacked the ruling czars and forced in a new way of governing—or something that was called a new form of government—on that country's population.

The reason Marx thought that Germany, England, or the United States would be best for a Communist revolution is that the proper social structures were already in place. This included strong tendencies toward modernization, mature manufacturing sectors, and a population that was somewhat versed in democratic forms of government. Czarist Russia was also moving toward modern manufacturing, but this was not a well-developed sector, as most of Russia was still agricultural. In addition, the country did not have a history of democratic governance. So, while the Bolsheviks were able to create the Union of Soviet Socialist Republics (USSR), that governmental structure collapsed in the 1980s due to internal inconsistencies, as Marx may have predicted.

WHEN OUR AGENCY FAILS AND MORE
DON QUIXOTE

The collapse of the USSR did not cause an absolute rejection of Marx, which points to one of the more interesting aspects of the links between structure and agency. For many of us, a person who holds onto a mistaken belief is crazy. However, when our own beliefs are called into question, we find reasons as to why we are right. Such reasoning makes us just like Don Quixote, who found a way to justify his own beliefs after being thrown off Rocinante while tilting against the first windmill.

"For God's Sake!" said Sancho. "Didn't I tell you to be careful what you were doing, didn't I tell you they were only windmills? And only someone with windmills on the brain could have failed to see that!"

"Not at all, friend Sancho," replied Don Quixote. "Affairs of war, even more than others, are subject to continual change. All the more so as I believe, indeed I am certain, that the same sage Frestón who stole my library and my books has just turned these giants into windmills, to deprive me of the glory of my victory, such is the enmity he feels for me; but in the end his evil arts will avail him little against the might of my sword" (Cervantes, *Don Quixote*: 64–65).

You may think this is overstating the need to hold on to certain beliefs, but the same kind of reasoning is found over 300 years later in Leon Festinger's (et al., 1956) study of a cult of stargazers who believed they were to be rescued by extraterrestrials before a large flood. Festinger and his group had heard stories about a woman who claimed to be receiving messages from an extraterrestrial being who was talking about the end of the world. The woman was able to collect a group of followers, some of whom quit their jobs and sold everything they owned, as the designated day for the alien cargo ship to appear drew closer. When the spaceship failed to show up, the group decided they had gotten the day wrong, as aliens would definitely be following a different calendar than earthlings. When the group decided on a different day and the spaceship still failed to materialize, they began to tell the story that it was their faith that saved the world, as the head alien had decided that if these humans could show this kind of dedication then there was hope for the human race. Concerns over the predictions offered by Harold Camping and the Mayan calendar show that many people still believe the world is about to end, and when the earth keeps on spinning they find ways to justify their beliefs and latch on to the next Judgment Day story.

Such reasoning is not only found among fictional characters and doomsday cults. When a student says that she is going to fail a test, she may also say there is no longer any reason to study for it. When she does fail, she says she was right all along, even though other students say that studying helped them pass the exam. If your belief in something is strong enough, it becomes very hard to change, even if it means being made fun of by others.

NATURAL STRUCTURES AND *MOBY DICK*

Social structures such as speed limits and ridicule are only one set of structures we face. Natural structures can also challenge human agency. The current debate over global warming and if humans have any role in such changes highlights how natural processes are impacted by humans and vice versa. This also happens when we purchase consumer goods. The newest version of a cell phone may lead people to get rid of their older, seemingly outmoded phones. These discarded phones often end up in landfills. Rain falls on the landfills, and the water runs through the discarded phones, carrying materials used in the phones into the ground. Those materials, some of which may be carcinogenic, wind up in the water system, and there is little humans can do about changing their bodies to absorb such materials without harm.

The agency in the above scenario is that people decided to buy new phones and discard their old ones—or did they succumb to advertising and hype from their friends? The natural structures in place include rain falling where the dump filled with old phones is located, and that water acts in a certain way, including wanting to move toward the center of the earth. The materials needed to make a new cell phone are also part of this structure, as it is currently very difficult to make a viable information technology product comprised of materials that are safe for the environment such as sugar, flour, and cornstarch.

This is referred to as reflexive modernization (Beck, Giddens, & Lash, 1994). Following Isaac Newton's Third Law of Motion, which states that for every action there is an equal and opposite reaction, reflexive modernization looks at how social and natural processes are triggered in a reflexive way by other social and natural processes. Simply stated, every time you make a decision to do or not to do something, there will be an equal and opposite reaction *because there are structures in place.* This is especially the case in modern society, where so much of our lives are controlled by social institutions, a topic we will look at more closely in the next chapter on families. Natural structures and their reflexes to human activities are also important to keep in mind. Captain Ahab found this out when he experienced the whale's reaction to being harpooned:

The harpoon was darted; the stricken whale flew forward; with igniting velocity the line ran through the grooves;—ran foul. Ahab stooped to clear it; and he did clear it; but the flying turn caught him round the neck, and voicelessly as Turkish mutes bowstring their victim, he was shot out of the boat, ere the crew knew he was gone. Next instant, the heavy eye-splice in the rope's final end flew out of the stark-empty tub, knocked down an oarsman, and smiting the sea, disappeared in its depths.

For an instant, the tranced boat's crew stood still; then turned. "The ship? Great God, where is the ship?" Soon they through dim, bewildering mediums saw her sidelong fading phantom, as in the gaseous Fata Morgana; only the uppermost masts out of water; while fixed by infatuation, or fidelity, or fate, to their once lofty perches, the pagan harpooneers still maintained their sinking lookouts on the sea. And now, concentric circles seized the lone boat itself, and all its crew, and each floating oar, and every lance-pole, and spinning, animate and inanimate, all round and round in one vortex, carried the smallest chip of the *Pequod* out of sight.

But as the last whelmings intermixingly poured themselves over the sunken head of the Indian at the mainmast, leaving a few inches of the erect spar yet visible, together with long streaming yards of the flag, which calmly undulated, with ironical coincidings, over the destroying billows they almost touched;—at that instant, a red arm and a hammer hovered backwardly uplifted in the open air, in the act of nailing the flag faster and yet faster to the subsiding spar. A sky-hawk that tauntingly had followed the main-truck downwards from its natural home among the stars, pecking at the flag, and incommoding Tashtego there; this bird now chanced to intercept its broad fluttering wing between the hammer and the wood; and simultaneously feeling that ethereal thrill, the submerged savage beneath, in his death-gasp, kept his hammer frozen there; and so the bird of heaven, with archangelic shrieks, and his imperial beak thrust upwards, and his whole captive form folded in the flag of Ahab, went down with his ship, which, like Satan, would not sink to hell till she had dragged a living part of heaven along with her, and helmeted herself with it.

Now small fowls flew screaming over the yet yawning gulf; a sullen white surf beat against its steep sides; then all collapsed, and the great shroud of the sea rolled on as it rolled five thousand years ago (Melville, *Moby Dick*: 428–29).

Captain Ahab made the decision, his agency, to hunt Moby Dick. In doing so, he risked the lives of everyone onboard the *Pequod*, as it was known that the great white whale had destroyed ships in the past, including one of Ahab's. The captain's agency goes deeper still, as he made the decision to board one of the harpoon boats after another crew member said that such a decision was foolish. The whale had been spotted swimming away from the ship that morning, and Ahab was told that the whale had given up its own quest of finishing off the one-legged captain. All of Ahab's decisions came up against the realities of a large whale not wanting to be harpooned, and when it was to dive to the depths with Ahab attached to the harpoon rope. Anyone who has ever gone fishing knows that ropes and lines tend to get wound around things, and once this happens, any force on either end only tightens the rope's grip. Ahab's rope was only following its nature of being between a rock (Moby Dick) and a hard place (Ahab). All of those natural structures that Ahab thought he could master ended up killing him, the crew, and the whale.

Is this, however, all of Ahab's own doing? We need to revisit the idea of people choosing a line of action. According to Erving Goffman (1922–1982), most of us understand the importance of performing in a particular manner within whatever context we are situated. Students tend to act one way when in their dorm rooms with other students, and give a much different performance when their grandparents come to visit. Captain Ahab may have decided that if he stopped the hunt, others would think he was a coward. He had to follow the script—a social structure—which he felt would show him in the best light to himself and others. To reiterate, we must be careful in deciding that all actions are structures, but must also be cognizant of how many of our actions are directed by scripts that have been put in place through a long history of human interactions, including the writing of novels that give us a sense of what is and is not appropriate in given circumstances.

PLAYING TO STRUCTURES AND *THE ADVENTURES OF HUCKLEBERRY FINN*

Much like Don Quixote and the windmills, Captain Ahab and Moby Dick have come to symbolize those aspects of society where structure and agency intersect, intersections that all of us have to navigate, including such historical figures as Vladimir Lenin and his Bolshevik followers who believed Karl Marx was right in saying that only revolution would bring about real social change. Much like Ahab challenging a large whale in its own environment, history has shown that structures do not change easily (as Melville notes in the last paragraph when he states that "the sea rolled on as it rolled five thousand years ago"), and that even after great battles structures often remain unchanged. Many who were rich under the Russian czars tended to be rich within the Soviet regime, though some of the noble families and other sympathizers literally lost their heads in the process.

These structures that shape our lives are often as much in our heads as in the physical environment. A professor at Louisiana State University told me that when he first moved from Colorado to Louisiana someone warned him that there were poisonous snakes in the area. This became part of his script when jogging, as every crack in the sidewalk began to look like a snake. The structures in our heads are there because we typically want a place to fit in with others, and these others want us to fit in, all of which can lead to behaviors that are not necessarily advantageous to ourselves. This happens when we open a door for another person on a cold day when we wanted to get into that warm building right away, or to signal a lane change on a crowded freeway when it would have been quicker to just dart into the other lane. There are few dire penalties such as being dragged to the bottom of the ocean on a dying whale if you decide not to follow these norms, but behaving this way is so powerful that we often act politely without thinking too much about it. If we forget to be nice others will penalize us for acting rude, and we may even browbeat ourselves once we realize how we behaved. Mark Twain's Tom Sawyer understood the power of social scripts and behavior when he and Huckleberry Finn were trying to find a way to free Jim, a runaway slave, who had been captured. The two boys had just learned that Jim was chained to a small bed in one of the slave cabins. In thinking about planning Jim's escape, Tom said that the bed could be lifted up to release the chain, but then asked about finding a saw. Huckleberry asks,

"What do we want of a saw?"

"What do *we want* of a saw? Hain't we got to saw the leg of Jim's bed off, so as to get the chain loose?"

"Why, you just said a body could lift up the bedstead and slip the chain off."

"Well, if that ain't just like you, Huck Finn. You can get up the infant-schooliest ways of going at a thing. Why, hain't you ever read any books at all?—Baron Trenck, nor Casanova, nor Benvenuto Chelleeny, nor Henri IV., nor none of them heroes? Who ever heard of getting a prisoner loose in such an old-maidy way as that? No; the way all the best authorities does is to saw the bed-leg in two, and leave it just so, and swallow the sawdust, so it can't be found, and put some dirt and grease around the sawed place so the very keenest seneskal can't see no sign of its being sawed, and thinks the bed-leg is perfectly sound. Then, the night you're ready, fetch the leg a kick, down she goes; slip off your chain, and there you are. Nothing to do but hitch your rope ladder to the battlements, shin down it, break your leg in the moat—because a rope ladder is nineteen foot too short, you know—and there's your horses and your trusty vassles, and they scoop you up and fling you across a saddle, and away you go to your native Langudoc, or Navarre, or wherever it is. It's gaudy, Huck. I wish there was a moat to this cabin. If we get time, the night of the escape, we'll dig one" (Twain, *The Adventures of Huckleberry Finn*: 331–32).

Tom Sawyer and Huckleberry Finn did take their time freeing Jim. This was due to the fact that they were sure to follow the above script as closely as possible, including having Jim come up with a coat of arms for himself and finding a way to cook a rope ladder into a pie that was delivered to Jim, whose cabin was not at the top of a castle's tower but in a field with windows no more than a few feet off the ground. Tom was even excited about being shot in the leg during the actual escape, though it meant finding a doctor who turned in Jim who was to be sold at the slave auction, until it was found out that his old master had set him free.

All three of these examples—Don Quixote, Captain Ahab, and Tom Sawyer—point to the fact that the scripts we follow are typically not of our own making. Goffman (1959) goes so far as to say that we are always on stage when interacting with others, and to be on stage means you are following a script that was written by someone else. Think of your own role as a student. Most students would rather not be in a classroom on any given day, and this goes for many instructors as well. We would rather be lying on a sun-drenched beach, backpacking in the Amazon, skiing in the Alps, or looking at statues of Dante in Florence, Italy. (Dante, by the way, was kicked out of Florence when he was alive, but is now considered one of the city's heroes due to the popularity of *The Divine Comedy*, a poem that was motivated by his exile from that city.) You are in class because you have been told college is important for landing a good job. This motivates you to pay for tuition and books, go to classes where you wonder about the point of the material, take tests, and worry about grades. This is all part of the role of a student. There are other actions you are also expected to follow, and I am guessing this started the first day of class. Only the instructor went to the front of the room and began lecturing. Most of you could have done that, but to do so would be to move away from the normal script and face ridicule from classmates and possible sanctions from the instructor and college administrators. Most of us do not like to be made fun of or get into trouble, so we stick to the scripts that we assume are in place in any given situation.

The rest of this book will follow the same basic structure as this chapter—introduce sociological concepts and how these can be found and used in fiction. The point is to show that sociology can be helpful in making sense of many situations, including reading a book, watching a movie, navigating a first date, or understanding what a potential employer is looking for in a job candidate. It is also hoped that some of the excerpts will make you decide to pick up one of these works of literature, and find your own examples of both great writing and the sociological imagination.

REFERENCES AND RECOMMENDED READINGS

Agger, B. (2004). *The Visual Self*. Malden, MA: Blackwell.

Beck, U., Giddens, A., and Lash, S. (1994). *Reflexive Modernization*. Stanford, CA: Stanford University Press.

Charon, J. M. (2012). *Ten Questions*. Belmont, CA: Wadsworth Publishing.

Cervantes, M. (2000). *Don Quixote* (trans. John Rutherford). New York: Penguin Books.

Festinger, L., Riecken, H. W., and Schachter, S. (1956). *When Prophecy Fails*. Minneapolis: University of Minneapolis Press.

Goffman, E. (1959). *The Presentation of Self in Everyday Life*. New York: Anchor Books.

Marx, K., and Engels, F. [1848] (2012). *The Communist Manifesto*. New Haven, CT: Yale University Press.

Melville, H. 2007 *Moby Dick*. Costa Mesa, CA: Plain Label Books.

Sewell, W. H., Jr. (1992). "A Theory of Structure: Duality, agency, and transformation." *American Journal of Sociology*, 98(1):1–29.

Twain, M. (1918). *The Adventures of Huckleberry Finn*. New York: Harper Classics.

2 FAMILIES

FAMILIES OF ORIGIN AND *THE ADVENTURES OF OLIVER TWIST*

We have all seen or heard stories of feral children who were locked away in attics or cellars for years by cruel, uncaring parents and guardians. When these children are found, they have no idea how to interact with others. They seem crazy and are referred to as animals, as they have never been properly socialized. Socialization is how we come to know what to do when interacting with others. It is how we learn to get through each and every day, as none of us wants to wake up each morning wondering what it is we are supposed to do, how to talk and act, and whom to talk to and interact with. George Herbert Mead (1962) argues that we are socialized by two sets of actors—those who are close to us such as parents, siblings, and teachers (what he referred to as significant others), and those who are more distant from us such as television actors and actresses, and societal rules, what he called generalized others. Both groups give us ideas of how to act in certain situations, though there are times when they may disagree (such as a movie star who is portrayed as cool while engaged in drugs and parents telling their children that drugs are dangerous). Mead makes the additional distinction between the "I" and the "me." The "I" is more compulsive. It is how we act before we become socialized, and is the basis for compulsive thoughts that run through our minds that we try not to act on, such as simply stealing an item that we cannot buy. The "me" is the socialized aspect of an individual, and the reason we act civilized around others. As we learn these various scripts, we begin to think of them as the proper or natural way to act (more "me" and less "I"), though there is very little that is natural or instinctual about it. It is the feral children who are acting instinctually, following their "I," and those are the people we think of as animals. This chapter will focus on one of the first institutions that starts us on the path to "me," and includes many of the significant others in our lives: the family.

Families are social units that are very important for understanding the sociological imagination. This term, which was introduced at the end of the last chapter, was coined by C. Wright Mills (1959: 5), who states, "[t]he sociological imagination enables its possessor to understand the larger historical scene in terms of its meaning for the inner life and the external career of a variety of individuals." While Mills's argument is complex, at this point you can think of agency as "the inner life" and "the external career" of people, and structure as the "larger historical scene" of society that includes what is happening around you at this moment. We cannot change history—though it is often reinterpreted—and history does influence our own inner selves and career trajectories (not many people can become a wainwright today, though this was a career for many, many people years ago). To have a strong sociological imagination, you must be able to take both the individual and society into account when thinking about why we do the things we do.

Learning about social structures and our own agency, and therefore creating an opportunity to develop a sociological imagination, typically begins with one's family of origin—the family you were born into, adopted, or brought into through a parent being remarried. A person learns very early in life that moms seem different from dads, sisters different from brothers, grandparents different from parents, and so forth. When we meet friends who have different family structures from our own, we sometimes question why there are different family experiences. Even within various types of families (both within cultures such as extended families living within the same household, single-parent families, mixed families, and between cultures where family expectations may vary widely from one person's culture to another's), we find structures in place that can partially explain the activities of a person, or at least their expected activities throughout life. We come to realize how important these structures are when they are taken away, which can help us understand the disadvantages a child like Charles Dickens's Oliver Twist faces when born into this world with no family. In the words of Dickens,

Although I am not disposed to maintain that the being born in a workhouse, is in itself the most fortunate and enviable circumstance that can possibly befall a human being, I do mean to say that in this particular instance, it was the best thing for Oliver Twist that could by possibility have occurred. The fact is, that there was considerable difficulty in inducing Oliver to take upon himself the office of respiration,—a troublesome practice, but one which custom has rendered necessary to our easy existence; and for some time he lay gasping on a little frock mattress, rather unequally poised between this world and the next: the balance being decidedly in favour of the latter. Now, if, during this brief period, Oliver had been surrounded by careful grandmothers, anxious aunts, experienced nurses, and doctors of profound wisdom, he would most inevitably and indubitably have been killed in no time. There being nobody by, however, but a pauper old woman, who was rendered rather misty by an unwonted allowance of beer; and a parish surgeon who did such matters by contract; Oliver and Nature fought out the point between them. The result was, that after a few struggles, Oliver breathed, sneezed, and proceeded to advertise to the inmates of the workhouse the fact of a new burden having been imposed upon the parish, by setting up as loud a cry as could reasonably have been expected from a male who had not been possessed of that very useful appendage, a voice, for a much longer space of time than three minutes and a quarter (Dickens, *The Adventures of Oliver Twist*: 1–2).

It is likely that many of us would take offense at the idea that the presence of loving grandparents and aunts—to say nothing of knowledgeable doctors and nurses—would end in a bad way for someone as sick as Oliver Twist upon being brought into this world. We are taught that such people will do anything to help the younger generation survive, especially during their first few days of life. In fact, many of us would expect just the opposite—that having no family would be much more detrimental to a young person's well-being than being surrounded by loving family members. Oliver does eventually become entrapped in a situation that many of us would expect of a child without a doting family—a homeless young boy who becomes a pickpocket's apprentice before being taken off the streets of London by a well-to-do family that, according to Dickens, would have killed him if they had been there in the beginning.

For many experts who study real families, it is very important for the well-being of children not to be born in workhouses or given to orphanages, but to have a stable household, which typically means the presence of a nurturing mother and employed father. This harkens back to Sigmund Freud's (1995) work on psychoanalysis, as he argued a mother was important for normal emotional development in a child. That idea has deep roots in the United States and other cultures, and continues to be the structure many of us use when thinking about a normal family. While the one-mother-one-father model is still considered ideal, numerous single parents and gay couples have raised well-behaved children. Additionally, many "intact" families have little to show for the behavior of their children in terms of staying out of trouble, if we use the same measures of good behavior as Dickens, in the sense that children who turn to crime or other deviant ways are problematic. This is why sociological theories of the family are often questioned, as there are always exceptions to the rule of what makes the best family. Sociologists typically seek to understand trends and patterns, and the exceptions are studied as we try to learn how and why a certain group or situation does not fit our ideas. Do we need to rethink our theories, or is there something different about the situation that does fit the mold? These questions can be answered in numerous ways, and this is why sociologists constantly study the world around them.

Whatever the form the modern family takes, many people agree that a stable family situation shows children how roles such as breadwinners, nurturers, protectors, etc., are successfully fulfilled. Those who play these roles successfully are said to lead a lifestyle more accepting than those who fall short of their expectations. When children are then asked to play their own roles—such as being a sibling, playmate, or student—the way the adults in their lives have played their roles becomes the model for the children's behavior. The ties that are developed through this socialization are so strong that many children find it difficult to completely separate from their parents as they move into adolescence. According to John P. Hewitt (1989), peer pressure and parental influence constantly come into conflict among teenagers who want to prove their independence to their friends, but worry about alienating their parents and losing their support. These are the people we have modeled ourselves after, and to challenge them means to challenge our own sense of self. This is why you will hear children who are beginning to explore their independence say, "that's not me," when caught acting in ways that are considered deviant (Mead might have them saying, "that's not my 'me,' that's my 'I'"). If they continue those same actions, they may come to the conclusion that these behaviors are part of their (new) true self, and will stop saying, "that's not me," when asked about their behaviors.

THE FUNCTIONS OF THE FAMILY AND *PRIDE AND PREJUDICE*

One of the major functions of the modern family is to determine reproductive rights among its members. This often entails the institution of marriage (the heated debates over reproductive rights such as abortion and birth control show that many people still believe only married people should engage in sex and have children). According to the Centers for Disease Control (CDC) (www.cdc.gov), there were approximately 2,118,000 weddings in 2011 in the United States, out of 311,591,917 people who could have been married. That means 6.8 percent of the marriageable population actually married in 2011 (though it usually takes two to have a wedding, but we will leave critiquing government statistics alone for now). That rate has fluctuated from a high of 8.2 percent in 2000 and 2001, to a low of 6.8 percent between 2009 and 2011. Not all marriages, however, last until death do them part. In 2011, there were 877,000 divorces reported by the

CDC, for a rate of 3.6 percent of the population that could be divorced (it should be noted that some states did not report divorce numbers for this report). If 8.2 percent of the population get married and 3.6 percent get divorced, then the CDC estimate that about half of all first marriages end in divorce is about right (http://www.cdc.gov/nchs/data/nhsr/nhsr049.pdf, page 1, accessed April 2013).

One reason family formations are so important is that more than just the married partners are impacted by marriage and divorce. Family and friends are often part of these unions, including kids who may have been born into the family or entered through earlier marriages. While nearly half of all marriages end in divorce, a majority of children (nearly two-thirds of all children under the age of 18) lived with married parents (original or step) in 2009, maintaining our notion of what makes a good family (http://www.census.gov/newsroom/releases/archives/children/cb11-117.html, accessed April 2013). Any situation that could challenge the marriage structure of the parents could impact the well-being of these children, though studies have shown that divorce is often a better situation than living with parents who are violent toward each other (Amato, 2001–2002).

These rates and trends, along with expectations of what parents are supposed to teach their children, are part of the structures of family life. While marriage and divorce rates may have changed over the years (according to the CDC there were 50 times more divorces in 1967 than 1867, http://www.cdc.gov/nchs/data/series/sr_21/sr21_024.pdf, accessed April 2013), the structures we often associate with modern marriages and families have been in place for a long time, including how we think and talk about husbands and wives, as in Jane Austen's *Pride and Prejudice*, first published in 1813.

> Mr. Bennet was so odd a mixture of quick parts, sarcastic humor, reserve, and caprice, that the experience of three and twenty years had been insufficient to make his wife understand his character. *Her* mind was less difficult to develop. She was a woman of mean understanding, little information, and uncertain temper. When she was discontented, she fancied herself nervous. The business of her life was to get her daughters married. Its solace was visiting and news (Austen, *Pride and Prejudice*: 3).

While notions of the complexities of men and women may have changed over the years—though that may depend on the vested interests of the person asking the questions—there is a sense of what the people involved in the union of marriage are expected to do, as well as the fact that most marriages are presumed to be between a man and a woman, a topic under much debate in 2013 in the United States. Mr. Bennet is expected to be informative and entertaining, while Mrs. Bennet is expected to be supportive of her husband and nurture the children. That there are many ways to be entertaining, supportive, and nurturing, and all family members can play these parts, societal expectations could hinder individuals like the Bennets from trying different roles, such as Mrs. Bennet leaving her family for five years to pursue a doctorate in German philosophy. If Mr. Bennet decided to study philosophy, and had enough money in the bank to support the family, people reading the book when it was written (and possibly even today) may have thought that was within his rights to do so. If he had given his fortune to a workhouse, taken up needlepoint, and led his family into poverty, there may have been less enthusiasm among readers regarding his choices as a husband and father.

While the elder Bennets seemed to fit a rather typical marriage, not everything went smoothly for their daughters. If it had, there would have been little reason to write the book, as we have a pretty good idea of what happens when everything is done properly (which rarely happens in real life or fiction). One of the issues Austen raises is a different set of expectations across characters, though this is not a concern when the daughters start pursuing a gentleman they find most intriguing: Mr. Bingley:

> Not all that Mrs. Bennet, however, with the assistance of her five daughters, could ask on the subject was sufficient to draw from her husband any satisfactory description of Mr. Bingley. They attacked him in various ways, with barefaced questions, ingenious suppositions, and distant surmises. He eluded the skill of them all. They were at last obliged to accept the second-hand intelligence of their neighbor Lady Lucas. Her report was highly favorable. Sir William had been delighted with him. He was quite young, wonderfully handsome, extremely agreeable, and, to crown the whole, he meant to be at the next assembly with a large party. Nothing could be more delightful! To be fond of dancing was a certain step towards falling in love, and very lively hopes of Mr. Bingley's heart were entertained (Austen, *Pride and Prejudice*: 6).

It should be noted that some readers might argue that this is a very sexist approach to males and females—i.e., women are gossips and men are stoic—but would it be fair to say that the passage is sexist only in today's terms, but maybe not so much when Austen was writing? That is a difficult question to answer, and once again, most likely depends on the person reading this rather than some intrinsic value to the words written. Whether sexist or not, there is a risk for the Bennet daughters in determining whether Mr. Bingley is Mr. Right (another sexist term) and if so, if one of them can get him to ask for her hand in marriage. That risk is overcome, though we come to find out that Mr. Bingley had a very different family experience from the Bennets, as he relays to one of the Bennet daughters who has just told him that she understands his frustration over a personal matter, but to only look for pleasure in things that have happened in the past:

"I cannot give you credit for any philosophy of the kind. *Your* retrospections must be so totally void of reproach, that the contentment arising from them is not of philosophy, but, what is much better, of innocence. But with *me*, it is not so. Painful recollections will intrude which cannot, which ought not, to be repelled. I have been a selfish being all my life, in practice, though not in principle. As a child I was taught what was *right*, but I was not taught to correct my temper. I was given good principles, but left to follow them in pride and conceit. Unfortunately an only son (for many years an only *child*), I was spoilt by my parents, who, though good themselves (my father, particularly, all that was benevolent and amiable), allowed, encouraged, almost taught me to be selfish and overbearing, to care for none beyond my own family circle, to think meanly of all the rest of the world, to *wish* at least to think meanly of their sense and worth compared with my own. Such I was, from eight to eight and twenty, and such I might still have been but for you, dearest, loveliest Elizabeth! What do I not owe you! You taught me a lesson, hard indeed at first, but most advantageous. By you, I was properly humbled. I came to you without a doubt of my reception. You showed me how insufficient were all my pretensions to please a woman worthy of being pleased" (Austen, *Pride and Prejudice*: 323).

Few of us get to choose our parents, yet our family structures frame much of what we learn about how families function, as well as the workings of other social structures. Moving from our family of origin to a marriage or other type of intimate relationship can be difficult if partners are not compatible on various issues, and much of this can be linked back to our socialization within a family. Mr. Bingley grew up as an only son, and was given more leeway to make his own way in life than Elizabeth Bennet. His personal experiences within his family, as well as being a male in a patriarchal society where men are considered more important than women in terms of power, influenced his behavior, put him at odds with the expectations of Elizabeth who grew up in a houseful of daughters. Jane Austen understands these social processes decades before Mills writes about the sociological imagination. Once we are made aware of Mr. Bingley's family structure and standing in history as a male with privileges, we come to a better idea of why he acts in certain ways in various situations. This is true of people coming to college as well, which is why there are often special programs for students whose parents did not attend college. Success involves much more than finding a compatible roommate and getting into the classes you want. It also involves understanding how to successfully navigate the whole experience, including attending large lecture classes, having little or no adult supervision outside the classroom, attending parties where alcohol is served to everyone in attendance regardless of age and experience with drinking, and deciding which sanctioned extracurricular activities will be most helpful, interesting, and fun. If your parents did not attend college and are unaware of how all this works, your own understanding of the college experience is likely to be missing a number of pieces. The role of families and the structures they build around us enters into many of our activities, even when we believe we are acting of our own accord.

THE STRENGTH OF STRUCTURES AND *THE SWISS FAMILY ROBINSON*

Authors such as Jane Austen use the structure of families to determine a character's actions, as well as the larger structures of society, including how to behave at social gatherings such as balls. These familial structures are so deeply ingrained that even when all other social structures are absent, the roles a person is expected to play within a family are hard to ignore. Such is the case in Johann David Wyss's *The Swiss Family Robinson*. The Robinson family was shipwrecked on a deserted island (much like a student dropped off at college with little understanding of the environment), forcing them to fend for themselves in terms of surviving wild animals, finding food, and building their own shelters. We get an indication of who is going to play what role within the first few lines of the book, when the father describes himself as having to stay brave as the ship is dashed upon the rocks during a storm and the wife is "weeping." Shortly thereafter, the father does admit to being at his wit's end, at which point the wife rallies the children to be strong. Even in this passage there is the sense that the father and older boys are the instigators of all that is good, and the wife and younger children are there to support them.

That the Robinsons end up living on a deserted island with no other people has very little impact on the family structures and the roles played by the various individuals. While the characters could have gone their own way, and do at times—which some would argue is an example of agency—the family tends to remain together. Gender roles are played out in typical, if not idealized, ways during many of their adventures, as are the age roles of what we would consider within the traditional family. Here is how one adventure begins from the father's perspective:

All was ready for a start at an early hour; my brave wife consented to remain in camp with Franz as her companion, while the three elder boys, and all the dogs, except Juno, went with me (Wyss, *The Swiss Family Robinson*: 125).

Many of us would find all of this to be unexceptional. The mother will keep the youngest child safe, as he is not yet ready for adventures that include coming face-to-face with ostriches and bears (no one demanded appropriate zoological information from Wyss, and many readers at the time of the publication would likely have found his choice of animals to be appropriate for an exotic location). These roles are reinforced through a telling of what took place during the day when the father and boys return to camp:

> When a full account of our adventures had been given, with a minute and special description of the bear-fight, my wife related what she had done during our absence. She and Franz had made their way through the wood up to the rocks behind it, and discovered a bed of pure white clay, which it seemed to her might be used for making porcelain. Then she had contrived a drinking-trough for the cattle out of a split bamboo.
>
> She had arranged a hearth in a sheltered place by building up large stones, cemented with the white clay; and, finally, she had cut a quantity of canes and brought them, on the cart, to be in readiness for the building we had in hand.
>
> I praised the thoughtful diligence which had effected so much that was of real and definite use. In order to try the clay I put some balls of it in the fire now kindled to burn during the night, and we then betook ourselves to rest under shelter of our tent.
>
> I awoke at dawn and aroused my little party. My first idea was to examine the clay balls, which I found baked hard and finely glazed, but too much melted down by the heat—a fault which, seeing the excellent quality of the clay, I knew it would be well worthwhile to remedy (Wyss, *The Swiss Family Robinson*: 130).

That the mother found and worked with clay while the father and older boys (the men) engaged a bear point to the woman's role as domestic provider. Even in the domestic sphere, however, the father is still the person to handle problems, especially since solving the problem of the clay would involve creative thinking. Much like the Bennet family, the Robinson patriarch is the one expected to have the characteristics of "quick parts, sarcastic humor, reserve, and caprice."

It may be helpful to understand the ways in which we think about the family by reversing the roles of the mother and father. If the father had stayed in the camp with the youngest child when the mother fought bears, we would have a very different opinion of what these characters were like. When we come across a male who holds a position of authority in the family we rarely question it, unless violence is used to maintain that position. When a woman holds the same position, even without resorting to violence, we begin to question the roles and values of the couple, and worry about the mental and physical well-being of the children.

It should be noted that at the time *The Swiss Family Robinson* was first published (1812), the family was thought of as an economic unit, much like today's small businesses. They were typically involved with agricultural work on the family farm, and to be efficient, everyone had to know their place. It would have done very little good to have two groups of planters fighting over a field, or to have everyone working on dinner throughout the day while neglecting the fields that would provide the food for the next day's meals. Since it was thought that men were stronger, they worked the fields, especially when it came to animals and equipment, while women worked in the home or did field labor considered suitable for their gender such as planting and picking certain crops. The matriarch of the Robinsons could very well have led the children into the jungle to face monkeys, ostriches, and bears, but it was thought that she would be better suited—and readers at the time would have a better understanding of the family—if she stayed in camp with the little one making utensils out of clay.

Sociologists of the modern family note that today's family in industrialized countries is much less likely to be considered an economic unit, as the resources needed to survive originates from outside the family structure (parents go to work for pay). If the adventures of the Robinson family were written today, we could still expect everyone to fall within structured gender and age roles, but the adventures would probably be about sex and sexuality, entertainment choices, and maintaining gender roles. These are the activities that modern sociologists who study families see as the most important functions within the institution of the family. The modern family is expected to determine who can have sex with whom, and given all the entertainment choices in a media-saturated society, what is considered entertaining is often decided at the family level. What is enjoyed by the father and mother will be consumed by the children, who learn to enjoy the same entertainment options as their parents. Bourdieu (1980) finds this to be the case in France, as people within the same social structures tend to like the same things (Bourdieu focuses on socioeconomic class more so than individual families, and we will talk about class in Chapter 9). In short, how could you know if you liked caviar or escargot if you were never given a chance to try these items? Our place in social structures not only determines our actions, but also our tastes in such things as food, clothing, and the music we like. Socialization with the family provides deep roots for who we are as individuals, and those roots become tied to many different individuals, groups, organizations, and institutions.

Before moving to the next institution (religion), I want to pause for just a moment to discuss two terms used above—typical and ideal. Many readers may think that by stating someone has played an ideal role I am saying that they did what was expected of them and did it well, but this is not the case. According to Erving Goffman (1959), people often try to fit into roles in two ways—by acting in an idealized or typified manner. Idealization involves someone trying to play a role that is exemplary and would make them stand out in that role. Typification happens when someone tries to play a role that would be considered normal and unexceptional. To say that Mrs. Robinson came off as an idealized mother is not to say that what she did was right, and that any mother who diverges from that path is problematic. Instead, we must consider Wyss's perspective. Wyss, who was a minister, most likely had an image of a mother in his head that he wanted Mrs. Robinson to emulate as closely as possible, including doing some things so well that others who thought of mothers would be envious of her abilities. Mrs. Robinson was idealized according to Wyss's expectations. We can assume that many women—as well as men—who read *The Swiss Family Robinson* would realize that even in the best of circumstances, a woman could not do all the things Mrs. Robinson was able to accomplish. She was idealized as a mother, as was the situation of being on an island inundated with strange animals. While we would recognize the idealized playing of the mother role in fiction, it provides a model for how others are expected to act. The typical mother would have acted very differently, such as asking why she was being left behind, or what the husband wanted for dinner, or that she was going to the beach to get a tan (all things many fathers would do in the same situation). The creation of the Robinsons as a family playing these roles becomes yet another social structure from which we use to make sense of our own lives.

As mentioned, Wyss was a pastor, and as such had a vested interest in creating and maintaining idealized, and at times typical, family roles. For many people within Wyss's circle, God was a father, Mary a mother, and Jesus a child; it would have been important to maintain such a structure within mortal families so that they would replicate what was being said from the pulpit. When something as powerful as religion informs a structure such as the family, it becomes difficult to challenge. The current divorce rate and literature such as *My Two Moms* shows that family structures are changing to some degree. Still, we expect children to grow up knowing certain things about the world around them, and that this information, much like Austen's Mr. Bingley, is passed down from generation to generation through the family. When that fails, we hope that other institutions will pick up the pieces, including religion, education, and the criminal justice system.

REFERENCES AND RECOMMENDED READINGS

Amato, P. R. (2001–2002). "Good Enough Marriages: Parental discord, divorce, and children's long-term well-being." *Virginia Journal of Social Policy & the Law*, 9: 71–94.

Austen, J. (1853). *Pride and Prejudice*. London, UK: Spottiswoodes and Shaw.

Bellah, R. N., Madsen, R., Sullivan, W., Swidler, A., and Tipton, S. M. (2007). *Habits of the Heart* (3rd ed.). Berkeley: University of California Press.

Dickens, C. (1866). *The Adventures of Oliver Twist*. Boston: Ticknor and Fields.

Freud, S. (1995). *The Basic Writings of Sigmund Freud*. New York: Modern Library.

Goffman, E. (1959). *The Presentation of Self in Everyday Life*. New York: Anchor Books.

Hewitt, J. P. (1989). *Dilemmas of the American Self*. Philadelphia: Temple University Press.

Mead, G. H. (1962.) *Mind, Self, and Society*. Chicago: University of Chicago Press.

Mills, C. W. (1959). *The Sociological Imagination*. New York: Oxford University Press.

Wahls, Z. (2013). *My Two Moms* (reprint ed.). New York: Gotham Books.

Wyss, J. D. (2005). *The Swiss Family Robinson* (trans. William H. G. Kingston). Lawrence, KS: Digireads.com.

3 RELIGION

INTRODUCTION AND *"LETTERS FROM EARTH"*

One of the first places people in the United States and in many other cultures visit after arriving home from the hospital (or leaving the workhouse, as Oliver Twist would have done) is a place of faith such as a church, temple, synagogue, or mosque. The socialization we receive within religion is so powerful that nearly 82 percent of all adults in the United States say that they are affiliated with a religion of one kind or another (Pew Institute, http://religions.pewforum.org/reports#, accessed May 2013). Even more say they believe in God (approximately 90 percent, according to a 2007 Gallup poll, http://www.gallup.com/poll/27877/Americans-More-Likely-Believe-God-Than-Devil-Heaven-More-Than-Hell.aspx, accessed May 2013), though the same poll shows that only about 70 percent believe in the devil or Hell. How one can believe in God and not the devil would be a mystery to many who follow religions based on the story of Abraham (such as Muslims, Jews, and Christians), but it does show that people are making choices. The complexity of such religious beliefs is noted by Mark Twain when he writes in "Letters from Earth" about a trip one of the more powerful angels made to Earth:

This is a strange place, and extraordinary place, and interesting. There is nothing resembling it at home. The people are all insane, the other animals are all insane, the earth is insane, Nature itself is insane. Man is a marvelous curiosity. When he is at his very, very best he is a sort of low grade nickel-plated angel; at his worst he is unspeakable, unimaginable; and first and last and all the time he is a sarcasm. Yet he blandly and in all sincerity calls himself the "noblest work of God." This is the truth I am telling you. And this is not a new idea to him, he has talked it through the ages, and believed it. Believed it, and found nobody among all his race to laugh at it.

Moreover—if I may put another strain upon you—he thinks he is the Creator's pet. He believes the Creator is proud of him; he even believes the Creator loves him; has a passion for him; sits up nights to admire him; yes, and watch over him and keep him out of trouble. (Twain, "Letters from Earth": 13).

The angel writing this story is Satan, who decided to visit Earth after God told him to take some time off and that he might enjoy a planet created many, many years ago. It is Satan's first visit to Earth, and, as noted, he finds the religious practices of humans to be very strange and nothing like the activities carried out in Heaven. One of the reasons for the discrepancy is that God has basically forgotten about Earth, given that he has many, many other projects to create and look after. This left humans to come up with their own ideas of religion. That is an example of both the agency and structure of religion—that humans created their religious practices over centuries (agency), and many of us follow the same routines and share the same beliefs (structure). In addition to following beliefs, most religions provide us with stories of creation, tell us to be nice to each other, and that there is a better life waiting for us after death if we follow all the rules placed before us by our religion. This is more structure, as these are issues for which few other institutions can provide insights, and we are uncomfortable devising our own ideas regarding the meanings of life and death.

If you were in the same position as Twain's Satan, in the sense that you had never visited Earth or been a member of an earthly faith-based organization, you may come away with similar thoughts. For example, if religion is about worshipping a creator and giving us some idea of the afterlife, then why are there so many interpretations of this seemingly simple thought? In addition, some of the religions that share many of the same beliefs are often at war with each other. Judaism, Islam, and Christianity all believe in a God that created Adam and Eve, of whom Abraham, Noah, and Moses were descendants (as are all of us from this perspective). These three religions and all their various sects view the role of these historical figures in much the same way. Interpretations of relatively more recent events are where everyone goes in different directions. People who follow Jewish traditions do not believe God sent a son, Jesus, to Earth, while Christians do believe that Jesus Christ was, and is, God's son. Those who follow Islam believe in Christ, consider him an important person and a man of faith, but not God's son. It is Muhammad who is God's true prophet. Not only are there conflicts between these groups, but even within the groups there are disagreements that have led to bloodshed. Catholics and Protestants both believe that Jesus Christ was the Son of God and have gone after each other in Ireland. Sunnis and Shiites both believe that Muhammad was the true prophet of God, yet have killed each other in Pakistan. While these conflicts are real and have cost many lives, they should not be thought of as absolute. There are many families comprised of individuals from these various religious groups, as well as a myriad of other combinations. A student told me after a lecture on religion that he was considered "sushi" because one of his parents was Sunni and the other Shiite, and that he grew up in a very loving household. Still, the lessons we learn in our religious institutions, which include who is considered good and who is thought to be bad, structure much of our lives, though most of us have very little input into what stories are told and how they are interpreted within the institution or within our own lives.

THE CREATION OF RELIGION AND *CAT'S CRADLE*

Religions may seem very formal and structured, especially those with long histories such as Christianity, Buddhism, Islam, or Judaism. Each has ways of thinking about such issues as gender, sexuality, age, etc., as we saw among the family members in *The Swiss Family Robinson*, a story written by a Protestant minister. When someone within one of these religions decides they do not like the way things are said about some issue or topic, they may seek to leave their established religion, join another religious group, or start something new. This can cause problems and upheavals, and the individuals and groups seeking change are often considered heretics. Their ideas are often short-lived and can end rather violently, as was the case in times such as the Spanish Inquisition, when people were tortured and killed for seeing things differently from Church officials. Sometimes, however, an idea can catch on and become very popular. This includes thoughts on the intersection of religion and economics, as pointed out in Max Weber's *The Protestant Ethic and Spirit of Capitalism*, published in 1904. According to Weber, the Protestant split from the Catholic Church, led by Martin Luther, enabled individuals to decide for themselves whether or not they were God's chosen ones by virtue of what they were able to accomplish and acquire while living. Prior to the split, entry into Heaven was only possible through the Catholic Church. The prosperous Protestant is a chosen person because God is rewarding her for leading a good life. She has every reason to believe that such good fortunes will translate into entry into Heaven after death, even if her church attendance is less than stellar. According to Weber, this approach to accumulation and prosperity is important in understanding the link between religious beliefs and economics in many Western societies. While many of these countries are still populated with large numbers of Catholics, many have adopted the Protestant ethic when it comes to wealth and income.

History provides us with numerous examples of congregations splitting from a church, which highlights the fact that religion—much like gender roles in families—are of our own making as a species. Splits are often very difficult and long processes, as once a religion becomes settled it becomes a way of life that is not to be questioned. Kurt Vonnegut, an author who often states that if a god did exist, it was too complicated for humans to understand, shows how this works in *Cat's Cradle*:

"There was at least one quality of the new conquerors of San Lorenzo that was really new," wrote young Castle. "McCabe and Johnson dreamed of making San Lorenzo a Utopia."

"To this end, McCabe overhauled the economy and the laws.

"Johnson designed a new religion" (Vonnegut, *Cat's Cradle*: 127).

McCabe and Johnson come to San Lorenzo after their boat capsizes during a storm. They are washed ashore, and both are completely naked, but manage to take control of the island by claiming to be the island's protector (McCabe) and savior (Johnson). Johnson's religion becomes known as Bokononism, which McCabe outlaws so that the people of San Lorenzo would have good and evil to choose from, though it is often hard to tell which is worse—the politics or the religion. Everyone claims to be anti-Bokononist so as to be law-abiding citizens, yet the whole island practices Bokononism in one form or another. This includes the president of the country, who takes over when McCabe dies, though he continues to outlaw any public displays of Bokononism. Even a horrific torture device does little to stop this:

Just before we reached the palace gate the ruts carried us through a rustic arch made of two telephone poles and a beam that spanned them.

Hanging from the middle of the beam was a huge iron hook. There was a sign impaled on the hook.

"This hook," the sign proclaimed, "is reserved for Bokonon himself" (Vonnegut, *Cat's Cradle*: 212–13).

Readers might think this is over-the-top even for a fictional account, as anyone in their right mind would give up silly religious practices in the face of such a cruel and gruesome death. Would the Romans have had the same thoughts while they were feeding the early Christians to the lions, knowing that others would give up their faith, since only crazy people would continue practices that could lead to such an unpleasant ending? Most religious practices have survived gruesome tortures and death. Christians even worship a torture device used by the Romans—not the lion, but the cross. Even Buddhism, which is thought of as a peaceful religion by many in the West, experienced wars between those priests and followers who believed that the path to Zen was found during long journeys of inner reflection, and those who argued that Zen was to be found during brief, intense moments of suspended self-awareness such as being scared or hit when not expecting it. The Sunni and Shia split is based on the former believing that leadership of Islam should be controlled by someone who is familiar with the prophet Muhammad's teachings, while the latter believe leadership should stay within Muhammad's family. These ideas have led to wars. These oversimplified explanations for schisms and violence within these religions point to the fact that violence has been part of most—if not all—religions at some point in their histories, even though most advocate peace in one form or another.

For a sociologist, the idea that there are many religions, and that these religions split into new groups for any number of reasons, means that all religions have been constructed, though we rarely try to decide if a religion is right or wrong. The account in *Cat's Cradle* of Johnson deciding to create a new religion after washing ashore on San Lorenzo could be much like the creation and expansion of other religions, though Vonnegut did it over a much shorter time period, a characteristic of cults relative to religions. This is not to say that all sociologists are atheists or agnostic, but that many who study religion try to make sense of how religions are founded and why some people follow one religion, while others feel that their spiritual needs are better filled by another religion, or in another way entirely.

WHY RELIGION IS SO IMPORTANT AND *THE DIVINE COMEDY*

Another early sociologist who studied religion was Emile Durkheim. Durkheim thought of society as a living organism (Durkheim was writing when Charles Darwin's theory of evolution was taking hold in many academic disciplines), with institutions acting as organs, including religion. According to Durkheim's (2001) way of thinking, religion grew out of rituals practiced by human groups. The rituals are important because they give individuals in these groups a sense of belonging through shared behaviors and activities. The institutionalization of rituals into religion legitimated those practices, as well as the power held by individuals who could either practice or talk about them—including talking to the supreme deities—better than others. These individuals eventually become the shamans, priests, ministers, prophets, etc., in society. Vonnegut was in much the same mind-set when he created Bokononism, as the main character in *Cat's Cradle* has to learn that religion's rituals such as touching feet as a sign (and ritual) of affection, before he can be a true practitioner and an accepted member of San Lorenzo society.

While Durkheim thinks of religion as a vital organ within society and Weber sees it as an institution that could be used for status attainment and individual salvation, Karl Marx (1983) argues that religion is a cultural institution that helps maintain the socioeconomic status of society. In other words, it helps the rich get richer and keeps the poor in their place. While there are a number of interpretations of Marx's comment about religion being the opiate of the masses, the most common is that religion, like opium, keeps parishioners lethargic so they would have no energy or reason to challenge those who are rich or the structures that make them rich. "The meek shall inherit the earth," was heard by the poor populating the pews so many times that it came to be considered true, and that their struggles with life on earth would transform into a glorious afterlife in Heaven. If Christ returned to Earth before they died, then they would finally get their just desserts and be put in charge of everyone who had taken advantage of them.

Dante (c. 1265–1321) was under the same impression, to some extent. After being exiled from Florence (the city is now filled with statues and tributes to him), Dante wrote a three-part epic poem known as *The Divine Comedy*, in which one of his heroes, the poet Virgil, guides him through Hell (the Inferno), purgatory (Purgatorio), and Heaven (Paradiso). Virgil, however, is not allowed into Heaven, as he is not a Christian, having lived well before Jesus was around. Dante's guide in Paradise is a woman named Beatrice, who was supposedly a love of Dante's when he was younger. As one might expect, those who were behind the efforts to exile Dante are found doing disgusting things in Hell. The following involves traitors to Dante's cause:

When I beheld two spirits by the ice
Pent in hollow, that the head of one
Was cowl unto the other; and as bread
Is raven'd up through hunger, the uppermost
Did so apply his fangs to the other's brain,
Where the spine joins it. Not more furiously
One Menalippus' temples Tydeus gnaw'd
Than on that skull and on its garbage he,
"O thou! who show'st so beastly a sign of hate
'Gainst him thou prey'st on, let me hear," said I,
"The cause, on such condition, that if right
Warrant thy grievance, knowing who ye are,
And what color of his sinning was,
I may repay thee in the world above,
If that, wherewith I speak, be moist so long."
His jaws uplifting from their fell repast,
That sinner wiped them on the hairs o' the head,

Which he behind had mangled, then began:
"Thy will obeying, I call up afresh
Sorrow past cure; which, but to think of, wrings
My heart, or ere I tell on't. But if words,
That I utter, shall prove seed to bear
Fruit of eternal infamy to him,
The traitor whom I gnaw at, thou at once
Shalt see me speak and weep. Who thou mayest be
I know not, nor how here below art come:
But Florentine thou seemest of a truth,
When I do hear thee. Know, I was on earth
Count Ugolino, and the Archbishop he
Ruggieri. Why I neighbor him so close,
Now list. That through effect of his ill thoughts
In him my trust reposing, I was ta'en
And after murder'd, need is not I tell
What therefore thou canst not have heard, that is,
How cruel was the murder, shalt thou hear,
And know if he wrong'd me" (Dante, *The Divine Comedy*: 134–36).

According to historical accounts, Count Ugolino and the Archbishop Ruggieri were members of an opposing party to Dante's Florentine Guelphs, so they are to spend eternity eating each other's heads in Dante's rendition of Hell. On the other hand, those Dante found to his liking were residing in Heaven, such as Cacciaguida degli Elisei, who took part in the Crusades and was Dante's great-great-grandfather.

"You are my sire, said I: "you give me heart
Freely to speak my thought: above myself
You raise me. Through so many streams with joy
My soul is fill'd, that gladness wells from it;
So that it bears the mighty tide, and bursts not.
Say then, my honour'd stem! what ancestors
Were those you sprang from, and what years were mark'd
In your first childhood? Tell me of the fold,
That hath Saint John for guardian, what was then
Its state, and who in it were highest seated!"
    As embers, at the breathing of the wind,
Their flame enliven; so that light I saw

Shine at my blandishments; and, as it grew
More fair to look on, so with voice more sweet,
Yet not in this our modern phrase, forthwith
It answer'd: "From the day, when it was said
'Hail Virgin!' to the throes by which my mother,
Who now is sainted, lighten'd her of me
Whom she was heavy with, this fire had come
Five hundred times and fourscore, to relume
Its radiance underneath the burning foot
Of its own lion. They, of whom I sprang,
And I, had there our birth-place, where the last
Partition of our city first is reach'd
By him that runs her annual game. Thus much
Suffice of my forefathers; who they were,
And whence they hither came, more honourable
It is to pass in silence than to tell"
(Dante, *The Divine Comedy*: 352–53).

Notice the number of times Dante makes Cacciaguida saintlike such as stating that his great-great-grandfather said, "Silence is more considerate than speech." Religion teaches us to hold our tongues unless it is absolutely necessary, and those who do it best are saints. There is no way of testing this idea, but it is what we believe. Even during the Sermon on the Mount, Christ says, "When you pray, go into your room, close the door, and pray to your Father, who is unseen. Then your Father, who sees what is done in secret, will reward you" (Matthew 6:6). Praying secretly, however, is not communal, so we continue to attend our religious organization to show others that we belong. Writing this poem was also not done in secret, and if we think more deeply about the construction of Heaven and Hell, we would assume if any of Cacciaguida's enemies from the Crusades wrote an epic poem, that person would not have put him in their Heaven, but would have him doing disgusting things in Hell. As with much of religion, there is no way to test which of these theories is right.

This idea of building worlds, whether earthly or otherwise, through religion is discussed at length by Peter Berger in *The Sacred Canopy* (1967). According to Berger, humans need to make sense of their surroundings which seem chaotic. This is done through a three-stage process of externalization, objectification, and internalization. Externalization involves actions. An individual thinks of something and acts on it. This action is then external to the individual who is thinking of doing it. Once the action is external, it becomes an object for others to see and interpret, as well as the individual who instigated the action. Once the action becomes an object and others begin interpreting it—including the actor who instigated the action and is now watching how others are interpreting it (as well as interpreting the action him or herself)—it becomes an internal component of those who are witnessing the action, as they can think about whether it is appropriate or not and whether or not they can or want to emulate it, reward it, expand on it, or punish it.

After numerous iterations of externalization, objectification, and internalization, certain actions become routine. Individuals and groups practice routines that help them make sense of their lives—this is the practice of building worlds—and any threat of returning to a less formalized and unpredictable existence is threatening. Some of these rituals become sacred in the sense that few, if any, of those practicing the rituals understand how the ritual began, or its power to make sense of some unknown event or other type of mystery. For example, science can tell us very little about what happens to us after we die besides the body starts decomposing. Stories of the afterlife told by those who have come back from that arena, either through reincarnation or near-death experiences, make sense of this experience, and these stories are rarely part of science except to study patterns within the accounts. Other unexplainable actions, such as being healed after a long illness or feeding the masses with a few loaves of bread and a handful of fish, become sacred stories, as no one can make sense of them through routine ways of thinking. Random events are defined as miracles and explained through religion and faith in beings more powerful than ourselves. These beings take on the roles of bringing about the things that we cannot explain when looking at our own actions, such as creating the universe and life. We cannot do those things, yet they exist, and so must be explained. Religion builds the world we see, as well as what we cannot see or explain. Many of us are unable to live in a state of not knowing how these things came about. We need explanations for our existence.

It should be clear by now that there is a number of social structures tied to the practices of religion—an institution that typically incorporates a creator, provides the norms, values, and beliefs its followers are to live by, and involves various realms for the souls of those who have died that are controlled by those very same norms, values, and beliefs. On Earth, people are to show appreciation of their god(s) by engaging in certain rituals, such as praying, going to services, and being kind to others; and that these will determine where one ends up after death. People like Mark Twain found this to be a very silly belief, especially since most accounts at that time likened Heaven to a never-ending church service. Most of the churchgoers Twain knew could not wait to get out of the service, but his words make little difference to the many who believe in something greater than themselves. How those otherworldly realms are interpreted and who belongs where, however, seem open to the interpretation and the agency of writers and poets such as Twain, Vonnegut, and Dante. To think that the formal structures we now find in established religions were once like Bokononism is hard for us to understand.

The structures linked to religion go beyond who will end up in Heaven or Hell (or come back as a professional athlete or snail), and whether one should attend

Friday prayers at the mosque, the synagogue on Saturday, the voodoo ceremony Saturday evening, or Mass on Sunday. As discussed by Weber, Marx, and others, religion permeates much of society. The rise of Protestantism provided added impetus to the growth of capitalism. The beliefs and practices of Islam and Judaism have made it possible for large halal and kosher food industries to gain a foothold in various communities like Dearborn, Michigan. Buddhist temples and shrines have become tourist destinations. Voodoo, a much-misunderstood religion in the United States, provides a sense of mystery for trinket shops in the French Quarter of New Orleans. Many of us pray before eating, while others ask God for a miracle when their favorite sports team is losing the big game. Like the family and other institutions we will investigate, religion is a socializing agent whose roots reach beyond the specific buildings in which it is practiced.

Let me end this chapter with a quick note about voodoo. According to Métraux (1959), voodoo is a polytheistic religion, which means its practitioners believe there are many gods (religions such as Christianity are monotheistic; practitioners believe in one god). Voodoo was brought to parts of the New World (such as Haiti and New Orleans) through the importation of African slaves. The gods of this religion can practice both good and bad magic, though some lean more heavily one way than the other. The gods can do the biddings of certain persons given the right incentives, but can also possess individuals and make them do its deeds. Humans who are in contact with the gods can get them to turn people into zombies, though these are nothing like the flesh-eating zombies of Hollywood. Voodoo zombies, at least according to Métraux, are basically mindless servants. Some are thought to have been dead for awhile before being turned into a walking corpse (still no appetite for human flesh), though others are thought to be normal during the day but become zombies at night to do the work of their masters. This can include activities as harmless as cleaning the house to criminal activities such as robbery and murder. Most, if not all, voodoo zombies are thought of as pitiful creatures, though they are also feared as their minds are not their own. People who are constantly tired or find possessions in their homes that do not belong to them often blame their bad luck on having been turned into a zombie by someone practicing black magic.

Dr. Kelly Hancock, who was my major professor at Portland State University, spent a good deal of time in Haiti, including some initial work on establishing a new university in the country. He was quick to state that voodoo was nothing to be afraid of, and, in fact, many of those who participated in the voodoo ceremonies on Saturday evenings went to Catholic Mass on Sunday mornings. When asked how they could practice—and believe—such different religious ways, the Haitians told Dr. Hancock that they wanted to make sure all their bases were covered. That voodoo is feared by many in the United States has more to do with the mass media than with the religion or its practitioners—though before we talk about the media, we have to go to school.

REFERENCES AND RECOMMENDED READINGS

Alighieri, D. *The Divine Comedy*. Accessed through the Gutenberg Project, www. gutenberg.org

Berger, P. L. (1967). *The Sacred Canopy*. Garden City, NY: Doubleday.

Della Fave, L. R. (1980). "The Meek Shall Not Inherit the Earth. Self-evaluation and the legitimacy of stratification." *American Sociological Review*, 45(December): 955–71.

Durkheim, E. (2001). *The Elementary Forms of Religious Life*, Carol Cosman, Ed. New York: Oxford University Press.

Eliade, M. (2000). *The HarperCollins Concise Guide to World Religions*. San Francisco: Harper San Francisco.

Largo, M. (2010). *God's Lunatics*. New York: William Morrow Paperbacks.

Marx, K. (1983). *The Portable Karl Marx*, E. Kamenka, Ed. New York: Penguin.

Métraux, A. (1959). *Voodoo in Haiti*. New York: Oxford University Press.

Twain, M. (1996). "Letters from Earth," in *The Bible According to Mark Twain*. New York: Touchstone.

Vonnegut, K. (2007) [1963]. *Cat's Cradle*, in *Three by Vonnegut*. New York: Dial Press.

Weber, M. (2011). *The Protestant Ethic and the Spirit of Capitalism*, Stephen Kalberg, Ed. New York: Oxford University Press.

4 EDUCATION

INTRODUCTION AND *HOCUS POCUS*

While we learn roles within the family and try to figure out what it is we are supposed to believe regarding the supernatural, many of us are introduced to another institution within the first years of life—education. For some, this begins very early with day care and preschool, where we are taught how to work with a few numbers and words, as well as how to get along with others. For others, the indoctrination begins around the fifth year of life with kindergarten. Much like religion, education is an institution with strong boundaries and seemingly little room for agency. Even college students are expected to pick majors within a specified range of choices (no options for those who might want to be sanitation workers, shoe salespersons, or restaurant waitstaff at the university where I teach, though there are majors for packaging, turf grass, and hospitality business). This process involves declaring a major, seeing advisers who will tell you what is needed to graduate, and filling out paperwork for loans, parking permits, and a meal plan. If a student is unable or unwilling to do these things, then good luck with graduation, even if you do meet all the requirements needed to leave in good standing.

Another similarity to religion is that education is thought of as a level playing field where all students are considered equal, or at least they are expected to have an equal chance of succeeding, regardless of the fact that only 36 percent of eligible people attended college in 2009, so the other 64 percent either could not or did not want to attend college. Still, education is thought as the one place that opens doors for rich and poor alike (religion has *open doors* for everyone, which is different from *opening doors*). This belief is so ingrained that in many Western countries education to a certain age is mandatory, and some parents will use any means necessary to find ways to continue education for their children for as long as possible. This includes sending older children to college even if they lack the necessary skills to read and write at the college level. Kurt Vonnegut portrayed this in *Hocus Pocus*, when his main character landed a job as a professor at Tarkington College located in Scipio, New York, which housed rich kids with learning disabilities:

The Moellenkamps were also Tarkingtons, since the founder of their fortune had married a daughter of the illiterate Aaron Tarkington. Eleven of them so far had been dyslexic, and they had all gone to college in Scipio, since no other institution of higher learning would take them (Vonnegut, *Hocus Pocus*: 17–18)

Vonnegut goes on to tell a story of how a mass escape at a nearby penitentiary leads to many of the prisoners walking across a frozen lake to the college. The escaped convicts take over the college, and one gets a sense that Vonnegut's underlying message is that the modern college experience is much like prison, where students learn so little that even those who cannot read or write can still succeed if they have the right connections, large amounts of money, or whine enough about their lot in life. This includes the student who follows Vonnegut's main character around so she can put together a case against this liberal—a liberal who happened to fight in the Vietnam War—who was living among the children of the rich and spreading progressive ideas.

My own story can also shed light on how the education system bounds our action. Much like Vonnegut's Moellenkamps and Tarkingtons, my parents had attended college (neither was dyslexic), so education was both important and unexceptional in the Ten Eyck household. I was the youngest of three children, and none of us did anything exceptional in our K–12 years, though some kind of continued education was expected. My brother graduated high school in 1979 and attended Southwestern Oregon Community College, but had no real direction. My sister graduated high school in 1981, and two years later graduated from cosmetology school in Eugene, Oregon. I graduated from North Bend (Oregon) High School in 1982 and enrolled at Portland State University, where I was accepted into the Sports Training program. I hoped to walk onto the baseball team.

There were signs during my junior and senior years of high school that may have predicted a hard time in taking that next step. The English portion of my SAT was so poor that I was told to take Introduction to Speech instead of Freshman English. My scores in math put me in college algebra, though I had decided to skip on math classes my senior year. What is more telling, however, is the level of dependency I had developed regarding educational structures. Homework was typically completed after arguing about it with my parents. Without their constant supervision, there was little motivation to study beyond the superficial reading of class material. In addition, all class registrations, photo cards, and other typical school things were given to students during their time in the North Bend Public Schools. There was very little I had to figure out for myself, and the assumption was that this was how all educational organizations worked.

As I mentioned earlier, my time as an undergraduate at Portland State University was short. While I rarely, if ever, skipped classes, I had no structure in place for managing my time outside the classroom or had any inkling of why it was important to study if I went to class. While I was allowed to play baseball with the junior varsity team my freshman year, I was asked to leave the Sports Training program, mainly because I was told I had to choose between sports training and baseball and I chose the latter, though nearly passing out while watching a first aid video in a sports medicine class did little to help my cause. Soon I was on academic probation with a GPA lower than 2.0. I was so out of my element that I even failed to acquire a photo ID, so was unable to check out books from the library. The dorm I lived in had no cafeteria, and we were expected to cook our own food; otherwise, I might have starved to death.

When I returned to Portland State my sophomore year, I registered for Animal Behavior, Public Speaking, and a few other classes for which I have no recollection. I received a 3.0 (B) in a few of the classes, and my favorite was Public Speaking. Not only was my partner attractive and intelligent, but the professor was fun, and I began to excel at giving speeches. Unfortunately, the intersection of agency and structure was not in my favor, as we were asked to give three speeches outside of class to receive a 4.0 (A). My partner took me to one of her student groups to give what I thought was to be one of our speeches. She went first, and after I gave my speech she jumped up again and gave another one. She asked me to give my second speech, which I refused to do, so she gave her third and final public speech. I told her that while her efforts did meet the requirements of the course, it did not seem to meet the underlying intentions of having us give three public speeches. I never did get around to scheduling two more speeches. It was another 2.0 on my Portland State University transcripts, though my overall GPA for that semester was over 2.5, and I had been traveling with the varsity baseball team during fall baseball practices and games. I truly thought my college experience had turned the corner.

Structure took over when I returned to Portland State after the 1983–1984 winter break. I had enrolled in a writing class and Animal Evolution before leaving, but when I returned to campus I was told that I had been dropped from both because of a lack of prerequisites. I had never talked to an adviser about my schedule (and still lacked a photo ID), and had made my own decisions on what courses to take. I was also out of money, had no idea how to apply for a student loan, and was told by the baseball coach that a scholarship was out of the question. The next day I wrote my parents a letter stating that by the time they received the letter, I would no longer be in college. The following morning, I pointed my car south and ended up in San Diego, where I landed a job in maintenance at Sea World.

Over the next few years, I would attend college at Lane Community College (Eugene, Oregon), the University of Wyoming, and Green River Community College (Auburn, Washington). I finally finished my bachelor's degree at Southern Illinois University–Carbondale on the McChord Air Force Base in Tacoma, Washington, in 1992—ten years after graduating from North Bend High School. While this is not the typical path for someone on the college track, it is not atypical that students enter and leave college before finishing. In fact, dropping out of college seems to be about as typical as completing in four years, according to Jeff Selingo in the *Journal of Higher Education* (http://chronicle. com/article/The-RiseFall-of-the/131036/, accessed May 2013), who notes that in one state alone—Pennsylvania—the graduation rate across colleges ranged from a high of 65 percent to a low of 24 percent, though graduation and dropout rates are often dependent on who is doing the counting and what their vested interests are. College administrators who would like to see higher completion rates to justify their efforts at running a college will find ways to boost numbers, while state legislators who must deal with budget issues may look for lower graduation rates as an excuse to cut state funding. Each group may use different means to develop their own standards and measures, but the actions of both can impact the quality of the education system.

Applying the sociological imagination to my own undergraduate college trajectory would take into account my parents' education: Both attended college, though only my father graduated after he, too, did poorly in academics at Oregon State University; he ended up at Oregon College of Education, which is now Western Oregon State University. I would also include the societal expectations for high school students with certain grades to attend college (I did graduate with honors from high school, though I was teetering on the edge by the end of my senior year), and my own performance in school, which would include grades and my attitude toward education more generally. The structures that are in place for high school students from middle-class families would have predicted that I would attend college. But a closer look at my own actions and behaviors during high school, especially the end of my junior year and throughout my senior year, may have given some indication that, without intervention, my trajectory through college would have been anything but straight. If you take all of these factors and use them to study other college students, you can begin to understand which factors have the greatest impact on the success of college students. You are now on your way to thinking like a sociologist.

EDUCATION, MONEY, AND *I AM CHARLOTTE SIMMONS*

Among parents, the tendency of expecting (even needing) children to go to college can often be linked to socioeconomic standing, as argued by Bourdieu (1984). Bourdieu found that education was one of the main institutions used to pass cultural and symbolic capital from one generation to the next. In many Western societies, what is learned in school is information that is most helpful for middle- and upper-class students. Think again of the majors that are and are not offered at most colleges and universities and the parental employment backgrounds of people from different socioeconomic classes. It is only in recent decades that some organizations of higher learning have offered classes on what are thought of as working-class jobs, and these places are often referred to as technical or vocational colleges. This is not a degradation of these organizations, and my undergraduate degree is in vocational education studies. The point is that technical skills such as logging, cooking, and auto mechanics were often thought of as something one did not need to attend college to learn. That has changed with advancements in the equipment used in many of today's manufacturing and natural resource jobs, so individuals who want those jobs have to spend time in the classroom learning how to diagnose an engine, use a computerized stamping or tool-and-die machine, or determine best logging management techniques and practices. Many graduates of traditional colleges would be completely lost in today's auto mechanic shop or on a forested hillside with a chainsaw in their hands. That may have been the case a hundred years ago, but the gap may have widened in some fields.

While new skills and technologies are now widely distributed in the home and classrooms, information technology can still divide a classroom and one student from another across schools (Wood & Howley, 2012). Many colleges and universities require students to have quick and ready access to computers, including laptops and tablets they can bring to the classroom. For students from well-funded suburban high schools, this seems normal, as computers have been part of both their home and school lives. There is, however, a digital divide along economic lines in the United States, within other countries, and even between countries. People from poorer families and poverty-stricken areas tend to have less access to information technologies, including something as seemingly basic and affordable as a desktop computer. Their families are too poor to afford one, and because they live in poor areas where the libraries and schools have few resources to purchase and maintain basic infrastructural resources. Such resources include information technology or subscriptions to Internet providers. These students quickly fall behind other students who do not face such challenges. The former students are most likely aware of computers, having seen them around town and in movies, but to be expected to learn how to use one while also navigating college can be a difficult task. Even if a college gives computers to underserved students, the students still need to understand how to connect to the Internet and what to do if the computer crashes or is dropped; these situations are outside their spheres of experience.

The digital divide is only one possible obstacle for the incoming student to overcome. Tom Wolfe's Charlotte Simmons was bright enough to do well in classes at DuPont, which is characterized as a prestigious college, but navigating her dorm mates early in her college career was a different issue, especially with family members in the general vicinity.

> The young men in the mauve T-shirts were pushing their heavy dollies through this cardboard chaos like icebreakers. On the landing of a stairwell near the elevator, there was a huge garbage can the color of drained veal with boxes, bubble paper, lacerated shrink-wrapping, Styrofoam peanuts, and other detritus gushing out of it. On the floor of the hallway, what you could see of it, were … dust balls … more dust balls than Charlotte had ever seen in her life … everywhere dust balls. Toward the far end of the corridor Charlotte spied two barefoot boys. One was clad only in a polo shirt and the towel he had wrapped about his waist. The other wore a longsleeved shirt with the tail hanging out over a pair of boxer shorts, and he had a towel slung across his shoulders. Boxer shorts? Both boys were scampering across the corridor into the men's bathroom, judging by the towels and the toilet kits they were carrying. But no pants? Charlotte was shocked. She glanced at Momma—and was relieved to see that she hadn't noticed. Momma would have been more than shocked. Knowing Momma … she would have brought God's lightning down on somebody's head. Charlotte hurried to her room, 516, which was fortunately just ahead of them (Wolfe, *I Am Charlotte Simmons*: 66–67).

DuPont was depicted in much the same way as Vonnegut's Tarkington, though more functional as far as the students being able to read, write, and do arithmetic. As with Tarkington, most of the students at DuPont were from wealthy families, while Charlotte and her Momma were poor and from a rural area. It was only because of an academic scholarship that Charlotte was at DuPont. It would be hard to write a story about a prestigious college in which only poor students attended, as few people would know what that would look like. We can also assume that parents from the middle or upper classes would not have "brought God's lightning down on somebody's head," after seeing boys running around the halls without pants. Chances are they had seen the same thing during their own time in college. This may help them understand that this is a time when many students are experimenting with sex and sexuality, and while the parents would like to see everyone dressed, they would know not to make a scene in front of their children. This would not only shame themselves but likely make it harder for their own sons and daughters to make friends.

Given all the difficulties students face in college, both inside and outside the classroom, maybe it would be better if more people passed on higher education. People like Glenn Beck (2012) would agree with such a statement. Education, however, does have its advantages. Take something as simple as knowing the difference between two people or things with similar names. Do you know the difference between Jean-Jacques Rousseau and Henri Rousseau? How about Charles Barkley and Gnarles Barkley? With both questions, I am asking you to distinguish between two things, so in that sense I am asking for the same *amount* of information. The *quality* of information, however, is treated much differently. We tend to be more impressed with the person who can tell us that Jean-Jacques Rousseau was a political theorist and Henri Rousseau a post-Impressionist painter than someone who knows that Charles Barkley was a basketball player and Gnarles Barkley a music group. Besides thinking the person who knows the difference between the Rousseaus is an insufferable bore, we are likely to think she is better educated than the individual who only knows the Barkleys. A potential employer who knows nothing else about these two individuals is likely to think the same thing. If you were that employer, whom would you be more willing to hire: a candidate with more education, or the one with less? While a good college experience provides more than just the tools needed to distinguish you from other job candidates, that is one of the outcomes we expect for putting up with half-naked students running around the dorms and attending boring lectures. The knowledge we gain and can use properly becomes part of the structures we experience and use throughout the rest of our lives.

TAKING A STEP BACK WITH *JANE EYRE*

Up to this point, I have focused mainly on the structures of higher education, so let me discuss how sociologists think about grades K–12. Herbert Spencer (1963) argues that laws for general education would slow down the truly exceptional students, as they would be in classes with others who would need more time and resources from teachers. C. Wright Mills, who writes about the sociological imagination, is also concerned about general education, contending that the United States could become a mass society through both the mass media and mass education. A mass society, according to Mills, is easily led by individuals such as Adolf Hitler and Joseph Stalin. The problem is that general education is taught through a common curriculum, and if that curriculum happens to carry messages of fascism or totalitarianism then everyone would come to want and expect such state structures (Gerhardt, 2011). Education is a great place to teach students what you want them to hear, a topic I will return to shortly.

Contemporary sociologists are also worried about our schools, though many do not see these organizations becoming hotbeds for Nazis or terrorist groups. Instead, they focus on concerns such as dropout rates and the continuing decrease in the rankings of U.S. schools within the global village. According to the National Center for Educational Statistics (nces.ed.gov), the percentage of kids between the ages of 16 and 24 who were not enrolled in high school and had not earned a high school diploma or General Education Degree (GED) ranged from a high of 12.1 percent in 1990 to a low of 7.4 percent in 2010 (the years in which these statistics were available).

However, not all ethnic groups are dropping out at the same rate. In 1990, for example, 32.4 percent of the Hispanic population in the age range were not in school and had failed to earn a high school diploma or GED, while the same could be said for only 4.9 percent of Asian/Pacific Islanders (9.0 percent of whites, 13.2 percent of blacks, and 16.4 percent of Native Americans fell into this category). The difference in dropout rates among these groups stems from various factors, including the neighborhood conditions where the kids lived. Crane (1991), for instance, found that children in poor neighborhoods were more likely to drop out of school and engage in other delinquent activities (e.g., teenage pregnancy) than kids in more affluent neighborhoods, regardless of where they went to school. This is what is known as the Epidemic Theory, and includes arguments that when children grow up in areas with few adults who finished school and work full-time jobs (what Crane referred to as professionals), they have little reason to believe that they are any different. In other words, social structures outside the classroom can play into a person's decision to drop out of school.

Sociologists have also looked at the efficacy of such policies as the No Child Left Behind Act (NCLB). This was passed in 2001 under President George W. Bush. According to its Statement of Purpose, "The purpose of this title is to ensure that all children have a fair, equal, and significant opportunity to obtain a high-quality education and reach, at a minimum, proficiency on challenging State academic achievement standards and state academic assessments" (http://www2.ed.gov/policy/elsec/leg/esea02/pg1.html#sec101, accessed May 2013). This would be accomplished, at least partly, by holding schools and teachers accountable for the progress of each and every student in their classrooms. If too many children were not meeting federal standards, then the school faced budget cuts.

The NCLB Act was supposed to close the gap between high- and low-achieving students by increasing the abilities of the latter group. Unfortunately, gaps can be closed by going the other way—lowering the expectations of high achievers so they are closer to those who are struggling, a concern voiced by Spencer over a hundred years ago. Lewis (2009) provides an example of this when he tells a story of an ancient Greek dictator cutting off the heads of any tall stalks of corn in a field, with the point being that no one should be preeminent in a democracy.

Another strategy is to change the test scores of low achievers, as was done by Atlanta school officials and teachers, as well as other school districts since the NCLB Act was passed (http://www.washingtonpost.com/blogs/answer-sheet/wp/2013/04/01/atlanta-test-cheating-tip-of-the-iceberg/, accessed May 2013). While policies such as NCLB are created with the best intentions, controlling an institution as large as the U.S. K–12 educational system is a monumental task, with many different ideas floating around concerning what is best. In fact, some commentators such as Glenn Beck (2012) would like to see all the teachers fired, the teacher unions disbanded before the better teachers are hired back, and to close most public universities due to their penchant for spreading progressive and liberal ideas.

Given all these concerns, it might be worth the time to think about what a general education—whether conservative or liberal—looks like. Many educators would say that schools are currently focused on the STEM disciplines—Science, Technology, Engineering, and Math—as these are the skills needed to succeed in the modern world. Our modern world is characterized by the technology treadmill in which everyone is clamoring to make and buy the newest gadgets. To compete against countries like China and India, U.S. students must learn how to work in labs, solve sophisticated mathematical formulas and logics, and engineer ever smaller, yet more powerful, technologies in various fields, ranging from making electric automobiles to constructing the newest cell phone. Such a society, according to Beck, Giddens, and Lash (1994), who wrote about reflexive modernity, is post-traditional in the sense that long-standing traditions—for instance, what students might learn from reading Homer and Socrates—become less important than "new" traditions like competing in technology and science fields to maintain our status as the world's superpower.

Whether students should be learning nanotechnology or Latin, poring over calculus books, or trying to complete pull-ups in gym is likely to be debated as long as there are schools, but students learn more than specific topics such as quadratic formulas and the three branches of the U.S. federal government. As with all organizations and institutions, schools have set structures that go beyond their manifest expectations of learning about various subjects. Students are also expected to learn how to properly act in social situations and to be truly middle or upper class, by realizing that they must be active consumers to help maintain our systems of production (Sarup, 1983). To do so, one must understand and be guided by the norms and expectations for behavior that reflect the values found among those groups. Understanding one's place in society is a latent function of education, while learning math and writing skills are the manifest functions of schools. Latent functions are the ones we might not be fully aware of, while manifest functions are clearly provided to us. This has changed very little over the years, as Charlotte Brontë depicts in *Jane Eyre*, first published in 1847:

"Would you like to go to school?"

Again I reflected: I scarcely knew what school was; Bessie sometimes spoke of it as a place where young ladies sat in the stocks, wore backboards, and were expected to be exceedingly genteel and precise: John Reed hated his school, and abused his master; but John Reed's tastes were no rule for mine, and if Bessie's accounts of school-discipline (gathered from the young ladies of a family where she had lived before coming to Gateshead) were somewhat appalling, her details of certain accomplishments attained by these same young ladies were, I thought, equally attractive. She boasted of beautiful paintings of landscapes and flowers by them executed; of songs they could sing and pieces they could play, of purses they could net, of French books they could translate; till my spirit was moved to emulation as I listened. Besides, school would be a complete change: it implied a long journey, an entire separation from Gateshead, an entrance into a new life (Brontë, *Jane Eyre*: 19).

For Jane Eyre, school was as much about learning new things as it was about gender roles (a topic that arises in most, if not all, institutions), including learning about music and painting, and how to sit in stocks, wear backboards, and practice being genteel and precise as a proper lady of the time should behave. None of this had anything to do with how to paint or translate French, let alone a topic like engineering. Such efforts continue today, as certain school administrators at eminent schools have been asked to step down from their posts after stating that there seem to be differences in the abilities of men and women in certain disciplines (such as the natural sciences versus the humanities). One of the more interesting aspects of such gender roles is that while historically we have expected women to learn to cook, paint, and write, it has been the men who have come to be known as leaders in many of these fields.

Part of the concern with what is taught and learned in U.S. schools is that the curriculum reflects the concerns of policy makers regarding how the United States ranks in terms of international education, instead of what is best for students. According to a 2010 ABC News report, the United States "ranks 25th in math, 17th in science, and 14th in reading out of the 34 Organization for Economic Cooperation and Development (OECD) countries" (http://abcnews.go.com/Politics/china-debuts-top-international-education-rankings/story?id=12336108, accessed May 2013). Schoolchildren in Shanghai ranked at the top of all three subjects, and while such rankings are always tenuous due to how educational standards are developed and measured, most rankings show that the United States is, at best, in the middle of the pack of developed nations in terms of education—and at worst, near the bottom. If education is truly the great equalizer, then it is fair to say that some countries, schools, and students are more equal than others. This is a critical perspective on education, as we realize that some students are in a better position to use the knowledge gained in school to further their own causes. How well we do in school in terms of the topics we choose to study, or are chosen for us, and our grades that are often as much about our lives outside of school as in the classroom, can have an impact on the next institution we encounter: work.

REFERENCES AND RECOMMENDED READINGS

Apple, M. W. (1996). "Power, Meaning and Identity: Critical Sociology of Education in the United States." *British Journal of Sociology of Education*, 17(2):125–44.

Beck, G. (2012). *Cowards*. New York: Threshold Editions.

Beck, U., Giddens, A., and Lash, S. (1994). *Reflexive Modernity*. Stanford, CA: Stanford University Press.

Bourdieu, P. (1984). *Distinction* (trans. Richard Nice). Cambridge, MA: Harvard University Press.

Brontë, C. (1922). *Jane Eyre*. London, UK: J. M. Dent and Sons.

Crane, J. (1991). "The Epidemic Theory of Ghettos and Neighborhood Effects on Dropping Out and Teenage Childbearing." *American Journal of Sociology*, 96 (5):1226–59.

Gerhardt, U. (2011). *The Social Thought of Talcott Parsons*. Burlington, VT: Ashgate.

Lewis, C. S. (2009). *The Screwtape Letters*. New York: HarperCollins e-books.

Sadovnik, A. R. (2010). *Sociology of Education* (2nd ed.). New York: Routledge.

Sarup, M. (1983). *Marxism/Structuralism/Education*. New York: Routledge.

Spencer, H. (1963). *Education*. Paterson, NJ: Littlefield, Adams.

Vonnegut, K. Jr. (1997). *Hocus Pocus*. New York: Penguin Books.

Wolfe, T. (2005). *I Am Charlotte Simmons*. New York: Macmillan.

Wood, L., and Howley, A. (2012). "Dividing at an Early Age: The hidden digital divide in Ohio elementary schools." *Learning, Media and Technology*, 37 (1):20–39.

5 WORK

INTRODUCTION: *THE JUNGLE*

Sociologists interested in labor issues have found that the kind of work you do is often related to your level of educational attainment (e.g., Blau, Brummund, & Liu, 2013), though going to college is no guarantee for finding a good-paying job. Factors such as what your parents did for a living, the color of your skin, your gender, and where you live can influence what jobs are available. When a person finds themselves coming from a working-class background, without an education and few other skills that are in demand, they may end up like Jurgis in Upton Sinclair's *The Jungle*. Jurgis has just gone through the death of a child in his family, so he is already dealing with difficult issues:

All this while that he was seeking for work, there was a dark shadow hanging over Jurgis; as if a savage beast were lurking somewhere in the pathway of his life, and he knew it, and yet could not help approaching the place. There are all stages of being out of work in Packingtown, and he faced in dread the prospect of reaching the lowest. There is a place that waits for the lowest man—the fertilizer-plant!

The men would talk about it in awe-stricken whispers. Not more than one in ten had ever really tried it; the other nine had contented themselves with hearsay evidence and a peep through the door. There were some things worse than even starving to death. They would ask Jurgis if he had worked there yet, and if he meant to; and Jurgis would debate the matter with himself. As poor as they were, and making all the sacrifices that they were, would he dare to refuse any sort of work that was offered to him, be it as horrible as ever it could? Would he dare to go home and eat bread that had been earned by Ona, weak and complaining as she was, knowing that he had been given a chance, and had not had the nerve to take it? And yet he might argue that way with himself all day, and one glimpse into the fertilizer works would send him away again shuddering. He was a man, and he would do his duty; he went and made application—but surely he was not also required to hope for success! (Sinclair, *The Jungle*: 151–52).

While many people could sympathize with Jurgis in not wanting to work at a fertilizer plant in the early 1900s (*The Jungle* was published in 1906), how dirty a job is might not be the most important aspect of whether someone likes what they do for a living. The dirtiness and safety of a job are important, as is pay. However, sociologists have found that control over one's work is often more important than how much one gets paid or the tasks one is expected to accomplish (Erikson & Vallas, 1990). If Jurgis could set his own hours, not worry about a supervisor looking over his shoulder, and set his own pace, the fertilizer plant may not have been as bad a place to work as it would seem, though many of us would still rather work a different job, even with lower pay and more supervision.

Control over our lives, including work, is very important when thinking about the world around us. Some of the top phobias, such as the fears related to flying, spiders and snakes, and public speaking, are as much about our lack of control as concerns with real physical dangers. Many more people die each year in automobile accidents than in airplane crashes, yet because we are not in control when we fly we are more likely to be worried about our safety. There may be a spider or snake crawling into your bed right now, and you have no control over that except to check the covers before you go home to take a nap, though the chances of that happening are less likely than food going bad in your kitchen (though we tend not to be so concerned about the food we handle). Few people die while giving public speeches, but when you step in front of a large group you have no idea what people think of your looks or way of talking, if there are people in the audience who know more than you, or whether all of your clothes are securely fastened (unbuttoned shirts, pants, dresses, etc.). In many of the factories portrayed in *The Jungle*, there are very few controls in place, ranging from workplace safety to the aesthetics of the building to setting your own hours and breaks. If nothing else, it would have been very hard to control the smell of a fertilizer factor in the early 1900s. Since Jurgis has little control over the workplace, he was going to experience a level of discomfort no matter what the task.

Efforts at control can also be found in small group tasks. The infamous Stanford Prison Experiment, in which groups of students were divided into prison guards and inmates showed how quickly we fall into the roles we are asked to play at work, even when the situation is fictional and everyone is aware of the randomness of the assignments (Haslam & Reicher, 2012). The students involved had signed up for the experiment, and on the morning it started, those who were randomly assigned to be guards took over a basement in one of the buildings on Stanford's campus that had been set up to look like a prison. The student inmates were arrested that same morning and brought to the basement in police cars (all arrests were fictional, and the students knew this). The student guards almost immediately began abusing the inmates, and most inmates quit within the first couple of days. The experiment was supposed to last a few weeks, but ended after six days. I have witnessed the same behaviors when asking students to lead a class. Even the quietest students can become dictatorial when given a position of power.

Much like families, schools, and other institutions, work provides us with scripts we are expected to follow to be successful in our roles as workers, managers, supervisors, teachers, etc. The Stanford Prison Experiment showed just how quickly we assume these roles when we are put in a work situation. These roles are so important in a capitalist society that many people find that their careers conflict with other roles they are expected to serve, such as a contributing member in a family. An individual who wants to be a successful financial adviser may find herself working 60 hours a week, spending fewer hours at home than either she or her family deems appropriate for a mother (the same could be said about a male who spends more time at work than at home, though as we have already seen that society has different expectations for men and women in both the workforce and in the home). This kind of role conflict can lead to such problems as physical illness from stress and marital discord from unmet expectations (Chassin et al., 1985).

Race and gender, both of which will be discussed in greater detail in Chapters 7 (Race) and 8 (Gender), were already mentioned as factors that can impact work opportunities and what is expected of someone once they land a job. Teachers in job-training programs tend to favor students of their own race, and hiring practices tend to show the same favoritism (Anderson, 1990). This includes looking at names on résumés, as employers often discriminate candidates whose names look to be attached to someone who is of a different race (such as a European American employer looking at a résumé from Latoya Johnson, as the name Latoya is often associated with African American females).

Gender can also impact an individual's access and success in the workplace (Thompson, 1982). Women are often thought to be best suited for "pink-collar" jobs such as secretarial work or selling cosmetics door-to-door, while men are more likely to be associated with blue-collar—manufacturing—and white-collar jobs—management and supervision. Once women are able to gain employment, they find that promotions stop at a certain point, while males hired at the same time with the same educational and experiential background continue to climb the corporate ladder. This is referred to as the glass ceiling, as women can see what is going on above them, but are unable to move beyond a certain level. Employers often point to femininity (unable to be strong in adverse situations) and aspects of a woman's biology (e.g., childbearing) to support their unwillingness to advance women beyond a certain level of authority. When women do break through the glass ceiling, their femininity and strategies for success are often called into question ("she's a bitch," or "she slept her way to the top"). Even when a woman is in the same position as a male, she often earns less money. As late as May 2013, the *Huffington Post* reported that on average, women would earn over $400,000 less than men over the course of a lifetime of work. To make up for such a shortfall, the average woman would have to work a decade longer than the average man (http://www.huffingtonpost.com/2013/05/09/gender-wage-gap_n_3245967.html, accessed May 2013).

OWNERSHIP OF LABOR AND *THE FOUNTAINHEAD*

Karl Marx (1965) argues that humans must work to gain a sense of self and belonging; that our labor separates us from other animals; and that history is created around the means of production. History, from this perspective, is generated out of the stories about how things are or were produced. Wars stem from unbalances in the means of production, as nations fight over the control of resources. We know that the societies of the ancient Greeks and Romans were made possible by agriculture production on a large scale largely through slave labor. Agriculture production and feudalistic ruling structures characterized Europe through the Middle Ages, and this began to change to capitalism with mercantilism. The Industrial Revolution brought about large factories and more economic prosperity to the business class. Capitalist societies are characterized by one group—the bourgeoisie—controlling the factories and means of production, and another—the proletariat—owning labor in the guise of their bodies and skill in doing certain jobs. Since those who make up the proletariat do not own the means of production, they must sell their labor to the bourgeoisie. The bourgeoisie are in business to make profits, so they will try to hire workers for as little as possible, including making them work long hours without compensation, such as more pay for overtime. These were the conditions throughout much of the 1800s and early 1900s, as factory owners paid very little to their workers. They hired children, and often did as little as possible to make sure that the work environment was safe and pleasant in factories and mines, and in building the nation's infrastructure. Such measures would have been costly and cut into the owners' profits.

The early labor unions and groups such as the Eight-Hour League were able to change some of these conditions, though most of us still like to think that we are the ones who control our work and would quit if treated poorly, or if our pay was cut. This is true for Ayn Rand's Howard Roark in *The Fountainhead*. Roark is a character with such strong convictions that he gets kicked out of architect school for not following the rules that students were expected to follow, as well as those who were entering the field:

> "Look here, Roark," said the Dean gently. "You have worked hard for your education. You had only one year left to go. There is something important to consider, particularly for a boy in your position. There's the practical side of an architect's career to think about. An architect is not an end in himself. He is only a small part of a great social whole. *Co-operation* is the key word to our modern world and to the professor of architecture in particular. Have you thought about your potential clients?"
>
> "Yes," said Roark.
>
> "The *Client*," said the Dean. "The Client. Think of that above all. He's the one to live in the house you build. Your only purpose is to serve him. You must aspire to give the proper artistic expression to his wishes. Isn't that all one can say on the subject?"
>
> "Well, I could say that I must aspire to build for my client the most comfortable, the most logical, the most beautiful house that can be built. I could say that I must try to sell him the best I have and also teach him to know the best. I could say it, but I won't. Because I don't intend to build in order to serve or help anyone. I don't intend to build in order to have clients. I intend to have clients in order to build."
>
> "How do you propose to force your ideas on them?"
>
> "I don't propose to force or be forced. Those who want me will come to me" (Rand, *The Fountainhead*: 14).

How many college students would be willing to talk that way to a dean, department chair, or professor if they knew their academic career was on the line? How many students would be willing to drop out of college with just a year or less left before earning a degree, especially with all the talk about how hard it is to get a decent job without a college education? How important are our convictions in the face of adversity? Roark ends up working in a rock quarry before he can get the right clients to support an architectural career that was off the beaten trail. The point Rand is trying to make through Roark is that more people need to be willing to sacrifice the easy life for even basic human principles, in the same way as the elites need to be left alone to make rules and to find the best ways to enforce those rules—no cutting off the heads of the fastest growing corn stalks. How would you choose between a job you enjoy doing and one that is frustrating but pays twice as much—especially if facing student loans, starting a family, and so forth? The answer may seem easy in fiction, but can be difficult in real life due to structures that are beyond our control.

Working in a rock quarry or as a highly esteemed architect will each have its advantages and disadvantages. The quarry worker does not have to worry about finding clients, but the work is hard and dirty to the point of being potentially life threatening. Possible dangers include an acute injury (being crushed by the rocks) and chronic illnesses such as contracting lung cancer through the inhalation of heavy dusts, as was the case of many of the men who worked on sculpting Mount Rushmore in the 1920s and 1930s (Smith, 1994). The architect's work is less physically demanding, though being able to create blueprints for a building will take more education and more student loans. Architects may have more freedom (agency) in their work, though that will be bounded by the ability to find clients and keep those clients happy.

The division of labor between physical work and mental work, as well as many other divisions based on socioeconomic standing, gender, age, and so forth, has interested sociologists for decades (Thompson, 1982). The goal behind some of these studies, often based on modern manufacturing and service industries, is to figure out how to be most efficient in a factory, office, on a delivery route, and so on. Henry Ford is thought to be one of the first individuals to bring into the factory management science, which he used to make assembly lines more productive. His approach came to be referred to as Fordism, and it is under this practice that workers are expected to repeat a certain task repeatedly, which, in turn, divides the workforce into various sectors. While each task was considered minimal during Ford's time (and this practice continues today), all the tasks combined result in a finished product, such as a car in the Ford factories.

While early assembly lines made work more efficient, they also led to numerous concerns with workers' welfare. Concepts such as alienation and anomie became part of the language of the sociology of work within capitalistic labor practices. Alienation is used to describe a person who feels they are no longer part of the production process—their work feels alien to them, especially if much of it is done by machines. Alienation is still useful in thinking about how workers try to make sense of their efforts in a technologically advanced society. Anomie is used to describe a feeling of disconnectedness from society on a larger scale. If humans are supposed to make sense of themselves through their work but their work is meaningless, they can feel as if there is no longer any reason to be part of the human race. Both alienation and anomie are reflexes to assembly lines and technological advancements in the workplace.

There is little reason to believe that a company would be concerned with its workers' well-being unless it is forced to do so. According to Marx, companies have to spend money in two ways—on fixed capital and variable capital. Fixed capital includes items such as buildings and machinery. A restaurant, for example, would find it hard to exist without a place for people to sit and eat, and even carry-out places need a place to cook and serve their customers and equipment to cook with (even food trucks need to have equipment to prepare food or ovens to keep food hot that has been cooked elsewhere). While employers may be able to cut costs related to fixed capital by purchasing used equipment or having suppliers bid for their business, these are costs that are integral to the running of a business.

Variable capital, on the other hand, consists of the inputs companies use for their product. In our restaurant example, variable capital would include the food that is purchased from other vendors (such as Gordon Food Systems) and wages for employees. The cost of food can range from purchasing quality food from local farmers who ask for a premium for their products, to buying in bulk from a national buyer who warehouses millions of gallons (or pounds) of product throughout the country and can have it shipped to the restaurant in the back of a refrigerated truck. A meal at the restaurant that serves only locally produced food will probably be more expensive than one that provides its customers with food wrapped in waxed paper.

Wages work in the same way. Marx pointed out that the only way the owner of a business can make money is to pay his workers less than what the products the workers make are selling for. If a worker puts in eight hours a day and makes eight widgets that sell for $10 dollars each in a store, the owner should be paying that worker $80. The worker makes the widgets that brought in $80 to the company. This, however, is a formula for bankruptcy in a capitalist system. Not only does the owner have to pay the workers a minimum wage as set by government policy, she must also pay for the buildings in which the widgets are made, the lighting that is used by the workers to see the widgets they are making, the raw material used for the widgets, and her own income. If an owner has 100 employees who make enough widgets to sell 800 widgets every day at $10 a piece, that would be equal to roughly $240,000 a month coming back to the factory. If we assume that half of that money is used for inputs, the costs of running the infrastructure, and the owner's profits, that would leave the company with $120,000 for employees. If each employee works four 40-hour weeks each month, that equals 16,000 employee hours—which means employees will be making about 75¢ an hour. The employer is way out of minimum wage compliance in the United States, and must either find cheaper inputs, cut back her personnel, charge more for widgets, or move the operation overseas, where such a wage would be acceptable.

Compliance with rules and regulations in the workplace brings up the topic of unions and their role in developing policies on issues such as wages, benefits, and workplace safety (e.g., Skurzynski, 2009). All of their efforts, however, have not kept some people from seeing unions as problematic in the United States. Unions are appreciated because they have helped protect workers from getting injured, stopped child labor practices, increased wages to where an individual can live while working in a factory, and so forth. They are vilified, or at least questioned, regarding suspected ties to government officials, crime syndicates, and even the business owners—including stockholders—from whom they are supposed to be protecting the workers. Workers pay dues to their unions so that union officials can have time to create and negotiate contracts with companies, an undertaking that is complex in terms of the legal expectations of contracts, as well as the desires of both the workers and the companies. Unions were once considered a major force in all levels of politics, though union membership has declined from 20.1 percent of all wage earners in 1983 to 11.3 percent in 2012 (http://www.bls.gov/news.release/union2.nr0.htm, accessed May 2013). Unions are still considered a political force in states such as Michigan and Ohio, but have become less powerful in other places, as jobs that were once a stable for unions (e.g., autoworkers and paper and pulp mill workers) have either disappeared or been moved overseas. Unions might structure workers' contracts, but the absence of unions leads to other structures being constructed by the companies.

BEING OUT OF WORK AND *THE POSTMAN*

Being alienated from work and feeling anomic may seem like the end of the line for many people as work becomes meaningless. There is, however, another divide that might be worse for some people, and that is the line between being employed and unemployed, as mentioned in the passage from *The Jungle*. From a sociological viewpoint, there are many dimensions to work, including the person without a salaried career but who does housework, and the individual who survives in an underground economy by selling pirated software and movies, selling drugs, or working as a prostitute (e.g., Richardson & Pisani, 2012). In fact, when work becomes nonexistent for a large portion of the population, the presence of someone who is working can make for a volatile showing, as in David Brin's postapocalyptic novel, *The Postman*:

The townsfolk blinked in astonishment. Most of them had not even moved, but stared at his uniform, and the shiny badge on his peaked hat. The true danger that faced them they could try to ignore, but *this* fantastic story had to be swallowed whole, or not at all.

For a long moment the tableau held—and Gordon stared them down until it broke.

All at once men were shouting at one another, running about to gather weapons. Women hurried to prepare the horses and gear. Gordon was left standing there—his poncho like a cape whipping behind him in the blustery wind—cursing silently while the Harrisburg guard turned out around him (Brin, *The Postman*: 126–27).

It is not enough to understand that Gordon is working as, or actually impersonating, a postman. The structures that the postal uniform symbolize go well beyond delivering mail for a group that believes civilization has ended. This is true of the uniforms worn by the police, military personnel, nurses, and religious leaders. These uniforms, and the people who wear them, encompass consistency, which is why some people have been able to use uniforms to pull off crimes. When we see a police officer, we expect that individual to be following a specific set of rules, and that we are to follow their lead. Their work is as much about a specific task as the structures they are helping to uphold. This is why impersonating certain people such as a police officer or a priest is considered a criminal act, even if the person is engaged in behaviors we would not normally consider deviant or criminal.

A uniform can also be symbolic of work and identity at a more abstract level. We typically do not have to ask an individual wearing a uniform what they do for a living, though that is a question we often ask when meeting an adult for the first time, or after coming across a friend we have not seen for years. The uniform provides both the wearer and the observer all the information necessary to know what that person does for a job. It is an objectification that precedes or coincides with externalization. It keeps one from having to answer the question of what one does for a living, and a uniformed person is rarely put in a position of having to say that he is unemployed or "between jobs." It is interesting to note that we often blame a person's character as the reason behind being out of work when we run across someone who is unemployed, but will blame the economy or some other social structure when *we* are out of a job.

Being unemployed and without a uniform that symbolizes being part of the workforce are both a matter of agency and structure, as one can look for jobs even in a bad economy or decide to sit at home and wait for the phone to ring, though the availability of jobs is likely outside any one person's control. According to Bellin and Miller (1990), part of employment and unemployment is the distribution of jobs; another factor is policies created to put people to work; and yet another is appropriate training and motivation among workers. Those looking for work have to take all of this into consideration, which can become daunting to the point of giving up. The official unemployment rate only takes into account those people who are still trying to navigate these structures by actively looking for work. Bellin and Miller argue that the true unemployment rate should be at least double the number reported in the news, as we need to understand that some people are out of work but have given up the quest to find employment, so are no longer counted by groups such as the Bureau of Labor Statistics, which keeps track of such numbers.

Once someone stops looking for work, as was the case for many of the people in Brin's novel (though there were no jobs in the sense we think of them), he must turn to other means for survival. Ferman (1990) points to seven different types of irregular employment used in various exchange relationships (some for money, some for food or other products) that are utilized by those without full-time employment or the means to pay their bills. These include making and/or selling products; for instance, selling pirated music or selling blankets out of the back of a van in an abandoned supermarket's parking lot, providing services in other people's homes such as cleaning services, personal services such as taking in clothes for alterations, getting paid "under the table" by an established business, renting property, providing entertainment for others, and criminal activities. One of the more interesting questions about these types of work is whether people feel more connected to their efforts in these types of tasks than if they were working for a large company at a repetitive task, even though the risks of staying in the irregular or underground economy can be much higher in terms of a steady income, being harassed by the police, or being drawn into criminal organizations from which can be difficult to disengage.

RETIREMENT

Most of us want to stop working at some point. So why would a sociologist be concerned about what we do once we stop working? Once someone retires, they can do anything they like, right? Not necessarily—there are many structures that are either still in play from when people were working or once they retire. This can be as commonsensical as having enough money to live comfortably, or having to find another line of work that will hire older workers, like the smiling face of the greeter at Wal-Mart, to the complex relationship between one's race and access to health care during old age. While I will discuss end-of-life issues in the next chapter, retirement is often thought of as both the golden age in a person's life and the time to start thinking about getting your affairs in order for those who will be left behind.

Returning to the sociological imagination, thoughts on retirement should take into account historical contexts and individual biographies. The former relates to issues such as how many people are retiring and what structures have been put in place to afford them a comfortable living. This is a concern in the United States as the baby boomers get older, retire, and expect the younger generation to help fund programs like Social Security and Medicare. If there are more retirees who were born between 1946 and 1964 than there are workers born in later years, government funding that supports the elderly through taxes could become overburdened. If every able-bodied worker has to support two retirees in addition to themselves and family members, such a situation will be difficult to sustain. In numerous developed countries such as Germany, the current birth rate is lower than the projected retirement rate, which could lead to funding crises within various government agencies. One solution that has been put forward in these countries is to increase the retirement age. Such policies are rarely welcomed with open arms.

Demographic shifts are only one component of history that we need to consider to understand retirement. Innovations in medical technology have led to longer life expectancies, so retirement programs that were put in place when workers were expected to die shortly after retirement are now having to support someone for a decade or more. The life expectancy in 2008 for males in the United States was 75 years and 81 years for females (http://www.cdc.gov/nchs/data/nvsr/nvsr61/nvsr61_03.pdf, accessed May 2013), which is a decade longer than the life expectancies in the 1950s. As companies restrict or cut their retirement programs as cost-cutting measures, the opportunities for retirees to enjoy their retirement become more restricted.

Individual situations should also be taken into account. If a person makes it to retirement age and still has young dependents at home, that individual may find it hard to be both retired and financially stable. This is also true of workers who have reached retirement age but are supporting elderly parents—a more common occurrence with longer life expectancies. Workers who are self-employed, work in low-income jobs, or small employers with no retirement plans may find that retirement is out of the question. These types of working conditions offer little support for those leaving the workforce, and so the worker becomes dependent on government funding. Living in an area with community support for seniors (community centers, active religious organizations, and entertainment options for the elderly) may make retirement more feasible and enjoyable. Those living in isolated rural areas or low-income urban areas may find that such opportunities are missing. Retirement in these areas can become an exercise in living alone, while staying at work would mean continued interaction with others. In short, sociologists are very interested in what is and is not available for those who are contemplating retirement, as well as why some people who do have options available to them continue to work. As with all the other institutions discussed, retirement is a combination of structure and agency that forms a complex social web for those trying to navigate a major transition in their lives.

REFERENCES AND RECOMMENDED READINGS

Adams, G. A., and Beehr, T. A. (2003). *Retirement*. New York: Springer.

Anderson, E. (1990). "Racial Tension, Cultural Conflict, and Problems of Employment Training Programs," pp. 214–34. In *The Nature of Work*, edited by K. Erikson and S. P. Vallas. New Haven, CT: Yale University Press.

Blau, F. D., Brummund, P., and Liu, Y.-H. A. (2013). "Trends in Occupational Segregation by Gender 1970–1980: Adjusting for the impact of changes in the Occupational Coding System." *Demography*, 50: 471–92.

Bellin, S. S., and Miller, S. M. (1990). "The Split Society," pp. 173–91. In *The Nature of Work*, edited by K. Erikson and S. P. Vallas. New Haven, CT: Yale University Press.

Brin, D. (2011). *The Postman*. New York: Random House Digital.

Chassin, L., Zeiss, A., Cooper, K., and Reaven, J. (1985). "Role Perception, Self-Role Congruence and Marital Satisfaction in Dual-Worker Couples with Preschool Children." *Social Psychology Quarterly*, 48(4): 301–11.

Erikson, K., and Vallas, S. P. (1990). *The Nature of Work*. New Haven, CT: Yale University Press.

Ferman, L. A. (1990). "Participation in the Irregular Economy," pp. 119–40. In *The Nature of Work*, edited by K. Erikson and S. P. Vallas. New Haven, CT: Yale University Press.

Haslam, S. A., and Reicher, S. (2012). "Tyranny: Revisiting Zimbardo's Stanford Prison Experiment," pp. 126–41. In *Social Psychology*, edited by J. S. Smith and S. A. Haslam. Thousand Oaks, CA: Sage.

Marx, K. (196)5. *Das Kapital* (edited by Friedrich Engels). Chicago: Henry Regnery Company.

Rand, A. (2005). *The Fountainhead*. New York: Penguin.

Richardson, C., and Pisani, M. J. (2012). *The Informal and Underground Economy of the South Texas Border*. Austin: University of Texas Press.

Sinclair, U. (1906). *The Jungle*. Doubleday, Page and Company.

Smith, R. A. (1994). *The Carving of Mount Rushmore*. New York: Abbeville Press.

Skurzynski, G. (2009). *Sweat and Blood*. Minneapolis: Twenty-First Century Books.

Terkel, S. (1987). *Working*. New York: The New Press.

Thompson, P. (1982). *The Nature of Work*. London: Macmillan Press.

Volti, R. R. (2011). *Introduction to the Sociology of Work and Occupations*. Thousand Oaks, CA: Sage.

6 DEATH AND DYING

INTRODUCTION AND *AS I LAY DYING*

You might think—maybe even hope—a chapter on death and dying would come at the end of a book, not somewhere near the beginning or even in the middle. In addition, you may be wondering how death and dying are an institution like family, religion, education, and work, as there can be little agency in death. Who could still be worried about social or natural structures after they are gone? Death, however, has always affected more than just the person who has died, and as such has been a major social institution that continues to grow in our consumer society. Take a look in a phone book or conduct an Internet search of any city, and you will find numerous listings for funeral homes, cemeteries, hospice facilities, monument construction, and services for the grieving, including counseling and support groups. There are also thousands, if not millions, of websites dedicated to the deceased (family members, celebrities, friends), as well as things (memorials to pets, cars, clothes, etc.). A quick Internet search on "Elvis Presley memorial" came back with nearly four million hits. Social network developers (such as Facebook) are currently reviewing policies related to the creation of memorial pages, as we have what sociology calls a "cultural lag" in terms of grief netiquette. Families and "friends" have had numerous conflicting opinions on whether social network formats are appropriate for death notification and support for those close to the deceased.

Besides being a social institution that structures our lives, as well as the ones around us who are reminded of their own mortality in the face of a family member or friend's passing, death also structures our bodies. As Strauss (1993: 110) states, "every action or interaction requires a body in action. ... " Strauss goes on to argue that because bodies act, they should be considered agential. At the same time, bodies are unable to do certain things, so they structure action. Human bodies cannot fly without assistance. A body cannot travel at the speed of light, and it cannot continue without a beating heart, working lungs, and all the things that sustain these activities (food, water, air). Disabilities, injuries, and death make us aware of our bodies' agency and structure.

The end of the functioning body and its agency and structure comes in many guises, and end-of-life issues have become of interest to scholars who find patterns in our behaviors at this time in our lives. Elisabeth Kübler-Ross (1969) argues that we go through five stages when facing death in a situation, such as being told we have a terminal illness. The process begins with denial, as we try to tell ourselves and everyone else that we are actually fine, while managing emotions to protect ourselves and those around us. This is followed by anger, as we come to realize that we are not fine. Once we realize that anger is not making us any better, we turn to bargaining with higher life forms. If God, Allah, Buddha, and others will spare us, we promise to do great things with the extra years we are given. If the miracle of recovery from a terminal illness does not take place, we become depressed before accepting our fate. This approach to grieving for ourselves was universal in the late 1960s, so much so that counseling protocols for terminally ill patients were developed to take into account each stage and to help people reach that final stage of acceptance, so that their bodies and minds could be at peace for as long as possible. Recent research points out that although Kübler-Ross's work was relevant at the time, and she brought an awareness to the importance of the study of the experience of dying, her work has been misinterpreted. We have learned, for example, that although death is universal, grief is not (Howarth, 2007), and that not all dying people go through "stages"; yet there are similar patterns experienced at the end of life as one works through their own death and the grief and loss it creates.

Sociologists also find these patterns interesting, as they point to trends in how a society deals with death. While each death is an individual experience, the fact that we tend to approach it in very similar ways indicates a socialization process concerning the meaning of death. When we are denied something in a consumer society, which means that we believe we can purchase things that will make us happy, we try to find ways to acquire what we have been denied, including getting angry or depressed. Death flies in the face of youthfulness and longevity—things we are told we can buy through gym memberships and plastic surgery—and news that our bodies are aging and dying tends to trigger a desire to purchase something that will make us better. Thus, we enter into our own "grief work," as first set out in the stages outlined by Kübler-Ross. It is only when we come to realize that all the bargaining that worked with other consumer products does not work with death that we finally accept our fate. While such a theory can be tested today—do people still go through stages as they approach the end of their lives?—it would be difficult to determine if this is a product of consumerism, or if people have always faced death in the same manner. We have little evidence of people's interpretation of death over history, besides being gloried in battle and so forth. In addition, if people were unaware of these stages, how would they know to think in this way? Is the meaning of death controlled by experts like Kübler-Ross and others since her time, or do we come to understand death through other forms of knowledge and experience that are captured by these experts? In other words, can I know that I will go through stages of emotions when facing death without reading about it, or do I start understanding my emotions in these specific ways because I have been told about them? Will there be stages, phases, and tasks to work through to effectively process my grief after I lose someone significant? These are interesting questions to sociologists studying death and dying, as well as to people who make a living by writing books and counseling people who face these issues.

Besides death and grieving becoming consumer goods in modern society, studies have found social structures linked to various forms of death. One such study on suicides was conducted by Emile Durkheim. *On Suicide* (2006), first published in 1897, focuses on how memberships in groups affect suicide rates. Protestants, for example, are more likely to commit suicide than Catholics. According to Durkheim, this could be explained by the understanding that Catholics are more closely tied to other Catholics, so ending their lives would be more devastating to the group than Protestants, who were more likely to believe in personal salvation. When a Protestant decides that he or she is no longer worthy of living, the links to other Protestants are loose enough that they do not have to be considered to the same extent as a Catholic when deciding one's fate. Durkheim also looks at married and unmarried persons, people in the military versus civilians, and so forth. While Durkheim's work has been criticized for various reasons, it shows that early sociologists were trying to figure out how something as seemingly personal as suicide is tied to larger social structures. His conclusions point to the fact that social circumstances can impact something as seemingly individualistic as taking one's own life.

More recent work on suicide has included the growth of information technology. Bollen and Phillips (1982) found that suicides in the United States tend to increase (i.e., copycat suicides) after a highly publicized suicide, even if the death is fictional such as a character committing suicide on a soap opera or in a movie. Along the same lines, Stack and Gundlach (1992) found links between listening to country music and suicide rates among European Americans in urban areas. Even though these studies have been questioned, they highlight the fact that much like Durkheim, contemporary sociologists continue to look for ways in which structures impact our decisions and actions.

The medical profession, often thought of as an institution focused on prolonging life, has also started playing a larger role in end-of-life decisions. Modern debates over the role of a physician have evolved from the notion of giving life to one of alleviating suffering. If a person is terminally ill and living with constant pain, who is to say whether or not that person has the right to die? At the time of this writing, only three states (Oregon, Washington, and Vermont) have legalized doctor-assisted euthanasia (even use of the terms "euthanasia" and "suicide" are part of this debate in many areas, as opponents of assisted deaths are more likely to call it suicide, if not murder, while proponents tend to refer to the issue as euthanasia and physician-assisted death), while other states have made it a criminal offense for anyone, including doctors, to assist another person in ending his or her life. Web sites have also been developed to help people with this process, such as the Hemlock Society.

While we often think that the person dying is the one most affected by death, members of other institutions and organizations are also impacted. When a state legalizes physician-assisted suicide, medical organizations within that state will most likely need to change some of their approaches to serving terminally ill patients. When this happens, the institution of medicine may also begin to change, as concerns regarding appropriate ethics will begin to be explored at conferences and in the news. Family members, as well as the institution of the family, are also likely to be affected by the death of a member, and rates of death that would impact our understanding of the institution of family. Within a family, a death may have dire consequences if that person is the sole breadwinner. If nonterminal suicide rates increase, people may begin to question the role of the family in helping people cope with crises in their lives. If fathers start dying in large numbers, we may start redefining the role of a father in the family.

The role of death in structuring actions is found in many novels and nonfictional accounts of people's lives. William Faulkner's *As I Lay Dying* provides an in-depth look at death and its effect on a group of people. The following excerpt gives the reader a sense of his thoughts:

> The girl is standing by the bed, fanning her. When we enter she turns her head and looks at us. She has been dead these ten days. I suppose it's having been a part of Anse for so long that she cannot even make that change, if change it be. I can remember how when I was young I believed death to be a phenomenon of the body; now I know it to be merely a function of the mind—and that minds of the ones who suffer the bereavement. The nihilists say it is the end; the fundamentalists, the beginning; when in reality it is no more than a single tenant or family moving out of a tenement or a town (Faulkner, *As I Lay Dying*: 43–44).

Whether death is a beginning or an end—a wall or a door—for the individual dying is open to interpretation, and science can do very little to prove what happens during and after death. Faulkner, however, was right in saying that a death is an end and a beginning for those who are left behind, and how much of each is open to negotiations at both the individual and societal level. The process of letting someone go is known as bereavement, and while it is universally observed among individuals and groups, it is not practiced uniformly across cultures. Bereavement ranges from a short time of sorrow for immediate family members, to isolating widows or family members from the rest of the community for a specified amount of time. When the grieving period is over, those who lost a loved one are expected to reenter society in a productive way. Those who cannot let go of the departed are often thought of as being mentally or physically ill.

One way family members and friends can maintain connections to the deceased is through memorials. In countries like the United States this historically was accomplished through grave markers and holidays such as Memorial Day, Veterans Day, or All Saints Day. Today, one can set up memorials on various websites, providing an opportunity to change ideas about the deceased as the days, weeks, months, and years pass (sites such as www. muchloved.com offer electronic memorials with numerous options of what can be posted and how people maintaining the memorial can make changes to their posts).

Virtual memorials are an example of how death has become a consumer product. The consumption of death, in fact, has become a big business. Besides websites, tours of places where death has occurred have been added to the consumer goods of cemetery plots, funeral homes, and counseling services. Such tours include places where genocide has occurred, or a concentration camp—or where a famous person was killed such as Dealey Plaza in Dallas, where John F. Kennedy was assassinated, or in Chicago, where bank robber John Dillinger was killed by police. The importance and expense of death is not new, as the pyramids and other enormous monuments have been built in honor of kings and other famous people upon their death. This practice continues in many forms. One of the more interesting funerals in recent U.S. history took place in Chicago in 1984. A gangster known as Willie the Wimp was buried in a coffin made to look like a car with his hands on the steering wheel and hundred dollar bills sticking out between his fingers. The funeral was described in a song titled "Willie the Wimp," by Stevie Ray Vaughn, who died in a plane crash a few years after recording that song. Such memorials become structures of how we think of our own lives and deaths, as well as how society treats the passing of its members. To prove that you were an important person in life, your death cannot be summed up by a cardboard box filled with ashes. Your remains must be placed in an urn that looks like it belongs on the hearth of a majestic castle. Media stories have shed light on some funeral home employees taking advantage of these desires, as well as the fragile emotional state of their clients, to find ways to make funerals and memorials more extravagant (and expensive), though this seems to be the exception rather than the rule of memorial services.

THE LEGITIMATION OF DEATH AND *ALL QUIET ON THE WESTERN FRONT*

Suicides and individual passing by natural causes or otherwise are not the only types of death that sociologists try to make sense of. Given that most religions, and even secular societies, frown upon the taking of another's life (as well as our own life, in many cases), it is somewhat of an enigma that society sanctions death in instances of self-defense, capital punishment, and war (to say nothing of the debate over abortion). Many of us would be horrified at the thought of stabbing another person under most circumstances, yet popular scenes from books and movies are based on such brutality, as when Paul Bäumer stabs a French soldier in Erich Maria Remarque's *All Quiet on the Western Front*:

Comrade, I did not want to kill you. If you jumped in here again, I would not do it, if you would be sensible too. But you were only an idea to me before, an abstraction that lived in my mind and called forth its appropriate response. It was that abstraction I stabbed. But now, for the first time, I see you are a man like me. I thought of your hand-grenades, of your bayonet, of your rifle; now I see your wife and your face and our fellowship. Forgive me, comrade. We always see it too late. Why do they never tell us that you are poor devils like us, that your mothers are just as anxious as ours, and that we have the same fear of death, and the same dying and the same agony—Forgive me, comrade; how could you be my enemy? If we threw away these rifles and this uniform you could be my brother just like Kat and Albert. Take twenty years of my life, comrade, and stand up—take more, for I do not know what I can even attempt to do with it now (Remarque, *All Quiet on the Western Front*: 106).

Such killings are legitimated or justified, by saying that we were only following orders, and that all is fair in love and war. Remarque, however, showed how even in the heat of battle, taking another's life can be extremely traumatizing—to the point of even being willing to give years of one's own life if it would bring back the fallen enemy. This scene was set in the trenches of the First World War, and the justified killings and subsequent trauma have not stopped. Kelman and Hamilton (1989) studied various accounts of the My Lai Massacre that took place during the Vietnam War. U.S. troops were told by commanding officers to enter the village of My Lai and engage hostile forces. When the troops reached the village, they found that it was populated mostly by women, children, and old men. At some point, soldiers began shooting the villagers—there are various and contradictory reports about how and why the shooting started—leading to the deaths of many unarmed civilians. When an investigation was conducted as to what went wrong, the soldiers said they were just following orders. According to the soldiers' perspective, the commanding officers and intelligence personnel said that there were hostiles in the area, the soldiers could be severely disciplined if they did not follow those orders, and anyone could have been carrying a bomb or weapon, including a child. Those who gave the orders for the excursion said that no orders were given to kill unarmed villagers. The soldiers were only supposed to see what was happening in the area. In other words, no one was responsible, though everyone could agree that innocent people died in My Lai, and that it could be blamed, at least partly, on the fact that a war was going on at the time. One of the more interesting findings during the investigation and subsequent court hearings was that those who refused to fire upon the villagers were likely to be new to the fighting in Vietnam. Much like Durkheim's work on suicides, the willingness to shoot people seems to be linked to how connected one is to the military. Those who have served longer are more likely to follow the orders of their commanders, no matter what the situation. Those who are new to armed conflict are more likely to question decisions being made by individuals sitting in offices far removed from the front lines. These new soldiers saw the people in the village as harmless.

War is not the only government-sanctioned death. Capital punishment is also legal and typically justified in two ways: that the person did something that was punishable by death (e.g., killing another person in a premeditated way, sedition, raping a helpless infant or other innocent individual like an elderly person), and that it is the state that carries out the killing. The use of capital punishment in the United States is not an issue we tend to agree on as a society, though a majority of the public would choose a different form of punishment for offenders; at least, that was the case in 2010 (http://www.deathpenaltyinfo. org/public-opinion-about-death-penalty, accessed May 2013). Regardless of public opinion, over 1200 people have been executed in the United States since 1976, though we are not the leading country when it comes to carrying out death penalties. According to a 2011 report in *The Guardian* (http://www. guardian.co.uk/news/datablog/2011/mar/29/death-penalty-countries-world, accessed May 2013), China leads the world in that category (the United States is often one of the top ten countries to carry out legal executions), and the forms of execution vary widely across the globe:

> Methods of execution included beheading, electrocution, hanging, lethal injection and various kinds of shooting (by firing squad, and at close range to the heart or the head). Public executions were known to have been carried out in Iran, North Korea, Saudi Arabia and Somalia. In Saudi Arabia, executions are usually beheadings with a sword. In one case recorded by Amnesty [International], a Sudanese man's head was sewn back onto his body and hung from a pole in a public place.

In each of these cases, government structures were used to find the person responsible for a crime, pass down a death sentence, determine the method of execution, and carry out the execution.

When such justifications among governments or groups of people are carried to an extreme, we find genocide (Kiernan, 2009). Genocide is the act of attempting to exterminate a group of people. Such atrocities have occurred for thousands of years, including the U.S. government's attempt to eradicate Native Americans while the government tried to expand into the Natives' territories. One of the more widely known acts of genocide is the Holocaust, which took place between approximately 1941 and 1945 during the Second World War. Nearly six million Jews and others deemed unfit for living were summarily executed or died by means of forced labor and starvation by the Nazi regime and its allies. Other modern genocides have occurred in Africa between Tutsis and Hutus, in central Europe between Serbians and Croatians, and in the Middle East between Iraqis and Kurds. Governments often try to deny or ignore their roles in genocide, and only recently have governments started to offer apologies and concessions. An example of this is the Australian government apologizing to the Australian Aboriginal community it began wiping out shortly after coming to the country to set up a penal colony in the late 1700s.

Sociologists who study these forms of death—capital punishment, war, genocide, etc.—often think about them in terms of the abuse or misuse of power. Why would a governing body like the Australian government be threatened by an aboriginal population that had only a few primitive weapons at their disposal? It may have been that their rituals seemed threatening, the fact that they did not practice religion in the same way as the invading British, that their language was strange, that they looked different, or any number of events or interpretations that led the British forces to see the aboriginals as a threat (Hughes, 1986). The same approach can, and has been, used to understand other genocide, as one group typically does not seek to exterminate another group unless it is feared on some level. In the end, the ability to hire one group (the military) to kill another group and have it considered legal puts one in a very powerful position.

FINDING MEANING IN DEATH AND *WHERE THE RED FERN GROWS*

Whenever someone or something we are close to dies, we often try to find meaning in that death. Why put in all the blood, sweat, and tears of life if, in the end, we simply become part of the earth through burials or cremation and are then forgotten? Is an altruistic suicide, in which someone forfeits his own life for the preservation of others, more meaningful in the afterlife than an egotistical suicide, where a person takes her life because of her own needs and desires? Does the altruistic person deserve a bigger monument in the cemetery, or more hits on their Internet memorial site? Those left behind may be equally devastated and look for reasons why their loved ones are no longer with them.

The desire to find meaning in death, and therefore meaning in life, has been captured in numerous ways by authors throughout history. Hollywood borrows from these authors, such as Remarque's *All Quiet on the Western Front*, to create movies that make audiences think more deeply about death. This is also true with losing pets, a powerful experience for those who have had to say good-bye to a nonhuman best friend. The following is from *Where the Red Fern Grows*, by Wilson Rawls, a story about the adventures of a young boy and his two dogs. The book was aimed at young adults, and made into a movie in 1974, with a remake in 2003. The following excerpt can teach many of us about the role of death in our lives, even when we are not the ones dying:

That evening when I came in from the fields, she was gone. I hurried to my mother. Mama told me she had seen her go up the hollow from the house, so weak she could hardly stand. Mama had watched her until she had disappeared into the timber.

I hurried up the hollow, calling her name. I called and called. I went up to the head of it, still calling her name and praying she would come to me. I climbed out onto the flats; looking, searching, and calling. It was no use. My dog was gone.

I had a thought, a ray of hope. I just knew I'd find her at the grave of Old Dan. I hurried there.

I found her lying on her stomach, her hind legs stretched out straight, and her front feet folded back under her chest. She had laid her head on his grave. I saw the trail where she had dragged herself through the leaves. The way she lay there, I thought she was alive. I called her name. She made no movement. With the last ounce of strength in her body, she had dragged herself to the grave of Old Dan.

Kneeling down by her side, I reached out and touched her. There was no response, no whimpering cry or friendly wag of her tail. My little dog was dead.

I laid her head in my lap and with tear-filled eyes gazed up into the heavens. In a choking voice, I asked, "Why did they have to die? Why must I hurt so? What have I done wrong?" (Rawls, *Where the Red Fern Grows*: 202–203).

Why does the death of a pet bring tears to our eyes (including my own as I was reading this passage), even when it is a fictional animal? Why do so many of us ask heaven to help us in understanding how a loved one can leave before we do, especially if the person asking believes in a better life after death? We have been dealing with death since we began walking the earth, so why all the emotion? Sociologists would say that we have been taught that death is a time of sorrow, and to be happy at a death would be considered deviant. In addition, we are taught that death is an end, regardless of what Faulkner wrote, and we do not want to find our lives or the lives of the ones we loved to be meaningless by ending without accomplishing a great deal. It may also be the case that we project our own fears onto those who have died, knowing that one day we will also be gone and fear the pain, as well as the knowledge, that we are unsure of where we go next. As Berger (1974: 149) states, "[t]he history of mankind is a history of pain," and much of that pain is captured in death. Berger discusses how history is often portrayed in wars and massacres, so death becomes the underlying meaning of our own existence from the standpoint of the sociological imagination. "At the foundations of every historical society there are vast piles of corpses, victims of the murderous acts that, directly or indirectly, led to the establishment of that society" (150). While our own notions of everyday life are questioned by death, societies and cultures are often grounded in the demise of their forefathers and others, such as all the people willing to fight and die during the Revolutionary War in the United States. The meaning of death goes far beyond the end of our own existence, and knowing that the world will continue on without us is also an unnerving thought.

Historians and sociologists are not the only writers who look for the meaning of death in larger social structures. Authors of fiction do the same thing, including Rawls, who finds meaning in the boy's pain through an old Native American legend:

After the last item was stored in the wagon, Papa helped Mama to the spring seat and we were ready to go.

"Papa, would you mind waiting a few minutes?" I asked. "I'd like to say good-bye to my dogs."

"Sure," he said, smiling. "We have plenty of time. Go right ahead."

Nearing the graves, I saw something was different. It looked like a wild bush had grown up and practically covered the two little mounds. It made me angry to think that an old bush would dare grow so close to the graves. I took out my knife, intending to cut it down.

When I walked up close enough to see what it was, I sucked in a mouthful of air and stopped. I couldn't believe what I was seeing. There between the graves, a beautiful red fern had sprung up from the rich mountain soil. It was fully two feet tall and its long red leaves had reached out and in rainbow arches curved over the graves of my dogs.

I had heard the old Indian legend about the red fern. How a little Indian boy and girl were lost in a blizzard and had frozen to death. In the spring, when they were found, a beautiful red fern had grown up between their two bodies. The story went on to say that only an angel could plant the seeds of a red fern, and that they never died; when one grew, that spot was sacred (Rawls, *Where the Red Fern Grows*: 209–10).

Many of us could visualize such an ending to our own existence—having our final resting place visited by an angel—which is why this telling can be so powerful. Maybe this is why we tend to believe in angels and continue to look to religion for answers about life and death.

To reiterate, sociologists cannot say what happens after we die, or even what we should believe as we move toward and through the end of life. They do not have the tools for such stories, but sociologists can make inroads into why so many of us do believe something, and that nearly every culture and individual tries to find ways of making sense of death. Sociologists can, through theories and concepts, bring clarity to our understanding of the experiences of both death and grief. Symbolic interactionists like Berger (1974) and Strauss (1993) help us to find meaning through language and symbols found in places like cemetery monuments and Internet memorial sites, while conflict theorists would examine the abuse or misuse of power in areas such as genocide, war, and capital punishment. Functionalists such as Durkheim might explore the end of the functioning body, or how death is used as a ritual to make sense of our communities. As with the ocean that takes Captain Ahab, the social structures that are in place when we are alive continue to play a part in our deaths, and will continue to do so in the foreseeable future.

REFERENCES AND RECOMMENDED READINGS

Berger, P. L. (1974). *Pyramids of Sacrifice*. New York: Anchor Books.

Bollen, K. A., and Phillips, D. P. (1982). "Imitative Suicides: A national study of the effects of television news stories." *American Sociological Review*, 47(6): 802–809.

Durkheim, E. (2006). *On Suicide*. New York: Penguin.

Faulkner, W. (2013). *As I Lay Dying*. New York: Vintage.

Howarth, G. (2007). *Death and Dying: A Sociological Introduction*. Cambridge: Polity Press.

Hughes, R. (1986). *The Fatal Shore*. New York: Knopf.

Kiernan, B. (2009). *Blood and Soil*. New Haven, CT: Yale University Press.

Kellman, H. C., and Hamilton, V. L. (1989). *Crimes of Obedience*. New Haven, CT: Yale University Press.

Kübler-Ross, E. (1969). *On Death and Dying*. New York: Macmillan.

Rawls, W. (1961). *Where the Red Fern Grows*. New York: Yearling Books.

Remarque, E. M. *All Quiet on the Western Front* (trans. A. W. Wheen, Fawcett Crest). From MyTeacherPages.com (accessed January 2013).

Stack, S., and Gundlach, J. (1992). "The Effect of Country Music on Suicide." *Social Forces*, 71(1): 211–18.

Strauss, A. L. (1993). *Continual Permutations of Action*. New York: Aldine de Gruyter.

Walter, T. (2008). "The Sociology of Death." *Social Compass*, 2(1): 317–36.

7 RACE

INTRODUCTION AND *THE LIFE AND ADVENTURES OF ROBINSON CRUSOE*

Within the formal institutions of the family, religion, education, work, and death, we learn about other social institutions and structures, and how these enhance and challenge our agency. The next two chapters—this one on race and the next on gender—are two of the more common social structures that sociologists use to make sense of why individuals and groups within the same situations often have very different experiences.

Current thoughts on race and race relations in the United States include thinking that either race has become institutionalized (individuals are no longer racist, but institutions and organizations are), or that we have become a color-blind society where everyone has an equal chance to succeed—for example, people such as Oprah Winfrey and Barack Obama. Anyone who is unsuccessful must be doing something wrong or is just plain lazy. Both approaches often overlook the realities of everyday discrimination and the prejudice faced by individuals from racial minorities.

I will return to these thoughts on race, but first I need to take a step back in time. Thomas Pettigrew (1980) put together a collection of sociological writings that were written between 1895 and 1980 and which focused on race relations. Through this collection, we can see how race went from something that was thought to instinctually affect a person's behavior, to a social label that is constructed within society and has nothing to do with natural forces. Richard LaPiere, for example, conducted research in the 1930s regarding the attitudes and actions of white people toward a young Chinese couple who traveled with

LaPiere in the United States. Only in one case—out of 251 encounters—did someone refuse to serve the couple and LaPiere. LaPiere found this interesting given the general attitudes toward Asians at the time, so he contacted one of the businesses that had served them and asked if they would serve Chinese patrons. LaPiere was told that the business would refuse to serve someone of Chinese origin. LaPiere decided to develop a more in-depth survey to ask the same thing of the other businesses they used, and found that of the 128 businesses that completed the survey, over 90 percent said they would refuse to serve people of different races, *even though they had served LaPiere and his Chinese companions.* We can only assume that Americans at the time thought of Chinese as devious and cunning, so those filling out the survey would refuse to serve someone with those characteristics, though when they met LaPiere's companions they found that they were nice and acted like white patrons. They may have thought that these were atypical Chinese people, and any other Chinese person would take advantage of American hospitality because their racial features would make them act that way.

You may be wondering at this point why a person would serve someone of a different race and then say they would refuse to serve that person in a survey, as well as why sociologists would be interested in knowing how someone thinks when what really counts is how they act. If these businesses were willing to serve the Chinese couple, that should be the end of the story. Sociologists are interested in interaction, not thoughts. We do, however, know that thoughts can influence action, and this is why we differentiate between prejudice and discrimination. Prejudice is defined as a strong feeling toward another person or object. It does not necessarily have to be a negative connotation, such as being prejudiced toward mint ice cream over strawberry ice cream. We do, however, tend to think of prejudice toward other groups or people as negative. To be prejudiced in terms of race typically means that we judge others based on a set of standards that we perceive to have been set by our own race. This is very often the foundation for stereotypes, which consist of characteristics that we link to certain groups. Stereotypes of Italians might include eating pizza and pasta and being linked to the Mafia, while someone from Australia is expected to wear dungarees, throw boomerangs, and say "ello, mate" to everyone they meet. Harsher stereotypes are tied to groups of African descent, those who practice Judaism or Islam, the homeless, the disabled, and countless others.

When we think of people in stereotypical ways, we treat those stereotypes as part of their human nature, which can lead to acts of discrimination. Discrimination is when actions—or lack thereof—are based on someone else's characteristics (their race, age, gender, religion, sexual orientation, etc.). During the Jim Crow era in the United States (roughly from 1876 to 1965), for example, people of African descent could not drink from water fountains, use bathrooms, sit at tables in restaurants, go to schools, or use the seats on buses that were used by people of European descent. These laws, and many more like them, were created and maintained by whites, and it was not until the civil rights movement of the 1950s and 1960s that the Jim Crow laws begin to disappear, at least from a legal standpoint. Changing a law, however, often does very little in changing people's attitudes and behaviors, especially when one group feels the laws protect their interests. Many whites saw the desegregation of schools and neighborhoods during the 1960s as problematic, so while they could no longer use the police and courts to maintain a distance from blacks, many were quick to either leave desegregated school districts and neighborhoods, or to make sure blacks knew they were not welcome in these areas.

Being prejudiced toward a group does not always lead to being discriminatory, and sometimes a person without any preconceived notions of a group can become prejudiced after watching a group being discriminated against, thinking that group must have done something wrong for the others to treat them that way. These two terms, however, are often linked to sets of behaviors tied to intergroup relations.

One of the more interesting twists to intergroup relations is that the individuals and groups toward whom we hold prejudice or discriminate against are often thought of as exotic, and therefore desirable on certain levels for specific reasons. Lalvani (1995) found this to be true of 19th-century Europe, when coffee tins were decorated with images of Middle Eastern harems. Such practices were considered crude and barbaric in most conversations, yet to see such images on a coffee tin made European consumers want to experience something linked to the exoticness of the Middle East. Such accounts can be found throughout literature, including Daniel Defoe's telling of Robinson Crusoe's depiction of the fellow who came to be known as Friday in his book, *The Life and Adventures of Robinson Crusoe*:

> He was a comely, handsome fellow, perfectly well made, with straight strong limbs, not too large, tall and well shaped; and, as I can reckon, about twenty-six years of age. He had a very good countenance, not a fierce and surly aspect, but seemed to have something very manly in his face; and yet he had all the sweetness and softness of a European in his countenance too, especially when he smiled. His hair was long and black, not curled like wool; his forehead very high and large; and a great vivacity and sparkling sharpness in his eyes. The color of his skin was not quite black, but very tawny; and yet not an ugly, yellow, nauseous tawny, as the Brazilians and Virginians, and other natives of America are, but of a bright kind of dun olive color, that had in it something very agreeable, though not very easy to describe. His face was round and plump; his nose small, not flat like the Negroes, a very good mouth, thin lips, and his fine teeth well set, and as white as ivory.

> After he had slumbered, rather than slept, about half an hour, he awoke again, and come out of the cave to me; for I had been milking my goats, which I had in the enclosure just by; when he espied me, he came running to me, laying himself down again upon the ground, with all the possible signs of a humble, thankful disposition, making a great many antic gestures to show it (Defoe, *The Life and Adventures of Robinson Crusoe*: 233).

The condemnation in this writing is clear in terms of both Friday and other races. Defoe has no problem talking about how the hair, skin tones, and noses of others did not fit his own standards of beauty. It was also Crusoe, a European, who saved Friday's life. Friday, in turn, shows his appreciation by acting like a small child who has been given a treat and understands that his pleasures, as well as basic survival, are dependent on the adult in the room. While such signs of appreciation among adults are acceptable in many cultures, one gets the feeling that Defoe is setting up Friday to be subservient to Crusoe in terms of both work and intellect.

It is also important to understand that Friday needed to be different from Crusoe. Not ugly, but pleasurable enough to interact with, but still different enough to serve a master. This includes an exoticness that makes him a mystery to readers who may have had little interaction with different races and played on the stereotypes of colored servants at the time. We can imagine readers being comfortable with Friday serving Crusoe, but less so if the tables were turned.

CONSTRUCTING RACE AND *TO KILL A MOCKINGBIRD*

Before we can consume the exotic other, we must construct him as both other and exotic. Constructing the other begins with construction of our own self and that we belong to a group of similar selves. Boys and girls tend to separate into groups on the playground. Within these groups are the nerds, jocks, and every other clique we experienced in school. The other is anyone who does not belong to the group we are in, and exoticness increases as differences grow between our group and others. Looking different, talking differently, and wearing different kinds of clothes become the basis for seeing another group as exotic. Defoe made the exotic by describing Friday's appearances and actions, a strategy used by numerous writers. Sociologists think about race somewhat differently, such as the following by Winant indicates (2000: 172):

> At its most basic level, race can be defined as a concept that signi-
> fies and symbolizes sociopolitical conflicts and interests in reference

to different types of human bodies. Although the concept of race appeals to biologically based human characteristics (phenotypes), selection of these particular human features for purposes of racial signification is always and necessarily a social and historical process. There is no biological basis for distinguishing human groups along the lines of race, and the sociohistorical categories employed to differentiate among these groups reveal themselves, upon serious examination, to be imprecise if not completely arbitrary.

If Defoe had used this kind of language, his book never would have made it past the first few readers or into the movies. What is also different between Winant and Defoe is that the sociologist questions any distinctions based on race, while the fiction writer sees outward appearances linked to inner characteristics. Most sociologists believe that racial differences are an excuse used by the majority who hold power to maintain dominance over minority groups.

Winant also contends that race is a modern concept, "although prefigured in various ways by ethnocentrism, and taking preliminary form in ancient concepts of civilization and barbarity … citizen … and outsider/slave" (170). Our modern constructions of race began in earnest at the end of the Middle Ages, when the African slave trade burgeoned, and societies steeped in Christianity had to find ways to justify their treatment of other humans. By referring to them as barbarians, savages, and less than human, white slave traders could go about their business of capturing and transporting Africans to plantations with few, if any, feelings of guilt.

That we are still dealing with vestiges of these systems is clear in our own lives, as well as the writings of sociologists and novelists. These structures run deep, as is evident in Harper Lee's *To Kill a Mockingbird*, published in 1960—over two hundred years after Defoe's novel (1719):

"It couldn't be worse, Jack. The only thing we've got is a black man's word against the Ewells'. The evidence boils down to you-did-I-didn't. The jury couldn't possibly be expected to take Tom Robinson's word against the Ewells'—are you acquainted with the Ewells?"

Uncle Jack said yes, he remembered them. He described them to Atticus, but Atticus said, "You're a generation off. The present ones are the same, though."

"What are you going to do, then?"

"Before I'm through, I intend to jar the jury a bit—I think we'll have a reasonable chance on appeal, though. I really can't tell at this stage, Jack. You know, I'd hoped to get through life without a case of this kind, but John Taylor pointed at me and said, 'You're It.'"

"Let the cup pass from you, eh?"

"Right. But do you think I could face my children otherwise? You know what's going to happen as well as I do, Jack, and I hope and pray I can get Jem and Scout through it without bitterness, and most of all, without catching Maycomb's usual disease. Why reasonable people go stark raving mad when anything involving a Negro comes up, is something I don't pretend to understand ... I just hope that Jem and Scout come to me for their answers instead of listening to the town. I hope they trust me enough ..." (Harper, *To Kill a Mockingbird*: 93).

Atticus is concerned that if his children see reasonable people acting in a certain way toward someone of African descent, they may look at themselves and say that they are also white like the people who are "stark raving mad when anything involving a Negro comes up." Jem and Scout are likely to think that is how they are supposed to act, and it would be considered strange to do otherwise. Such processes can be found in real life beyond the 1950s and 1960s, as I saw the same thing happen in my hometown of North Bend, Oregon. I was born in 1964 and graduated in 1982 with 214 other individuals, of which fewer than ten would have been considered a different race or ethnicity by many of my peers. One student from my class was of African descent and had been adopted as an infant by a white couple; others were of mixed race; and a few had darker skin than mine, but I was unaware of their racial or ethnic backgrounds. Given the lack of diversity, race was not something that was discussed very often in North Bend, and I rarely heard anyone say they were racist or bigoted. I have no doubt there were people who thought themselves as racist, but I never heard that in open discussions. Most of the people I knew went to church on Sundays, where they were told to love their neighbor with no qualifications about race, and watched sports or other forms of entertainment in which blacks and other racial groups were prominently displayed. This, in fact, was how most of us came to understand how nonwhites behaved—through the media.

At some point during my time in junior high school, a black family moved into the area, and the place was abuzz—"stark raving mad"—because the high school–aged son was tall and played basketball. Everyone asked if he could dunk, and when we found out that he could, we decided that North Bend was going to win the next basketball state championship because we finally had someone who looked and acted like those professional basketball players on television. The rest of the family, however, found it hard to find work as well as friends, and left the area within a year. I do not recall any discussions of race at that time.

The second black family to move into the area that I was aware of came during my freshman year in high school. They had a son who was a sophomore, and when he showed up to school we asked him if he could dunk a basketball. When he proved to us that he was not much of an athlete, we asked if he could dance or tell jokes like the other blacks we saw on television. When he failed at those tasks, some of the other students picked fights with him. In addition to the violence at school, the parents had a hard time finding work or friends, and that family also left North Bend within a year. There were still no discussions of race in the area, though it would have been interesting to pass out LaPiere's survey about serving minority groups after that family left.

While the situation in North Bend was likely much more complex than this story (told from memories over 30 years old and from a kid between the ages of 13 and 15, when life seems pretty simple), it does show how we come to understand people and their (perceived) actions based on the color of their skin. Racism and stereotypes are not something that only one group holds, but seems to be practiced in many contexts by most groups. This takes us back to the sociological imagination and the social construction of reality.

Winant (2000) states that there is no evidence that skin color makes people different in terms of action. He also states that wars such as the Crusades were fought between Europeans and Middle Easterners, who likely came to judge each other in terms of phenotypes, and while plenty of wars were also being fought at that time between groups similar in phenotypes, we began to see skin color as symbolic of certain ideas that were opposed to each other. Through inductive reasoning (looking at a specific event and deciding anything even remotely similar must be the same), we would begin to think that all people who look a certain way must believe in a specific set of values and act in prescribed ways. Given that there were great distances between these groups, people in both societies would have had few opportunities to question their notions of the other. From the sociological imagination, we can understand why overcoming negative race relations is difficult, given the history of violence between groups that just happened to look different.

While we are given few opportunities to choose our race, notions do change about what makes a group a minority. Irish immigrants to the United States were once considered black, and in some countries, a person's racial status changes as their economic status rises or falls. If ideas of race can change, and people and groups can move into and out of racial categories, then we begin to realize that race truly is socially constructed. Berger and Luckmann's (1966) work on this is helpful in understanding the process. To reiterate, the social construction of reality involves externalizing an action or symbol, that action or symbol becoming an object for others to see and judge, and internalizing their reactions. When racial groups are geographically separated and only come into contact during wars or through the mass media, the actions and symbols objectified in those situations will come to be thought of as "what that group does." If a black person sees white males like Bernie Madoff being taken to jail for running financial scams, they may come to expect all white males to be criminals. When they finally meet someone who is a white male and not in handcuffs (or rich), they will often think that it is just a matter of time before the person acts like the other white males they have seen on television. When the person fails to act in those preconceived ways, the typical response is something along the lines of, "you're not like the other white males." This kind of reaction is often reversed in the United States, as the exposure to blacks among whites is often through news reports portraying young black males in handcuffs being put into police cars. Whites come to think of blacks as criminals (or athletes, etc.). As with my experiences in North Bend, when someone of a different racial category does appear in our midst, we wait for them to behave in stereotypical ways, as that is how our realities have been constructed for us. When they do not act as expected, we either try to force them into our preconceived notion or say that they are somehow different from all the other people who look like them.

The narrative provided by Lee also points to another aspect of modern race relationships—institutional racism. While the above exchange focuses on one person's word against another, the decision regarding who is right will be decided in a courtroom. If Tom Robinson is found guilty or the Ewells found to be lying, everyone can say it was the court (judge or jury) that made the decision, and any specific person, whether the witnesses, jurors, lawyers, or judge, can wash their hands of any responsibility for the verdict (including if the verdict is proven wrong at a later time). Institutional racism plays into many decisions, including hiring employees and housing decisions at a college. Such situations were at least partially responsible for affirmative action policies that set quotas for racial groups within institutions such as higher education and government jobs, and made it illegal for realtors to show only certain neighborhoods to different racial groups. College admissions committees and hiring groups were able to say that they were only following the standards of their organizations—standards often set by whites—and that those who were let in came with the highest qualifications. Such an approach disregarded issues such as access to better primary schools, higher rates of poverty among minority groups, and gaps in cultural knowledge that manifested themselves in standardized tests. Whites have argued that affirmative action now discriminates against them, as less deserving individuals from underserved groups take their positions in prestigious schools and the offices of top companies. This reverse discrimination is difficult to prove at a level beyond a few individuals, since as a group, whites continue to enjoy greater access to resources in most social spheres.

POSTMODERN RACE RELATIONSHIPS AND *THE HELP*

My mother told me that when she was a kid in the 1930s and 1940s in Montana, her mother was very clear that she and her sisters were not to tell anyone they were Jewish. That her father, who was a Jewish immigrant from Russia, had renounced his religion at 17 before running away from home and joining the army made no difference. One did not have to attend Jewish services or observe religious holidays to be considered Jewish. It was basically a modification of the "one drop" rule, in which anyone who could trace any African ancestry in their family was considered black. In Montana in the 1930s, if anyone in your family had ever been Jewish or had Jewish ancestors, then you were Jewish.

I began teaching sociology courses at Portland State University in 1993, taught a few more at Louisiana State University between 1996 and 1998, and started teaching at Michigan State University in 2000. When race has been discussed in classrooms at these organizations of higher education, I often hear that it is no longer a problem. "That was something my parents (or grandparents) dealt with," is the typical answer I get when asking today's students about race relations among their peers. According to today's students, my mother's experiences are a thing of the past. In fact, some feel that race is only an issue because instructors keep bringing it up.

According to Byng (2012), such an attitude is typical within a color-blind society that sees individuals such as Barack Obama and Oprah Winfrey as evidence that anyone can make it. Students who say race is no longer an issue or that anyone can make it need only look at contemporary studies of employment, housing, access to medicine, and education to come to the conclusion that race still matters. According to a Centers for Disease Control report published in 2008, "[t]he infant mortality rate for non-Hispanic black women was 2.4 times the rate for non-Hispanic white women. Rates were also elevated for Puerto Rican and American Indian or Alaska Native women" (http://www.cdc.gov/nchs/data/databriefs/db09.htm, accessed May 2013). A report from the U.S. Census Bureau concerning income in 2010 showed that 12.4 percent of all white children lived in poverty, while 38.2 percent of black children and 35 percent of Hispanic children experienced the same fate (http://www.census.gov/prod/2011pubs/p60-239.pdf, accessed May 2013). If race is no longer an issue, then why do these gaps exist? I hear two justifications from students. First, that it is not their fault that these gaps exist, because they have never discriminated against anyone. Secondly, we begin to fall back on stereotypes to explain these differences, saying that it has nothing to do with race, but with the people within those racial categories. All they need to do is work hard and prove that they are productive citizens. Saying that moving into higher socioeconomic status for someone of minority status can be difficult is an understatement, as played out in Kathryn Stockett's *The Help*:

"I was … well, I was raised by a colored woman. I've seen how simple it can be and—how complex it can be between families and the help." I cleared my throat. I sounded stiff, like I was talking to a teacher.

"Continue."

"Well," I took a deep breath, "I'd like to write this showing the point of view of the help. The colored women down here." I tried to picture Constantine's face, Aibileen's. "They raise a white child and then twenty years later the child becomes the employers. It's that irony, that we love them and they love us, yet … " I swallowed, my voice trembling. "We don't even allow them to use the toilet in the house."

Again there was silence.

"And," I felt compelled to continue, "everyone knows how we white people feel, the glorified Mammy figure who dedicates her whole life to a white family. Margaret Mitchell covered that. But no one ever asked Mammy how she felt about it." Sweat dripped down my chest, blotting the front of my cotton blouse.

"So you want to show a side that's never been examined before," Missus Stein said.

"Yes. Because no one ever talks about it. No one talks about anything down here."

Elaine Stein laughed like a growl. Her accent was tight, Yankee. "Miss Phelan, I lived in Atlanta. For six years with my first husband."

I latched on to this small connection. "So … you know what it's like then."

"Enough to get me out of there," she said, and I heard her exhale her smoke. "Look, I read your outline. It's certainly … original, but it won't work. What maid in her right mind would ever tell you the truth?" (Stockett, *The Help*: 105–106).

Not only is the history of race replete with stereotypes of the other, it is also a story of lies and miscommunication. This includes whites giving blankets infected with smallpox to Native American tribes, whites using black men as subjects in studies of syphilis, and not letting blacks and whites serve together in the military until 1948. Mistrust at a cultural level is not easily overcome, and any event that supports that mistrust becomes yet another barrier to closing the gap between groups. A black maid might be more than willing to talk to a white employer, but Missus Stein pictures that as a conversation in which the maid will tell the employer what she thinks the employer wants to hear, and not what it is really like to be black and serving a white family.

Another important aspect of the excerpt from Stockett is the inclusion of qualifiers such as Elaine Stein being a Yankee. It is not enough that these women share a common bond of being white and both having lived at some point in the South—Stockett grew up there while Stein lived in Atlanta for six years. Their stories go beyond race, with Stein putting all black women into one category because of a few experiences. This could be considered a postmodern approach to race. One postmodern perspective, and there are many, is the idea that we now live in a society where factors such as race, gender, age, and so forth can be used to make any narrative possible and plausible. To a postmodernist, saying that two people are black gives us very little information. When we learn that one is from Detroit and the other from Los Angeles, we begin to look for differences regarding music tastes, clothing styles, foodways, and so forth. Race is only one variable that can be used to construct stories. It also becomes a card to play or not to play depending on the situation, though there is no reason to believe that just because one person decides to use her race that others will see it as unimportant or played wrong. An individual who finds herself in a group in which all other members are of another race may downplay her race ("I'm just like everyone else") or use it to get the attention of others ("Does anyone want to know what someone like me thinks about this situation?"). The possible narratives are endless in a postmodern society, though power still plays into what is and what is not acceptable behavior, as well as what stories are to be believed.

While this chapter focuses on race, many of the same approaches can be used regarding ethnicity. While ethnicity is not a phenotype and so can be more easily hidden in some circumstances, various groups within a society view certain ethnic groups as threatening. The Ku Klux Klan is thought of as a white supremacy group focused on the harassment of blacks, but the group also harasses Jews, Catholics, and immigrants. Violent ethnic conflicts, in fact, tend to be as prevalent, if not more so, as racial conflicts throughout the world's history (Cordell & Wolff, 2010).

Race and ethnicity are structures that impact our agency. While anyone of any race can act in ways that are not stereotypical, the expectations of ourselves and others that we carry in our heads can and will impact what we do in certain situations, as well as how we perceive the actions of others. How others feel about our race will likely influence how they act around us as well. When I heard a black poet say he was scared of white people, and my initial reaction was "no, we're scared of your group," I realized how deeply fears and expectations tied to race goes, and how they can affect even someone trained in sociology.

REFERENCES AND RECOMMENDED READINGS

Berger, P. L., and Luckmann, T. (1966). *The Social Construction of Reality*. New York: Anchor.

Byng, M. (2012). "You Can't Get There from Here: A social process theory of racism and race." *Critical Sociology*, published online July 16, 2012 (accessed May 2013).

Cordell, K., and Wolff, S. (2010). *Ethnic Conflict*. Malden, MA: Polity Press.

Defoe, D. (1870). *The Life and Adventures of Robinson Crusoe*. Philadelphia: Porter and Coates.

Lalvani, S. (1995). "Consuming the Exotic Other." *Critical Studies in Mass Communication*, 12: 263–86.

Lee, H. (1960). *To Kill a Mockingbird*. New York: HarperCollins.

Murphy, J. W., and Choi, J. M. (1997). *Postmodernism, Unraveling Racism, and Democratic Institutions*. Westport, CT: Praeger.

Pettigrew, T. F. (1980). *The Sociology of Race Relations*. New York: Free Press.

Stockett, K. (2009). *The Help*. New York: Amy Einhorn Books.

Winant, H. (2000). "Race and Race Theory." *Annual Review of Sociology*, 26: 169–85.

8 GENDER

INTRODUCTION AND *MADAME BOVARY*

Students in introductory courses are often told that sex and gender, while connected in society, are two different things. A person's sex is biologically determined, and while we typically think of sex in the binary terms of male and female, there are at least five biological sexes. Besides male and female, there are hermaphrodites (individuals who carry a functioning ovary and testes), "the male pseudohermaphrodites (the 'merms'), who have testes and some aspects of the female genitalia but no ovaries; and the female pseudohermaphrodites (the 'ferms'), who have ovaries and some aspects of the male genitalia but lack testes" (http://facweb. northseattle.edu/ratkins/ClassMaterials/PSYSOC230/230Activities-Instructor/ MSLib_Faus_The_Five_Sexes.pdf, accessed May 2013). Much like race, we think that individuals have little choice in determining sex at birth, though medical procedures have made it possible to change a person's sex. In addition, when a newborn falls into one of the "other" categories, parents tend to decide on either a male or female sex for their children. A person's sex, therefore, seems relatively straightforward—we are male, female, or a freak. Recently, sociologists have come to understand, often through anthropological work, that in some cultures, merm, ferms, and herms are considered unique and given privileged status. In other words, we have begun to understand that sex is not biologically determined, but influenced by social factors. For a sociologist, a person's biological features are less significant than how society gives meaning to bodies.

Gender, on the other hand, has been considered socially constructed for decades. The typical sociological approach to gender states that it ranges from the hypermasculine male to the hyperfeminine female, with most males and females falling somewhere on the continuum between these two extremes (there are also hypermasculine females and hyperfeminine males). We can change our gender through actions, though too radical of a change or practicing gendered activities that are thought of as belonging to the opposite gender can bring about ridicule and violence. A boy who plays with dolls might be called a sissy, while a girl who wants to play tackle football is thought of as a tomboy. Adult males and females who follow the scripts of the opposite gender (feminine men and masculine women) are often thought to be homosexual, regardless of their professed sexual preferences. (We will look more closely at sexuality in Chapter 10.).

The fact that gender is a continuum and that we have the ability to choose where we land on that continuum might make one think that gender is agent centered. It was my choice, we would conclude, to play football, basketball, and baseball as a kid, as well as bring home nearly every animal I came across no matter how slimy or how many legs it had. It was also my mother's choice to worry about me while I was playing sports and to shriek whenever I brought something home that wriggled. After all, I could have shrieked every time I saw something fuzzy in my path and my mother could have walked around in a football helmet.

That my mother did not wear a football helmet on a consistent basis and that I played male-centered sports are part of the structures that are grounded in gender and impact our actions on a regular basis. Men and women are expected to act in certain ways, and few of us would have any problem understanding the following passage from Gustave Flaubert's *Madame Bovary*:

> Madame Bovary, senior, had not opened her lips all day. She had been consulted neither as to the dress of her daughter-in-law nor as to the arrangement of the feast; she went to bed early. Her husband, instead of following her, sent to Saint-Victor for some cigars and smoked till daybreak, drinking kirsch-punch, a mixture unknown to the company. This added greatly to the consideration in which he was held (Flaubert, *Madame Bovary*: 28).

That a woman of society would be quiet and go to bed early while her husband engaged in social activities until morning seems appropriate for their genders. In fact, we might be unmoved if we found that Mr. Bovary was seeing prostitutes during his nightly excursions, though we may feel sorry for the wife while asking why she was unable to fully satisfy her husband. Think, however, of your reaction if the roles were switched—that Madame Bovary Senior was going out after her husband had gone to bed and was sleeping with other men. We are more likely to see that as problematic than a male acting in the same way. That was the reaction that readers gave to Flaubert when the novel depicted affairs that the younger Madame Bovary is having, even though her husband is boring.

Another way to think about how we come to act in gendered ways is through socialization. Boys are told they are supposed to come home dirty, while girls are expected to be neat and clean. We might feel some sympathy for a parent who forces a child to act in gendered ways, knowing that in the end the child will find it easier to fit into society. If parents scold their sons every time they play with dolls and pat them on the back when they pick up sporting equipment, those sons will likely decide that playing sports is what they are supposed to do, and therefore would come to see it as the way to have fun. If the opposite happens to daughters, they will come to see playing with dolls as the best way to have fun.

West and Zimmerman (1987) referred to these types of activities as "doing gender." Being masculine or feminine is not something inherent in an individual, but something we strive for based on our notions of what social institutions and important others expect of us. Much like Don Quixote believing he had to conquer the windmills because of what he read in the tales about knights, young boys and girls see other boys (men) and girls (women) acting in certain ways, and come to believe that to be a boy (man) or girl (woman) means acting in those specified ways. The senior Madame Bovary and Mr. Bovary did what was expected of them. As a woman, her behavior was feminine, and as a man, he projected masculinity. In and of themselves, these behaviors often cause few concerns within mainstream, heteronormative society, as men are expected to be dominant (and dominating), and women are expected to be subordinate (and subordinated). This began to change with feminist movements, a topic we will return to at the end of the chapter.

SOCIALIZATION AND *LITTLE WOMEN*

The socialization into gender begins early. The popular (now infamous?) nursery rhyme states that boys are made of "snips and snails and puppy dog tails," and girls are made of "sugar and spice and everything nice." That this rhyme is approximately two hundred years old shows how long we have been telling boys and girls what they are made of and how much different one is from the other. Would the world look any different if the lines in the rhyme had been reversed, or would there still be dominant and dominated gendered groups?

One of the more interesting aspects of a patriarchal society is that women tend to be the parents who stay home and raise the children. Why then, do women not raise boys and girls to see each other as equals, or to have girls see themselves as more powerful than boys? Mainly because the women who are raising the children were also socialized to think along gendered lines in which men are powerful and women are nurturing. Louisa May Alcott wrote in this way in the 1800s when describing a mother talking about her daughters in *Little Women*:

"I want my daughters to be beautiful, accomplished, and good. To be admired, loved, and respected. To have a happy youth, to be well and wisely married, and to lead useful, pleasant lives, with as little care and sorrow to try them as God sees fit to send. To be loved and chosen by a good man is the best and sweetest thing which can happen to a woman, and I sincerely hope my girls may know this beautiful experience. It is natural to think of it, Meg, right to hope and wait for it, and wise to prepare for it, so that when the happy time comes, you may feel ready for the duties and worthy of the joy. My dear girls, I am ambitious for you, but not to have you make a dash in the world, marry rich men merely because they are rich, or have splendid houses, which are not homes because love is wanting. Money is a needful and precious thing, and when well used, a noble thing, but I never want you to think it is the first or only prize to strive for. I'd rather see you poor men's wives, if you were happy, beloved, contented, than queens on thrones, without self-respect and peace."

"Poor girls don't stand any chance, Belle says, unless they put themselves forward," sighed Meg (Alcott, *Little Women*: 84).

Meg understands that women had to be aggressive to be noticed by certain men, and that continues to this day. hooks (2000) argues that this was the case for her as a black female student at Stanford in the 1960s, even though she had reached the same educational level as her fellow students. Being forward as a woman, however, can have its drawbacks in terms of how others see you. In Findlen's (2001) collection of writings from women, there are numerous stories of young girls being told to let boys win, or of being scolded for being too forward on the playground or with friends. These incriminations come from parents, aunts and uncles, teachers, friends, and the boys the girls want to have notice them. All of these individuals are important significant others, and young girls may find it hard to continue disappointing them, especially if the disappointment turns to anger or withdrawal by the other. These statements about being more feminine are often reinforced by the generalized others a young girl sees on television or in the movies, who also appear feminine through their looks, career choices, and the fact that they need a male companion to be complete. Even a strong character like Laura Croft (played by Angelina Jolie) has love interests that make her complete as a woman. Without a male, she might be considered butch, even without any female-female love scenes.

Much of the early work in gender was focused on these issues of women having to navigate their way through a male-dominated society, and so gender studies were synonymous with women's studies. However, females are not the only group who does gender, and instructors and students have come to recognize this. Like females acting in ways to show the world they are made of sugar and spice, males are expected to act in ways that show they truly are made of snips and snails and puppy dog tails. This begins in childhood, as boys are taught to be rough by significant others, and images connected to violence such as GI Joe action figures (notice the term is not "dolls," as that would be for girls) and the faces and bodies of men on the packaging carrying toy weapons. When we turn on the television between September and February, we are reminded that the men are supposed to hit each other and the women, who are wearing few clothes, are cheering them on.

Masculinity and what it means to be male has come under more scrutiny over the past few decades. Haywood and Mac an Ghaill (2003) report this is happening in the home, as men are now expected to be more involved in child rearing. The authors are not convinced that this change in the discussion of the domestic roles of men has turned into actual practices. In addition, they argue that any discussion of gender is still framed within a patriarchal society. From this vantage point, men will only be involved in child rearing if that is what other men expect them to do. In short, changes are based on narratives of masculinity—not on what is right, wrong, or equal in terms of helping with the family.

While men may be taking on new positions in the home, learning traditional masculine traits continues to be pervasive in schools. Pascoe (2012) reports on how two high school males showed him a social media video in which one of the males had to confess to being homosexual in order to have another friend pay for dinner. He also provides insights from a high school talent show, where male students were rewarded for a sketch where they transform from nerdy males to strong, heteronormative males with girlfriends. Haywood and Mac an Ghaill (2003) point to how both male and female teachers tend to be stricter and more violent with male students, and that curriculum choices for schools are typically determined in conjunction with masculinity. For example, changing a curriculum based on college-bound students to one with an equal focus on vocational training will often be assimilated into male culture much easier—and in more nuanced ways—than female culture, as the vocations taught will be male centered. The push toward the STEM disciplines—science, technology, engineering, and math—is a push toward areas of study historically dominated by males, and the inroads made by females in these fields are slow in coming. These are important disciplines and should not be ignored because of their history, but contemporary teachers and school administrators must work harder to provide equal opportunities for success among all their students, regardless of gender, race, religion, and so forth.

It is important to understand, as Haywood and Mac an Ghaill argue, that curricula are not deterministic in the sense that every male and female will go to school and learn how to do gender in specific ways. Curricula are resources that can be used to make sense of one's intellectual abilities, but moving too far afield within the curriculum can be as damaging to one's reputation as participating in certain sports. A male student who decides to pursue studies in child development will be ridiculed and called gay, while a female student who focuses on automotive engineering may be considered butch or weird. That some of these attitudes are changing is unquestioned, but instances of bullying in class, on the playground, on the bus, and on social media sites continue to be part of our world, and highlight the fact that we still expect boys and girls to act in certain ways.

Once males and females leave school and enter the workforce, they find that they must still do gender, and this is true across numerous cultures. While definitions of masculinity and femininity differ from one place to another, most modern cultures have determined gender roles (Haywood & Mac an Ghaill, 2003). One argument for why gender is so important is that societies need individuals to function in certain ways—to fight battles, rear children, provide food, build houses, etc. Since men cannot give birth and they tend to be stronger pound-for-pound than women in terms of upper body strength, certain tasks (such as traveling and fighting) have come to be considered part of the male realm. Child rearing and collecting food close to home seems more adaptable to a woman's physiology, as she is the one who gives birth and is typically stronger in their lower bodies relative to men (so squatting is easier for them).

Functionalist approaches such as these are viewed as deterministic. If you or a group provide a needed function, then it is best for all concerned if you stick to providing the services needed to fulfill that function. This is why gender socialization continues throughout one's lifetime, as even in retirement men and women are expected to play different roles. Additionally, we believe that life and society would become unbalanced if things shifted. That some men and women have begun seeking new ways to think about gender is the focus of the next section.

FEMINISM AND *THE GIRL WITH THE DRAGON TATTOO*

Efforts to gain more rights for females began centuries ago with women asking for the right to vote, which was granted at the federal level in the United States in 1920 (women in Switzerland were not given the right to vote until 1971). Control over reproductive rights has also been a long-running theme among women's groups, with the Supreme Court decision of *Roe v. Wade* legalizing abortions in 1973 at the center of continuing debates. These efforts have been part of a larger feminist movement, though it should be understood that this "movement" is fractured, and has gone through a number of different stages.

Popular images of the feminist movement in the United States typically involve women of the 1960s, who burned their bras, wanted more sexual freedom, and hated men. This is what some writers refer to as Second Wave feminism, as the First Wave was comprised of the (mostly) women who sought more equal justice and rights beginning around the early 1900s. (Many women who were involved in feminist issues in the 1960s and 1970s could also be considered part of the First Wave, in terms of their values). Third Wave feminism, which began approximately in the 1990s, focuses on culture and the role of women in modern society; it goes beyond voting and reproductive rights. Levy (2006), for example, provides insights into how women are becoming more like men, in the sense that they frequent strip clubs that display female strippers, enjoy pornography, and engage in activities such as bar hopping and "hooking up" on a regular basis. It is a lifestyle she refers to as "raunch culture." It should be understood, as discussed by hooks (2000), that none of these movements or waves has included all women, and that even among those who do subscribe to feminist beliefs, there have been disagreements and splits between white and nonwhite, rich and poor, and straight and queer women. Some of the most vocal opponents of any of the women's movements have been other women.

Once we move past the notion of the bra-burning and man-hating feminist—who are an incredibly small minority of the female feminists—we see a complex array of discussions of what a feminist and a feminist movement should look like. hooks (2000), for instance, states that feminism is not just about gaining the same rights as men in the political arena or career fields, but being treated equally, which means having the same life choices as men. It is not enough to say that women can work in factories, be CEOs, or run for public office, but that they have the *choice* to pursue such goals if they desire to do so, and will face the same opportunities and barriers as men. Sexuality is another aspect of the feminist movements, with feminists split between pro- or antiabortion and pro- and antipornography groups, but writers such as hooks argue that feminists should realize that all of the above are women's choices. Men can and should be part of the conversation, but in the end a woman must make the final decisions regarding her body, including sexual partners and any fetus she might be carrying. Within the abortion debate, hooks points to the fact that some women find abortion to be one of the few birth control strategies they can use, because the men they sleep with are unwilling to use condoms, and birth control pills are either too expensive or carry too high a risk for the woman's health. This is an excellent example of both the structure and agency of gender and the body, as women can make the decision to have sex with men (agency), but they are the ones who become pregnant (structure).

This modern approach to gender as being more liberating can be found in fictional portrayals of modern society, such as in *The Girl with the Dragon Tattoo* by Stieg Larsson. Lisbeth Salander is a female who seeks independence from the world, but finds she still needs money, which is given to her by men. In the following passage, we see the efforts of a male to dominate her:

Advokat Bjurman was relieved when Salander called again and explained that she needed more money. She had postponed their most recent scheduled meeting with the excuse that she had to work, and a vague sense of uneasiness gnawed him. Was she going to turn into an unmanageable problem child? But since she had missed the meeting, she had no allowance, and sooner or later she would be bound to come and see him. He could not help but be concerned that she might have discussed what had happened with some outsider.

She was going to have to be kept in check. She had to understand who was in charge. So he told her that this time the meeting would be at his home near Odenplan, not at the office. Upon hearing the news, Salander was silent for a long time on the other end of the telephone before she finally agreed.

She had planned to meet him at his office, exactly like the last time. Now she was forced to see him in unfamiliar territory. The meeting was set for Friday evening. She had been given the building code, and she rang his doorbell at 8:30, half an hour later than agreed. That was how much time she had needed in the darkness of the building's stairwell to run through her plan one last time, consider alternatives, steel herself, and mobilize the courage she would need (Larsson, *The Girl with the Dragon Tattoo*: 196–97).

Many of us can recognize the first two paragraphs—an older male with money controlling a younger female in need of his resources. We can also imagine Bjurman being upset that Salander came to his house late, much like the owner of a dog when the dog comes to the front door after being let out the back door into a fenced yard. The last paragraph shows that Salander may be ready to fight for her money, or tell Bjurman that he can live out his fantasies with someone else. Instead, just like a dog, she is let inside with her tail between her legs, at least for the time being:

Bjurman was wearing a bathrobe when he opened the door to his apartment. He was cross at her for arriving late and motioned her brusquely inside. She was wearing black jeans, a black T-shirt, and the obligatory leather jacket. She wore black boots and a small rucksack with a strap across her chest.

"Haven't you even learned to tell the time?" Bjurman said. Salander did not reply. She looked around. The apartment looked much as she had expected after studying the building plans in the archives of the City Zoning Office. The light-coloured furniture was birch and beechwood.

"Come on," Bjurman said in a friendlier tone. He put his arm around her shoulders and led her down a hall into the apartment's interior (Larsson, *The Girl with the Dragon Tattoo*: 197).

Salander is forced to have sex—including the use of an anal plug—with Bjurman, who uses his physical bulk to overcome her attempts at getting away (this is the second time Bjurman forces Salander to have sex with him). He slaps her, handcuffs her to the bed, and asks her to return on a later day for more sexual favors. She does return, but this time we see a different outcome, one that is more in tune with modern ideas about feminism and power:

Salander returned at the agreed-upon time to Bjurman's apartment near Odenplan. He let her in with a polite, welcoming smile.

"And how are you doing today, dear Lisbeth?"

She did not reply. He put an arm around her shoulder.

"I suppose it was a bit rough last time," he said. "You looked a little subdued."

She gave him a crooked smile and he felt a sudden pang of uncertainty. *This girl is not all there. I have to remember that.* He wondered if she would come around.

"Shall we go into the bedroom?" Salander said.

On the other hand, she may be with it. ... Today I'll take it easy on her. Build up her trust. He had already put out the handcuffs on the chest of drawers. It was not until they reached the bed that Bjurman realised that something was amiss.

She was the one leading him to the bed, not the other way around. He stopped and gave her a puzzled look when she pulled something out of her jacket pocket which he thought was a mobile telephone. Then he saw her eyes.

"Say goodnight," she said.

She shoved the taser into his left armpit and fired off 75,000 volts. When his legs began to give way she put her shoulder against him and used all her strength to push him down on the bed (Larsson, *The Girl with the Dragon Tattoo*: 203).

When Bjurman comes to, he finds himself tied to the bed with his mouth taped shut. Salander uses the anal plug on him, and then shows him that she had a video camera with her the time before, so he cannot have her arrested for battery and rape, as she could use the recording of his treatment of her against him. Madame Bovary, on the other hand, never has to resort to these actions to control the men she sleeps with.

At this point, you may be thinking that all male-female sexuality is violent and unequal—certainly an argument made by some feminists—but Larsson provides insights into sexual relationships that seem much more consensual:

At 8:00 Blomkvist switched off his computer and put on his outdoor clothing. He left the lights on in his office. Outside the sky was bright with stars and the night was freezing. He walked briskly up the hill, past Vanger's house, taking the road to Ostergarden. Beyond Vanger's house he turned off to the left, following an uglier path along the shore. The lighted buoys flickered out on the water, and the lights from Hedestad gleamed prettily in the dark. He needed fresh air, but above all he wanted to avoid the spying eyes of Isabella Vanger. Not far from Martin Vanger's house he rejoined the road and arrived at Cecilia Vanger's door just after 8:30. They went straight to her bedroom.

They met once or twice a week. Cecilia had not only become his lover out here in his place of exile, she had also become the person he had begun to confide in. It was significantly more rewarding discussing Harriet Vanger with her than with her uncle (Larsson, *The Girl with the Dragon Tattoo*: 197).

Is all of this part of Levy's (2006) raunch culture? In fact, later in the book, Blomkvist and Salander have consensual sex, though it is darker than what is described here between Blomkvist and Vanger.

Whether these sex scenes are simply gratuitous or part of the larger story (which climaxes in having Blomkvist and Salander discovering that one of the male Vangers is killing women), we see gender playing out in these scenarios. We have the stereotypical older male involved in business, who is forcing a younger female to have sex with him because she needs his resources. The younger female turns to modern technology and sex to neutralize the male and take her revenge. We also have the male hero, whom women of all ages cannot resist (though all seem somewhat embarrassed by the encounters or at least try to hide them), and the women who spy on him, though some of the Vanger males are also interested in his activities, but are typically more upfront or violent in wanting to know why he is on their property.

It should also be noted that gender is not a social structure that is isolated from other structures. Moraga and Anzaldua (1981) have collected stories from women of color who point out the difficulties of being both nonwhite and non-male. This is referred to as an intersectional perspective, and will be discussed further in the next chapter when I introduce the concept of class. At this point, it is enough to say that simply knowing that someone is male or female, masculine or feminine, is not enough to understand their life situation. It is another structure that must be navigated by the individual and taken into account by the sociologist, while also trying to understand how other structures influence our life chances and decisions.

REFERENCES AND RECOMMENDED READINGS

Alcott, L. M. (2009). *Little Women*. Rockville, MD: Arc Manor.

Findlen, B. (Ed.). (2001). *Listen Up*. Seattle: Seal Press.

Flaubert, G. (1919). *Madame Bovary*. New York: Brentano's.

Haywood, C., and Mac an Ghaill, M. (2003). *Men and Masculinities*. Philadelphia: Open University Press.

hooks, b. (2000). *Feminism Is for Everybody*. Boston: South End Press.

Larsson, S. 2008. *The Girl with the Dragon Tattoo* (trans. Reg Keeland). New York: Random House Digital.

Levy, A. (2006). *Female Chauvinist Pigs*. New York: Free Press.

Moraga, C., and Anzaldua, G. (Eds.). (1981). *This Bridge Called My Back*. Watertown, MA: Persephone Press.

Pascoe, C. J. (2012). *Dude, You're a Fag*. Berkeley: University of California Press.

West, C., and Zimmerman, D. H. (1987). "Doing Gender." *Gender & Society*, 1(2): 125–51.

9 CLASS

INTRODUCTION AND *THE BONFIRE OF THE VANITIES*

America is the home of the free, a place where anyone can make it, which means anyone can become rich and powerful. The name of Horatio Alger is often conjured up when talking about moving from the poorhouse to a New York penthouse. Alger wrote stories about poor boys working hard, and through their hard work they became wealthy. According to this kind of wisdom, anyone who does not make it in America just needs to try a little harder.

America is also thought of as a society in which socioeconomic class is non-existent. There are definitely rich and poor people, a middle class, working class, and so forth, but all the boundaries between classes are basically porous. People can and do move in and out of income brackets, unlike nations such as India where castes are relatively stable. Even the poorest immigrant kid in the United States can grow up to have a place like Sherman McCoy's from Tom Wolfe's *The Bonfire of the Vanities*:

> At that very moment, in the very sort of Park Avenue co-op apartment that so obsessed the Mayor ... twelve-foot ceilings ... two wings, one for the white Anglo-Saxon Protestants who own the place and one for the help ... Sherman McCoy was kneeling in his front hall trying to put a leash on a dachshund. The floor was a deep green marble, and it went on and on. It led to a five-foot-wide walnut staircase that swept up in a sumptuous curve to the floor

above. It was the sort of apartment the mere thought of which ignites flames of greed and covetousness under people all over New York and, for that matter, all over the world. But Sherman burned only with the urge to get out of this fabulous spread of his for thirty minutes.

So here he was, down on both knees, struggling with a dog. The dachshund, he figured, was his exit visa (Wolfe, *The Bonfire of the Vanities*: 9).

McCoy is trying to escape his Park Avenue apartment so that he can meet his mistress, another aspect of life we often think of as being part of the wealthy class—secret, kinky sex with lots of different people. There are also the luxury sedans and expensive sports cars. In fact, McCoy and his mistress end up in one of his expensive cars when they hit a black teenager from a poorer part of the city. As we follow the trials and tribulations of everyone in the book, we find that many people are trying to be like McCoy, yet so few ever make it.

Wolfe is obviously writing fiction, because everyone gets rich when they work hard in the United States. Just ask the garbage collectors who are working before most of us even wake up. While we like to think that anyone can make it, upward social mobility is difficult. This is true of the United States as well as most other developed countries (Erikson & Goldthorpe, 1985), and even harder in developing countries, where economies are typically less developed and so there are fewer opportunities to advance.

Not only is upward mobility difficult, so are leaving the people and habits we learned growing up if we do happen to move up (or down). Bourdieu (1984) refers to this as habitus. While we may have some agency in deciding to stay in school or focus on landing a job that pays more than our parents earned, the cultural structures we grow up with tend to inform our decisions into and through adulthood. If we learn to eat certain foods as a kid and then have the opportunity to try new things, most people might try those foods but typically end up back with their old habits. People who experience downward mobility will often try to find less expensive options of the foods, clothing, and other artifacts they grew up with. In short, our tastes are shaped by the socioeconomic class in which we were raised. Not everyone agrees that class background is so deterministic. Halle (1992) argues that changing tastes in some areas such as liking or not liking abstract art may not be as complex as having to learn more about the art and artists, but through simple exposure to this kind of art. This, however, still requires resources (moving to a city with a museum, buying a computer and Internet access so someone can see various paintings, etc.) that may be difficult for some groups to afford.

Bourdieu's research was conducted in France, which is said to be more concerned with class status than the United States. While we can find similar tendencies in U.S. society as in French society, there is a difference in the sense that many U.S. citizens believe themselves to be middle class, or hold middle-class values—even if they are above or below middle-class incomes and wealth. This appears in numerous ways, including food habits. It is often thought that people who are hungry will take anything given to them, but that does not seem to be the case. I have been involved in research regarding food procurement in poor neighborhoods, where we found that people who were having a hard time finding enough food for their families often ignored free fresh produce from local farms (complete with dirt and spots), and instead desired white bread and other highly processed foods. In their minds, a dirty carrot did not look like something a middle-class person eats or feeds their kids after school. Instead, a frosted cupcake from the local supermarket looks and tastes like a middle-class snack. That is what they desire, and are told so by television commercials, their friends, and their relatives. We may find ourselves saying that if the poor are unwilling to take free food then they deserve to be hungry, but many people would pass up items that do not fit their values if they were facing the same dilemma. I am guessing there are many college students without the money to buy new clothes, but would rather keep wearing the same outfits they do have than be given something from a charity store (Goodwill, Salvation Army, etc.) or a secondhand shop.

Karl Marx (1983) calls this kind of thinking false consciousness. From an abstract standpoint, false consciousness is the idea that we think we are happy with our lot in life when we should be upset with the social environment. This includes believing that you are part of the middle class when your bank account and tax bracket say otherwise. Credit and government assistance programs have been created to maintain both our false consciousness and the stability of the upper class by allowing consumers from the lower classes to buy the things that make them happy and feel that they are maintaining an appropriate lifestyle. As long as there are food stamps that can be used to buy highly processed foods, people are less willing to challenge the system that provides for them. In addition, people living in poor areas tend to think that they will eventually get out of their situation, though their choice of pathways is often tied to highly competitive jobs such as becoming a singer, actor, or professional athlete (McLeod, 2009).

CLASS AS A POINT OF INTERSECTIONS AND *LES MISÉRABLES*

Most of us understand that social stratification has been part of society for a long time (that it still exists in places like the United States is more difficult for people to see or acknowledge). Even a cursory glance through a history book shows kings and other nobles living in opulence, while others have meager belongings and toil in the fields from dawn until dusk, growing food for the king and his court. This has been part of humanity since we began growing crops and in need of a warrior class to protect our farms, though such living conditions have never been easy for the majority of the population. Victor Hugo understood this in his preface to *Les Misérables*:

> So long as there shall exist, by reason of law and custom, a social condemnation, which, in the face of civilization, artificially creates hells on earth, and complicates a destiny that is divine, with human fatality; so long as the three problems of the age—the degradation of man by poverty, the ruin of woman by starvation, and the dwarfing of childhood by physical and spiritual night—are not solved; so long as, in certain regions, social asphyxia shall be possible; in other words, and from a yet more extended point of view, so long as ignorance and misery remain on earth, books like this cannot be useless (Hugo, *Les Misérables*: 1).

Over a hundred years after Hugo wrote those words, there are still concerns with poverty, starvation, and dwarfing, with only a few violent uprisings to challenge the unequal distribution of power in terms of the lower classes attacking the upper classes. That was Marx's point when discussing false consciousness. For Marx, workers need to understand that they can take control of the government. All they need to do is come together for a common cause and rise up against those who own the factories (Marx's means of production in a capitalist economic system) and the politicians who protect them. The workers would then govern through communism—everyone has access to all things—and socialism—small government, as everyone is equal so there is little need to maintain a government that puts rules in place to maintain inequalities.

Proudhon (1994), who was known to argue with Marx regarding the plight of the working people and the root causes of poverty, contends that equality could only be gained by abolishing private property. According to Proudhon, many of the constitutions being developed at the end of the 1700s and beginning of the 1800s protected four rights—liberty, freedom, security, and property. The first three can bring about equality, but property negates those processes. Once people are allowed to own things, they become distrustful of their fellow citizens, who either own more or less than they do. In short, we become insecure knowing that others are gunning for our things.

If ownership causes so many problems and negates so many rights we hold dear, why does it exist, especially given the levels of inequality we see throughout society? Weber (2009) has an answer to that: status. Income and wealth not only allow you to purchase things, but they provide a measuring stick with which to compare yourself to others. A higher income typically means higher prestige and status, which in turn provides you with more opportunities to meet people who want to be linked to those with high status and prestige. People will even try to show their wealth (or hide their lack of it) by purchasing certain goods considered part of the higher-class lifestyle (luxury cars, expensive clothes, gold jewelry, meals at fine restaurants, etc.). Veblen (1912) studied this phenomenon, and concluded that vicarious consumption—showing one's wealth through purchases—was a habit of the leisure class, something we will see more of in Chapter 15 when I take on the issue of art.

There are, however, more poor than rich people in society. Many of those poor people try to get the things they want through legitimate means, but that does not always work out. When a person feels they deserve to be part of the leisure class or have nicer things but are denied access, they end up like Thénardier and his wife from *Les Misérables*:

It is understood that the word *innkeeper* is employed here in a restricted sense, and does not extend to an entire class.

In the same year, 1823, Thenarier owed about fifteen hundred francs, of pressing debts, which rendered him moody.

However, obstinately unjust destiny was to him, Thenardier was one of those men who best understood to the greatest depth and in the most modern style, that which is a virtue among the barbarous, and a subject of merchandise among the civilized – hospitality. He was, besides, an admirable poacher, and was counted an excellent shot. He had a certain cool and quiet laugh, which was particularly dangerous.

His theories of innkeeping sometimes sprang from him by flashes. He had certain professional aphorisms which he inculcated in the mind of his wife. 'The duty of the innkeeper,' said he to her one day, emphatically, and in a low voice, 'is to sell to the first comer food, rest, light, fire, dirty linen, servants, fleas, and smiles; to stop travellers, empty small purses, and honestly lighten large ones; to receive families who are travelling, with respect; scrape the man, pluck the woman, and pick the child; to charge for the open window, the closed window, the chimney corner, the sofa, the chair, the stool, the bench, the feather bed, the mattress, the straw bed; to know how much the mirror is worn, and to tax that; and, but the five hundred thousand devils, to make the traveller pay for everything, even to the flies that his dog eats!'

This man and this woman were cunning and rage married – a hideous and terrible pair.

While the husband calculated and schemed, the Thenardiess thought not of absent creditors, took no care either for yesterday or the morrow, and lived passionately in the present moment.

Such were these two beings. Cosette was between them, undergoing their double pressure, like a creature who is at the same time being bruised by a millstone, and lacerated with pincers. The man and the woman had each a different way. Cosette was beaten unmercifully; that came from the woman. She went barefoot in the winter; that came from the man.

Cosette ran up stairs and down stairs; washed, brushed, scrubbed, swept, ran, tired herself, got out of breath, lifted heavy things, and puny as she was, did the rough work. No pity; a ferocious mistress, a malignant master. The Thenardier chop-house was like a snare, in which Cosette had been caught, and was trembling. The ideal of oppression was realized by this dismal servitude. It was something like a fly serving spiders.

The poor child was passive and silent.

When they find themselves in such condition at the dawn of existence, so young, so feeble, among men, what passes in these souls afresh from God! (Hugo, Les Misérables:54)

There is something else to understand about flies serving spiders. We are told that we enjoy giving to those who have more than us. According to Marx (1983), social stratification consists of two components—the economic infrastructure that is the basis of inequality, and a cultural superstructure that legitimates the economic infrastructure and its inequalities. The cultural superstructure consists of stories and images that support the rich being rich and the poor wanting to be rich. Della Fave (1980) shows how we come to see those who are richer as more deserving through institutions like religion, education, and the mass media. These institutions provide narratives for why society is the way it is, and that this is best for all concerned. This is the cultural superstructure at work, as it provides justifications for inequalities. As we watch shows and commercials that tell us that all we need is to own an expensive car, fine clothes, and tell time on a specific type of watch, we come to think that this is what it takes to be happy. That some people are happy is great to know, because we can see ourselves as rich and happy like the people on television. To fight against such messages is to be an ungrateful consumer and radical. It would mean being uninformed on issues, for as Horkheimer and Adorno (2013: 71) state, "[t]he whole world is made to pass through the filter of the cultural industry," and as audience members we come to see the images on movie and television screens as simply extensions of our everyday lives. To fight such images is to say that your life is a lie, and many people do not want to think that everything they have worked for is false. It should be noted that Horkheimer and Adorno think that staying away from the mass media would help a person become enlightened, as they see the media as the quickest way to dumb down an audience. People who want to move above the masses need to read critical works such as Marx and listen to complex music like Wagner.

The cultural industry also plays a role in maintaining the intersections that are played out in Thénardier's inn. In looking again at the above passage, we see that the man is in charge of keeping the bills and that the women are expected to entertain (the Thénardiess) and clean (Cosette). Things were bad enough for Cosette, but they may have been even worse if she had been an immigrant from Africa or Asia. Stratification is rarely one-dimensional, but builds on various inequalities. While poverty is difficult for anyone dealing with it, a white male experiences poverty differently from a black female. An English-speaking immigrant experiences it differently from someone who speaks Chinese. This is true in most social spheres, whether we refer to a person living in poverty or in the middle class. People are treated differently not only because of their economic resources, but also on their cultural (what we know) and social capital (who we know), the color of their skin, their age, sex, sexual orientation, religion, and so forth. While this may seem to be enough to begin thinking about new ways to construct society—and some individuals and groups are doing exactly that—many of us would be lost without these structures in our lives.

THE NEED FOR ORDER AND *LORD OF THE FLIES*

The need for order has already been touched upon with the Robinson family that Wyss marooned on a deserted island filled with ostriches and bears, and sociologists have also found that the absence of social structures is often met with hurried attempts to reconstruct them (Garfinkel, 1967). The statuses of ourselves and others are not something that many of us can live without, as we need to know where we stand relative to those with whom we are interacting. Am I a leader, or are you? Am I responsible for finding us dinner, or can I count on you for that? William Golding played out this kind of scenario in *Lord of the Flies*, in which a group of young boys find themselves on an uninhabited island after their plane crashes into the ocean:

A storm of laughter arose and even the tiniest child joined in. For the moment the boys were a closed circuit of sympathy with Piggy outside: he went very pink, bowed his head, and cleaned his glasses again.

Finally the laughter died away and the naming continued. There was Maurice, next in size among the choir boys to Jack, but broad and grinning all the time. There was a slight, furtive boy whom no one knew, who kept to himself with an inner intensity of avoidance and secrecy. He muttered that his name was Roger and was silent again. Bill, Robert, Harold, Henry; the choir boy who had fainted sat up against a palm trunk, smiled pallidly at Ralph and said that his name was Simon.

Jack spoke.

"We've got to decide about being rescued."

There was a buzz. One of the small boys, Henry, said that he wanted to go home.

"Shut up," said Ralph absently. He lifted the conch. "Seems to me we ought to have a chief to decide things."

"A chief! A chief!"

"I ought to be chief," said Jack with simple arrogance, "because I'm chapter chorister and head boy. I can sing C sharp."

Another buzz.

"Well then," said Jack, "I—"

He hesitated. The dark boy, Roger, stirred at last and spoke up.

"Let's have a vote."

"Yes!"

"Vote for chief!"

"Let's vote—"

This toy of voting was almost as pleasing as the conch. Jack started to protest but the clamor changed from the general wish for a chief to an election by acclaim of Ralph himself. None of the boys could have found good reason for this; what intelligence had been shown was traceable to Piggy, while the most obvious leader was Jack. But there was a stillness about Ralph as he sat that marked him out: there was his size, and attractive appearance; and most obscurely, yet most powerfully, there was the conch. The being that had blown that, had sat waiting for them on the platform with the delicate thing balanced on his knees, was set apart.

"Him with the shell."

"Ralph! Ralph!"

"Let him be chief with the trumpet-thing."

Ralph raised a hand for silence.

"All right. Who wants Jack for chief?"

With dreary obedience the choir raised their hands.

"Who wants me?"

Every hand outside the choir except Piggy's was raised immediately. Then Piggy, too, raised his hand grudgingly into the air.

Ralph counted.

"I'm chief then."

The circle of boys broke into applause. Even the choir applauded; and the freckles on Jack's face disappeared under a blush of mortification. He started up, then changed his mind and sat down again while the air rang. Ralph looked at him, eager to offer something.

"The choir belongs to you, of course."

"They could be the army—"

"Or hunters—"

"They could be—"

The suffusion drained away from Jack's face. Ralph waved for silence.

"Jack's in charge of the choir. They can be—what do you want them to be?"

"Hunters."

Jack and Ralph smiled at each other with shy liking. The rest began to talk eagerly.

Jack stood up.

"All right, choir. Take off your togs."

As if released from class, the choir boys stood up, chattered, piled their black cloaks on the grass. Jack laid his on the trunk by Ralph. His grey shorts were sticking to him with sweat. Ralph glanced at them admiringly, and when Jack saw his glance he explained.

"I tried to get over that hill to see if there was water all around. But your shell called us."

Ralph smiled and held up the conch for silence (Golding, *Lord of the Flies*: 18–21).

In this scenario, size and age become the infrastructure that leadership, and therefore inequalities, was based upon, while ownership of the conch shell legitimated the newly formed political structure. I am not familiar enough with Golding to know whether or not he was a Marxist, but he was following a very similar formula that Marx saw as problematic.

While Jack and Ralph are two of many boys on the island, and Jack abuses his power as the story progresses, their ability to maintain their status points to how larger societies are also able to remain relatively stable. According to Parkin (1971), dominance can be maintained in a number of ways. Some regimes rely on fear and violence, though this approach is hard to maintain over a long period of time. Others, like the United States, legitimate stratification by providing opportunities to move into higher classes, though we have seen that this is very difficult for most. In addition, much of the movement is very short, such as the daughter of a well-paid factory worker having enough economic capital to go to college and land a middle-management job within the same type of company that her father works for. This is also true of downward movement, as we rarely see the sons and daughters of the upper echelons living in their cars on the streets of Chicago (and when we do it makes the news and the parents come and take the child back to the mansion). A third approach is for the poor to accept their fate (as the younger and weaker children do in *Lord of the Flies*), which is typically done through messages about how they are tough survivors or just did not work hard enough or in the right career fields to make it. Religious institutions are important in this respect, as most teach its members to love thy neighbor, be strong during hard times, and turn the other cheek when facing trouble.

Besides offering stability in an unstable world, stratified systems provide meanings for their members. Upper-class cultures, middle-class cultures, working-class cultures—all mean something to those who carry the labels (Parkin, 1971). Social inequality provides a model for smaller organizations that consist of members who are unable to take care of themselves (such as a family with small children), and it is within stratified systems that thoughts concerning social change are created and evolve. As stated by Parkin (1997), "attachment to the ideals of socialism can provide men with a sense of personal dignity and moral worth which is denied them by the dominant value system." To reiterate, in such writings, socialism is a social order in which all individuals are treated equally. Socialism as a political ideology will be discussed in the next chapter.

Dahrendorf (1979: 27) echoes this idea when he states, "[t]he greatest happiness of the greatest number may have something to do with a free society, but it leaves us with an elusive, individual and ahistorical concept." Humans are social animals, yet happiness is an individual feeling, though it comes from outside influences, as its pursuit is often done at the expense of others. To be truly human, then, is to seek progress that brings about feelings of community. The boys on the island could have spent their days searching for more conch shells or tracking down wild animals on their own, but such endeavors have little meaning when done in isolation.

Such need for structure goes beyond the individual. Organizations within institutions often seek order, and a great deal of time and effort are put into raising one's status in comparison with peer organizations. Colleges and universities continue to focus on how they are ranked by such media outlets as *U.S. News & World Report, Princeton Review,* and *Forbes.* Rising in one of these publications is grounds for celebration, while falling can lead to firings and rearrangements among administrators and instructors. If another plane had crashed near the island and a new set of boys who were older and stronger appeared, we can assume that Jack and Ralph would have been supplanted. If all the new boys were younger and smaller, Jack and Ralph's status would most likely increase. If the new plane was filled with females of the same age, we could assume there would be more control efforts on the part of the boys.

Once a group gains control of a situation, it typically wants to maintain its position, which is why modeling smaller organizations on larger social structures can be problematic. It is assumed that men were once thought to be better suited to hunt animals and go to war than women, and this led to patriarchal societies in which women are treated as less worthy than men in most social spheres, including the family, education, religion, and the workplace. There are few reasons to think that hunting is more important than childbearing, but power leads to control, which can lead to bullying. If subordinated groups begin to challenge those in power, the latter will often form alliances to maintain their positions of authority. Mizruchi (1996) provides a critique of one such strategy that takes place within large businesses—interlocking directorates. An interlocking directorate is when the board of directors of corporations such as AT&T, Disney, PepsiCo, and CitiBank share members. In other words, a member of the board at AT&T might also sit on the board at Disney. Both organizations own numerous corporations. Disney, for example, owns ESPN. If a reporter for ESPN were to find out that professional athletes were abusing AT&T services, the person who sits on the AT&T board may ask Disney to put off any news stories until more information is gathered. While Mizruchi points to a number of problems with this approach, strategies like these are used by powerful people and organizations to maintain their power, including seeking the resources of other powerful entities, as with interlocking directorates. This can backfire, as the other actors may not be as powerful or actually be more powerful than first thought, or become so through the alliance. Nazi Germany, for instance, ended up providing Mussolini's Italy with resources, as Italy's industry and war efforts were much weaker than Germany's; this is said to have cost Germany momentum in fighting the Allies.

Whether stratification and power are good or bad, these are likely to be part of our society for the foreseeable future. We may look for ways to close some of the gaps between economic, racial, gender, and other groups, but we make sense of society and our own places within it by understanding our relationship to power. If we want to bring about change, it begins with an understanding of how we treat others, as well as our own abilities and coming to understand how socioeconomic classes are created and maintained. If you find yourself degrading another person or group or telling yourself you are unable to do something, then you are maintaining structures of stratification.

REFERENCES AND RECOMMENDED READINGS

Bourdieu, P. (1984). *Distinctions* (trans. Richard Nice). Cambridge, MA: Harvard University Press.

Dahrendorf, R. (1979). *Life Chances*. Chicago: University of Chicago Press.

Della Fave, L. R. (1980). "The Meek Shall Not Inherit the Earth: Self-evaluation and the legitimacy of stratification." *American Sociological Review*, 45(6): 955–71.

Erikson, R., and Goldthorpe, J. H. (1985). "Are American Rates of Social Mobility Exceptionally High? New evidence on an old issue." *European Sociological Review*, 1(1) 1–22.

Garfinkel, H. (1967). *Studies in Ethnomethodology*. Englewood Cliffs, NJ: Prentice-Hall.

Golding, W. (2011). *Lord of the Flies*. New York: Riverhead Books.

Halle, D. (1992). "The Audience for Abstract Art: Class, culture, and power," pp. 131–51. In *Cultivating Differences*, edited by Michele Lamont and Marcel Fournier. Chicago: University of Chicago Press.

Horkheimer, M., and Adorno, T. (2013). "The Cultural Industry: Enlightenment as mass deception," pp. 65–79. In *Cultural Sociology*, edited by Matt Wray. New York: W.W. Norton and Company.

Hugo, V. (1863). *Les Misérables* (trans. Charles E. Wilbour). New York: Carleton.

Marx, K. (1983). *The Portable Karl Marx* (trans. Eugene Kamenka). New York: Viking.

MacLeod, J. (2009). *Ain't No Makin' It*. Boulder, CO: Westview Press.

Mizruchi, M. S. (1996). "What Do Interlocks Do? An analysis, critique, and assessment on interlocking directorates." *Annual Review of Sociology*, 22: 271–98.

Parkin, F. (1971). *Class Inequality and Political Order*. New York: Praeger.

Proudhon, P.-J. (1994). *What Is Property?* (edited and translated by Donald R. Kelley and Bonnie G. Smith. New York: Cambridge University Press.

Weber, M. (2009). *From Max Weber: Essays in Sociology* (trans. Hans H. Gerth and C. Wright Mills). New York: Routledge.

Veblen, T. (1912). *The Theory of the Leisure Class*. New York: Macmillan.

Wolfe, T. (2002). *The Bonfire of the Vanities*. New York: Macmillan.

10 SEX AND SEXUALITY

INTRODUCTION AND *LADY CHATTERLEY'S LOVER*

D o we make choices when falling in love? In Western societies, we often think that love is all about agency. You find someone you care about, realize there are common interests you share, and before you know it, the two of you are in love. Or maybe it involves a third person. What about four? We are socialized to challenge these last two scenarios, as true love is between two people. What about love within a family? Can the parents only truly love each other and not their children? Well, that kind of love is different. It is true love, but true in another sense. What about falling in love with someone from another time? It might be hard to convince your friends that you are truly in love with a person who lived in 12th-century India. What about someone who shares the same sexual organs as you? Can you love that person? Maybe you can love them, but in the eyes of many people, the two of you you should not be having sex. Do you have to have sex with a person to be truly, truly in love?

Before going much further, it is important to distinguish between love and sex, though both are social constructs and can be described in numerous ways. Most of us would accept the fact that we can love someone without having sex with them, though fewer would agree that you should have sex with someone you do not love (many people believe you can have sex with someone you do not love, just not as many who think it is fine to love someone and not have sex with them). Love is often thought of as a feeling, an emotion—however complex—while sex is a physical activity. You can show your love to someone by buying them presents or saying things, though it is more difficult to feel sex without engaging in it (besides memories or dreams of sex, which are thoughts and not physical actions, and thus would not be considered sex, but sexual). Much of this is splitting hairs. Readers may find ways to disagree with my approach, but that is the frame I will be using. This chapter focuses on sex and sexuality as an institution, and how we become socialized into that institution through both significant and generalized others. Love is and is not part of this discussion, and the reader is welcome to add that word and the emotions attached to it at any time. Just pay attention to when you think love should be part of the discussion; see if you can figure out why you feel that way, while your roommate or significant other disagrees.

Society often ties sex, sexuality, and gender very closely together, with males being the aggressors and females being more submissive when it comes to sex, and everyone is expected to be heteronormative with males liking females, and vice versa. While we have seen changes in this area over the past few decades (Levy, 2006), we still tend to think of males as more dominant when it comes to sex, which might be partly responsible for D. H. Lawrence's novel, *Lady Chatterley's Lover*, being so controversial when it was first published in the 1920s:

Both Hilda and Constance had had their tentative love affairs by the time they were eighteen. The young men with whom they talked so passionately and sang so lustily and camped under the trees in which freedom wanted, of course, the love connection. The girls were doubtful, but then the thing was so much talked about, it was supposed to be so important. And the men were so humble and craving. Why couldn't a girl be queenly, and give the gift of herself?

So they had given the gift of themselves, each to the youth with whom discussions were the great thing: the love-making and connection were only a sort of primitive reversion and a bit of an anti-climax. One was less in love with the boy afterwards, and a little inclined to hate him, as if he had trespassed on one's privacy and inner freedom. For, of course, being a girl, one's whole dignity and meaning in life consisted in the achievement of an absolute, a perfect, a pure and noble freedom. What else did a girl's life mean? To shake off the old and sordid connections and subjections.

And however one might sentimentalize it, this sex business was one of the most ancient, sordid connections and subjections. Poets who glorified it were mostly men. Women had always known there was something better, something higher. And now they knew it more definitely than ever. The beautiful pure freedom of a woman was infinitely more wonderful than any sexual love. The only unfortunate thing was that men lagged so far behind women in the matter. They insisted on the sex thing like dogs (Lawrence, *Lady Chatterley's Lover*: 3–4).

When it came to sex, Lawrence's placement of women above men in all accounts landed *Lady Chatterley's Lover* on numerous banned-books lists, as well as what were considered graphic sex scenes for the time period. Not only was sex a forbidden topic in public, but to say that women loved the men less after making love to them went against the typical Victorian principles of the time, though the so-called Roaring Twenties were beginning to challenge a number of sexual norms and beliefs. Lawrence pushes this even further when Lady Chatterley begins having sex with someone other than her husband:

Connie was in love with him, but she managed to sit with her embroidery and let the men talk, and not give herself away. As for Michaelis, he was perfect; exactly the same melancholic, attentive, aloof young fellow of the previous evening, millions of degrees remote from his hosts, but laconically playing up to them to the required amount, and never coming forth to them for a moment. Connie felt he must have forgotten the morning. He had not forgotten. But he knew where he was … in the same old place outside, where the born outsiders are. He didn't take the love-making altogether personally. He knew it would not change him from an ownerless dog, whom everybody begrudges its golden collar, into a comfortable society dog.

The final fact being that at the very bottom of his soul he *was* an outsider, and anti-social, and he accepted the fact inwardly, no matter how Bond-Streety he was on the outside. His isolation was a necessity to him; just as the appearance of conformity and mixing-in with the smart people was also a necessity.

But occasional love, as a comfort and soothing, was also a good thing, and he was not ungrateful. On the contrary, he was burningly, poignantly grateful for a piece of natural, spontaneous kindness; almost to tears. Beneath his pale, immobile, disillusioned face, his child's soul was sobbing with gratitude to the woman, and burning to come to her again; just as his outcast soul was knowing he would keep really clear of her.

He found an opportunity to say to her, as they were lighting the candles in the hall:

'May I come?'
'I'll come to you,' she said.
'Oh, good!'

He waited for her a long time … but she came.

He was the trembling excited sort of lover, whose crisis soon came, and was finished. There was something curiously childlike and defenceless about his naked body: as children are naked. His defences were all in his wits and cunning, his very instincts of cunning, and when these were in abeyance he seemed doubly naked and like a child, of unfinished, tender flesh, and somehow struggling helplessly.

He roused in the woman a wild sort of compassion and yearning, and a wild, craving physical desire. The physical desire he did not satisfy in her; he was always come and finished so quickly, then shrinking down on her breast, and recovering somewhat his effrontery while she lay dazed, disappointed, lost (Lawrence, *Lady Chatterley's Lover*: 27–28).

Connie becomes Michaelis's teacher in sexuality, another affront to many male readers in the early 1900s, and most likely female readers who might have agreed on principle but found the topic indecent or obscene. To reiterate, women were supposed to be passive and fulfilled by men, no matter how quickly the latter finished with the former. Even today, we think of a woman who knows enough about sex to teach a man how to handle himself as too experienced. This is obvious in the ways we talk about men, women, and sex, as there are very few flattering words for women who are promiscuous (slut, whore, bitch, floozy, hussy, skank, loose, etc.), while even supposedly negative terms for promiscuous males (player) will often gain one favor with other males as they try to learn the secrets for attracting the opposite sex. Some of the same dynamics are also found in gay culture, showing us how deeply held these social values are tied to sex.

SEX, THE SOCIOLOGIST, AND "HOWL"

Sociologists are not in a position to describe the sexual act (that is what the *Kama Sutra* and other how-to guides are for), but we are interested in how society treats the subject. Besides a few artificial inseminations, each of us appeared after sexual intercourse, which seems important enough to take into account when discussing the topic of sex, prostitution is the oldest profession, and pornography is a multibillion-dollar business. Still, sex is a taboo topic in most public spheres, as evidenced by the reception to *Lady Chatterley's Lover* and the selection for this section—Allen Ginsberg's "Howl," which was considered obscene enough to have those selling it arrested. The best place to start figuring out this puzzle is with the institutions we are exposed to early in life: family, religion, education, and the media.

As mentioned in Chapter 2, the modern family is expected to determine who has sexual access to whom, in part because sex has come to be viewed as a pleasurable activity—though not talked about—as compared to a more traditional value of procreation (Chambers, 2012). Given that the rights of children in the modern family have expanded, sexual access to appropriate partners needs to be maintained. Incest is frowned upon in most, if not all, societies, and some believe that it is only through such deeply held cultural values that sexual urges among siblings and between parents and children are deflected. There are enough stories about certain families, such as inclusive nobility, to understand that sex can and is practiced among those closely related to each other in certain circumstances.

Religion also regulates sex. Many orthodox religions believe that sex should only be between a man and a woman who have been married under the guidance of a religious leader. Fundamentalist Christians will point to the Bible as proof of this, saying, among other things, that there are no instances of same-sex relationships (though there are plenty of out-of-wedlock sexual encounters), or of sex with animals. The Seventh Commandment states that no Christian shall commit adultery, and the Tenth states that you shall not covet your neighbor's wife. Various religious institutions are also against any kind of birth control, so engaging in sexual behavior outside a committed relationship can be risky in terms of having an unwanted pregnancy that cannot be terminated. A willingness to overlook the edicts of one's religion can be detrimental to one's standing in the eyes of a watchful deity, as well as fellow parishioners.

While families and religious institutions typically forbid sex outside a committed relationship, the role of education in sexual activity is much more difficult to determine. Sex education classes range from abstinence-only curricula, to showing students how to put on a condom. Some schools provide free condoms, while others forbid any discussion of birth control. Some sex education teachers lecture only on the risks of sex—sexually transmitted diseases, unwanted pregnancies, rape, human trafficking—while others discuss the pleasures of consensual intercourse. Given that many children reach puberty between the ages of 9 and 13, what they are told at school will likely have an impact on how they think about their own bodies as well as those of other students, and sex education is not the only place they hear about bodies and what can be done with them.

One of the most implicated institutions regarding sex is the media (an institution I will discuss in more detail in Chapter 13). The easy access to media messages has led many observers to argue that these messages must be regulated. Such concerns led to the creation of the Federal Communications Commission (FCC) which is asked to monitor, with the help of audience members, obscene and indecent broadcasts. According to the FCC website (www.fcc.gov, accessed June 2013),

> [o]bscene material is not protected by the First Amendment to the Constitution and cannot be broadcast at any time. The Supreme Court has established that, to be obscene, material must meet a three-pronged test: An average person, applying contemporary community standards, must find that the material, as a whole, appeals to the prurient interest; the material must depict or describe, in a patently offensive way, sexual conduct specifically defined by applicable law; and the material, taken as a whole, must lack serious literary, artistic, political or scientific value.

Who, however, is an average person? Take the city in which I am writing this. East Lansing, Michigan, is home to a large college campus housing a few thousand individuals between the ages of 18 and 35. The campus is surrounded by typical families (mom, dad, and the kids) who attend religious services; there is an active queer community; numerous immigrant groups with different cultural values; and so forth. If one person is offended by a broadcast but another finds it entertaining and therefore valuable, who can really say which one is the average person applying contemporary community standards?

Such a situation is not unprecedented. The following excerpt from Allen Ginsberg's "Howl" led to the arrests of Shigeyoshi Murao and Lawrence Ferlinghetti who were selling the book at the City Lights Bookstore in San Francisco in the 1950s. Ginsberg was not in the country at the time, and likely would not have been arrested, as there are no laws against writing something with obscene words or indecent imagery. The concern is with distribution.

I saw the best minds of my generation destroyed by
    madness, starving hysterical naked,
dragging themselves through the negro streets at dawn
    looking for an angry fix,
angelheaded hipsters burning for the ancient heavenly
    connection to the starry dynamo in the machinery of night
…
who broke down crying in white gymnasiums naked
    and trembling before the machinery of other skeletons,
who bit detectives in the neck and shrieked with delight
    in policecars for committing no crime but their
    own wild cooking pederasty and intoxication,
who howled on their knees in the subway and were
    dragged off the roof waving genitals and manuscripts,
who let themselves be fucked in the ass by saintly
    motorcyclists, and screamed with joy,
who blew and were blown by those human seraphim
    the sailors, caresses of Atlantic and Caribbean love,
who balled in the morning in the evenings in rose-
    gardens and the grass of public parks and
    cemeteries scattering their semen freely to
    whomever come who may,
who hiccupped endlessly trying to giggle but wound up
    with a sob behind a partition in a Turkish Bath
    when the blond & naked angel came to pierce
    them with a sword

who lost their loveboys to the three old shrews of fate
    the one eyed shrew of the heterosexual dollar
    the one eyed shrew that winks out of the womb
    and the one eyed shrew that does nothing but
    sit on her ass and snip the intellectual golden
    threads of the craftsman's loom (Ginsberg, "Howl": 9, 13–14).

The trial over the distribution of "Howl" highlighted the difficulty in trying to determine who is an average citizen and what is a community standard when it comes to the topic of sex. The defense team for Ferlinghetti (charges against Murao had been dropped) called in literary critics and fellow poets to testify on the literary value of Ginsberg's poem, while the prosecutors asked high school teachers if they would assign the poem in their courses (Morgan & Peters, 2006). The defense team's strategy was to show that the whole poem provided insightful social commentary, while the prosecution pulled out specific words and lines that were considered problematic, and why high school teachers found the poem to be obscene. In the end, Judge Clayton W. Horn determined that the poem did not appeal to the prurient interest, and Ferlinghetti was found innocent of distributing indecent material.

Do we, however, learn about sex from reading about it in a poem? What about in the lyrics of a song such as ZZ Top's "Pearl Necklace," or Eminem and Rihanna's "Love the Way You Lie?" What about pornographic images on the Internet or in the back of a video store? Or is sex something we naturally come to understand? Easy access to sexual material is a relatively recent phenomenon, yet humans have been able to engage in sexual activities for a few thousand years. According to Terry (2012), sex is considered natural and part of adult life; it is the cessation of having sex that is a learned behavior.

Foucault (1990: 78, emphasis in the original) states that, "[i]n the space of a few centuries, a certain inclination has led us to direct the question of what we are, to sex. Not so much to sex as representing nature, but to sex as history, as signification and discourse. We have placed ourselves under the sign of sex, but in the form of a *Logic of Sex*, rather than a *Physics*." For Foucault, human sex and sexuality are learned behaviors that have changed over time. The act of sex might be a naturally occurring desire, but not how we think about sex or how it is practiced. Those things are learned and have changed over time, especially in the last few centuries, as we moved from sex for procreation (prior to modern times, the average woman would give birth to five children) to sex for recreation (the average fertility rate for women in the United States was 1.9 and 7.0 in Niger in 2011, http://data.worldbank.org/indicator/SP.DYN.TFRT.IN, accessed June 2013). Foucault even argues that we have had to learn how sex can be a pleasurable activity used for entertainment.

This still does not answer the question of how we learn about sex, but such an answer is complex, as it must take into consideration a number of institutions. As mentioned, knowledge of sex is found in the family, religion, school, workplace, media, serendipitous touching of ourselves and others, and so forth. How we learn about sex is much like how we learn about math or how to work on cars, though these activities are not tied to bodily functions in the same way as sexuality. From this standpoint, learning about sex is no more or less natural than other topics. Lenny Bruce (1965), a popular and controversial comedian in the 1950s, said that he learned about it from watching his aunt bring home boyfriends (Bruce's father and mother were separated), as well as from the older boys in school. Older siblings teach younger ones about sex, and we watch people kiss and roll around in bed on television shows. Beginning in 1997, the website whitehouse.com was a pornographic site, and we can assume that many reports about presidents led unsuspecting children and their parents to that site (in June 2013, whitehouse.com contained links to governmental, lingerie, and personal contact sites). In short, we are surrounded by sex, and as Terry mentions (2012), the trick might be learning not to have sex.

The learning of pleasure as it relates to sex often coincides with notions of morality (Foucault, 1990). Morality, in turn, is tied to other institutions such as religion, transportation (better transportation leads to people moving to new areas, where they experience new situations and may not be under close scrutiny of home institutions), and the media. This can be seen in changes toward sex and sexuality through time. According to Foucault, the ancient Greeks and Romans had sexual codes related to practices, but as Christianity became the religion of choice in the Western world, codes regarding sexuality became focused on forbidding certain practices and restricting sexuality. The rise of the adult film industry, which has become a multibillion dollar endeavor, is based on sexual pleasure and gratification, with very little discussion of pregnancy and other potential problems associated with unprotected sex. All of this has changed our way of thinking about sex and our moralities, though the act is basically the same as it has been over the centuries. This includes not only sex, but notions of sexuality as well.

SEXUAL ORIENTATION, SEXUAL VIOLENCE, AND *THE LIAR*

Sexual preferences—homosexual, bisexual, or heterosexual (as well as transgendered and so forth)—are at the center of debates over the roles of nature and nurture in the development of the self. If the desire to have sex is tied to our genes, does that mean whom we want to have sex with is part of our nature as well? Or do we see others in same-sex relationships and decide that would be best for us as well? If homosexual kids come out of heterosexual homes, can heterosexual kids be raised in homosexual homes? Can a parent steer a child toward a sexual preference?

Sullivan (2003) traces the history of medical and societal definitions of homosexuality, which has ranged from seeing it as nothing special, to considering it as dangerous mental and physical health issues. The notion of homosexuality—as well as bisexuality—being an illness was the typical approach from the 1800s until the 1960s, when some attitudes began to change, due to incidents such as the Stonewall riots in 1969. These riots were precipitated by police officers harassing patrons at the Stonewall Inn in New York's Greenwich Village, many of whom were known to be homosexuals or drags. Very rarely does one incident, even a riot, change societal conditions, and Sullivan points out that queer(ing) sexuality before, during, and after Stonewall has been a complex and delicate issue that will not change easily or readily. The following exchange in Stephen Fry's *The Liar* shows how even the highly educated can be at odds over sex and sexual orientation:

'If an undergraduate were compromised in this fashion,' said Menzies, 'we would have no hesitation in sending him down. Professor Trefusis is a member of the college just like any student. I submit that under the college ordinance of 1273 and subsequent statutes of 1791 and 1902 we are duty bound to take disciplinary action against any Fellow who brings the good name of the college into disrepute. I move that this meeting of the Fellows immediately invite Professor Trefusis to relinquish the post of Senior Tutor and furthermore I move that they insist he withdraw from any active teaching post in this college for one year. At the very least.'

'Nice subjunctives,' murmured Adrian.

'Now steady on, Garth,' said the President. 'I'm sure we're all as shocked as you are by Donald's ... Donald's ... well, his behaviour. But remember where we are. This is Cambridge. We have a tradition of buggery here.'

'Bottomy is everywhere, you know,' the ninety-year-old treble of Emeritus Professor Adrian Williams sang out. 'Wittgenstein was a bottomist, they tell me. I read the other day that Morgan Foster, you remember Morgan? Next door, at King's. Wrote *A Passage to India* and *Howards End*. Wore slippers into Hall once. I read that *he* was a bottomite too. Extraordinary! I think everyone is now. Simply everyone.'

A red-faced statistician thumped the table angrily.

'Not I, sir, not I!' he thundered.

'I don't think we should be unafraid not to discuss the gay dialectic as an energy and the homophobic constraints that endorse its marginalisation as a functionally reactive discourse,' said Tim Anderson.

The cameraman in the corner tilted his camera from one end of the table to the other, quite unable to decide on whom to concentrate his lens.

'If I can speak,' said Adrian.

He had just unwrapped a packet of cigarettes and now scrunched up the cellophane so loudly that the microphone boom, which had just reached him, swung away like a startled giraffe and struck Menzies on the head.

A production assistant with a clipboard giggled and was rewarded with a look of foul contempt from the President.

Menzies was not to be put off.

'The fact is this, Master. There are laws. Homosexual acts are only permitted amongst consenting adults in private.'

'Are you allowed in law, Dr. Menzies,' asked Adrian, 'to defecate in public?'

'Certainly not!'

'How would I be charged if I did?'

'Gross indecency, beyond question, the case of the Earl of Oxford.'

'Exactly. But would I be arrested for taking a crap in the public lavatory?'

'Don't be ridiculous.'

'So a public lavatory is, in law, a private place?'

'You're twisting words again, Healey.'

'But again, the words are already twisted. Either a municipal bog is a private place or it isn't. If it is a private place in which to shit, how is it not a private place in which to fellate?'

'Oh, it was fellatio, was it?' the President seemed surprised.

'Well, whatever.'

'Who was doing it to whom, I wonder?'

Menzies' hold on his temper was weakening.

'Either the law is the law or it is not! If it is your intention to campaign for a change in that law, Healey, very good luck to you. The fact remains that Professor Trefusis has brought into disrepute the good name of this college.'

'You never liked him did you?' Adrian couldn't help saying. 'Well, here's your chance. He's down. Kick him good and hard' (Fry, *The Liar*: 139–41).

Queering sexuality means queering our look on everything in a patriarchal and heteronormative society (Sullivan, 2003). If we consider a bathroom stall to be private for one act, why is it not for others? If the determination is based on laws, those laws are based on human interpretations of events and situations, all of which change over time and circumstances. In addition, most laws have been created and are maintained by heterosexual males who see society in a very specific way. Foucault (1990) argues much the same thing when discussing sexuality throughout history, as many of the laws we have today regarding sex and sexual orientation were not part of the social landscape in other societies at other times. This is true of homosexuality as well as acts of marital rape, the latter of which most queer theorists would say is problematic. However, the male-dominated heterosexual society did not see it that way until approximately the 1970s, and it was not until 1993 that all U.S. states determined that marital rape was a crime (http://www.crisisconnectioninc.org/pdf/US_History_of_Marital_Rape.pdf, accessed June 2013). Today, marital rape is said to account for approximately 25 percent of all rapes in the United States.

Rape is not the only violence that takes place during sex, some of which is consensual, as has been made popular by writers such as E. L. James in *Fifty Shades of Grey*, a novel in which the world of sexual sadomasochism is explored. Some scholars, however, would say that all sex is violent because it involves dominance of some kind. Even in consensual masochistic relations, authors such as Sullivan (2003) argue that at first glance, dominance, especially female dominance, can seem to be queering the boundaries of typical sexual relationships—until one realizes that the interaction is still based on power, and that it is assumed that the male, or physically stronger, partner can retake control at any time. Interpersonal sex is rarely defined by complete equality, and it is not until partners feel that they are under no obligation regarding the performance that sex will become completely queer relative to what sex involves today. If performances are no longer judged, books like *Lady Chatterley's Lover* become just another historical artifact.

Fry's scene not only captures the complexity of homosexual relationships, but the added layer of institutional power. In addition to whether or not the sexual act discussed above happens in a private or public setting, one of the members openly wonders who was providing oral sex to whom. We typically think of the person penetrating the other as dominant and the one being penetrated as subordinate (this definition is based on the word "penetration," though the same could be said about the word "envelop," as being enveloped can be as threatening as being penetrated). Given that this is a college setting, we could also assume that a professor would have power relative to a student. Many, with some arguing all, forced sex acts (sexual crimes) are also based on power. In a patriarchal society such as the United States, that usually means that men force women to have sex with them (approximately ten percent of all rapes involve men as victims, and some of those are perpetrated by men), with a majority of rapes, not just marital, involving individuals who know each other (acquaintance rape). While forced sex can lead to pregnancy or sexually transmitted disease that can be life threatening, it can also cause extreme mental anguish. If either of the characters involved in the fellatio of Fry's novel were either straight or did not want to have sex with the other person, their sense of who they are will be tested. Tyler Clementi, a student at Rutgers University, committed suicide in 2010 after his roommate posted videos of Clementi being intimate with another male. The sex was consensual, but Clementi had not told others about his sexual orientation. The clandestine filming was not a typical rape, but violent all the same, and led to Clementi's death. If social institutions had not made sex and sexuality such a taboo topic, Clementi, and many others, might still be with us. Whether more sexual freedom is the answer, however, is an open question, especially if we are waiting for all those other social structures connected to sex to change, and let us know that it is fine to talk openly about sex and one's sexual orientation. That would be a true queering of sex in the United States, which would have nothing to do with the sexual act or one's sexual orientation.

REFERENCES AND RECOMMENDED READINGS

Bruce, L. (1965). *How to Talk Dirty and Influence People*. Chicago: Playboy.

Chambers, D. (2012). *A Sociology of Family Life*. Malden, MA: Polity.

Foucault, M. (1990). *The History of Sexuality, Volumes 1 and 2* (trans. Robert Hurley). New York: Vintage.

Fry, Stephen. (1993). *The Liar*. New York: Soho Press.

Ginsberg, A. (1959). *Howl*. San Francisco: City Lights Books.

Lawrence, D. H. (1959). *Lady Chatterley's Lover*. New York: Signet Classics.

Levy, A. (2006). *Female Chauvinist Pigs*. New York: Free Press.

Morgan, B., and Peters, N. J. (Eds.). (2006). *Howl on Trial*. San Francisco: City Lights Books.

Sullivan, N. (2003). *A Critical Introduction to Queer Theory*. New York: New York University Press.

Terry, G. (2012). "I'm Putting a Lid on That Desire: Celibacy, choice, and control." *Sexualities*, 15(7): 871–89.

11 CRIMINAL JUSTICE AND DEVIANCE

INTRODUCTION AND *SHERLOCK HOLMES*

The popular approach to crime is typically that bad people (criminals) do bad things, while good people (law-abiding citizens) do good things. Laws are meant to make life easier and safer for the latter and harder for the former. This was probably the mind-set when it was decided that a pickpocket could be hung for practicing his craft in England around 1800. There were, however, consequences for passing such laws. First, the murder rate increased, as pickpockets decided that killing their marks meant there was one less person who could catch them and send them to the gallows. In addition, much of the pocket-picking took place during the execution of fellow pickpockets (including a 13-year-old accused of stealing a spoon), as these events were fairly well attended (http://www.time.com/time/magazine/article/0,9171,894775,00.html, accessed June 2013). There would have been a great deal of pushing and shoving among spectators as they tried to get a better look at the execution, so being jostled by a pickpocket likely felt the same as being bumped into by an overeager neighbor. Changing the laws did little to change the circumstances of pickpockets, and it is unlikely that any of them were given an opportunity to discuss their living conditions with members of Parliament.

Thinking that good people do good things and bad people do bad things is what Stinchcombe (1968) refers to as a psychological rut. This rut stems from the idea that people's actions are based on their own thoughts and have little or nothing to do with their environment. As you have come to realize by now, sociologists would argue that behaviors are framed by social structures, of which there are many in the criminal justice system. The sociological imagination is helpful in this regard, as we begin to look at crimes and deviant behavior from a larger, societal vantage point. Alcohol consumption is a good example of how our ideas of crime and deviance are shaped by society. For much of history, alcohol was the beverage of choice regardless of age, given the quality of water and other liquids that were in and around human settlements, as sewer systems and sanitation are relatively new ideas in many parts of the world (e.g., Abraham Lincoln's mother died from tainted milk). Fermentation kills much of the harmful bacteria that can be found in liquids, so it was considered safe to drink. History is also full of groups that understood the effects of alcohol when used in excess, and tried to stir clear of it, some even saying that it was a product of the devil or some other evil being. The perspective that alcohol was a problem on a large scale began to really take hold in the 1800s in the United States, culminating in the passage of the Eighteenth Amendment to the U.S. Constitution in 1920. This amendment, commonly called Prohibition, outlawed the manufacturing and selling of alcohol—but not its consumption—which in turn led to a growth in criminal activity around bootlegging (this was the era of criminals such as Al Capone). In 1933, the Twenty-First Amendment to the Constitution was passed. It repealed the Eighteenth Amendment, and alcohol manufacturing and sales were once again legal. In a span of 14 years, the same activity went from being legal (prior to the Eighteenth Amendment) to being illegal (after the Eighteenth Amendment) to being legal again (after the Twenty-First Amendment), even though very little changed about alcohol or its effects on a person who consumes it. It was the structures of the criminal justice system and its intersections with other institutions that determined the status of alcohol usage, not the substance itself or most of the people who consumed it.

Contemporary alcohol laws in the United States also point to the importance of social structures in determining what is and what is not considered criminal activity. Those same actors (distillers) who were criminals during Prohibition are not held responsible for most alcohol-related crimes today. Instead, behaviors are linked to the person consuming the alcohol and/or distributing it at the retail level (bar or store) or at a party. If a person in a vehicle is accused of hitting someone while driving under the influence of alcohol, the driver and whoever provided the liquor to the driver can be arrested, but not the company that originally produced the alcohol. If the criminal justice system treated illegal drugs the same way, those manufacturing the drugs would be considered legitimate, but not those who are selling or using on the streets. However, one of the main targets in the War on Drugs, a federal program aimed at getting illegal drugs off the streets, are the manufacturers. William Burroughs, a known drug user who wrote *Naked Lunch*, said going after manufacturers and dealers would have little affect on the situation because as long as there were users, there would be manufacturers and dealers. The process of holding some people responsible for a crime but not others who can be linked to that crime is what Denzin (1977) refers to as a criminogenic market—one set of legal behaviors (such as the making of alcohol) can lead to illegal behaviors (driving drunk). Others have uncovered the same processes in businesses such as car sales (Leonard & Weber, 1970), where the money made from new-car sales is not enough to maintain a business, so dealers provide unneeded services to customers and find ways to hide profits in their used-car sales.

The complexity of the structures that surround the criminal justice systems can actually make it difficult to determine if an act is a crime, even if a law exists that states that it is. This not only changes throughout time, but within and across societal contexts. What is criminal in one society might be perfectly acceptable in another, such as businesses giving gifts to each other (considered illegal bribes in the United States, but considered appropriate activities in many countries). Even after an act has been determined to be criminal, those involved in the investigation have to take into account the rights and responsibilities of victims, the accused, those doing the prosecuting and defending, and their own actions. This is especially true in societies such as the United States, where we take pride in supporting basic human rights. An act that violates another person's rights is typically considered criminal, but are we then expected to treat that individual in the same way that we found revolting enough in the original act to say it was a crime? "Turnabout is fair play," some would argue, while others would say that, "two wrongs don't make a right." When a character like Arthur Conan Doyle's Sherlock Holmes can solve crimes through ingenuity and guts, we often breathe a sigh of relief knowing that someone—even a fictional character—can cut through all the red tape and difficulties to bring a bad person to justice:

Sherlock Holmes closed his eyes and placed his elbows upon the arms of his chair, with his finger-tips together. "The ideal reasoned," he remarked, "would, when he had once been shown a single fact in all its bearings, deduce from it not only all the chain of events which led up to it but also all the results which would follow from it. As Cuvier could correctly describe a whole animal by the contemplation of a single bone, so the observer who has thoroughly understood one link in a series of incidents should be able to accurately state all the other ones, both before and after. We have not yet grasped the results which the reason alone can attain to. Problems may be solved in the study which has baffled all those who sought a solution by the aid of their senses. To carry the art, however, to its highest pitch, it is necessary that the reasoned should be able to utilize the facts which have come to his knowledge, which, even in these days of free education and encyclopedias, is a somewhat rare accomplishment. It is not so impossible, however, that a man should possess all knowledge which is likely to be useful to him in his work, and this I have endeavored in my case to do so. If I remember rightly, you on one occasion, in the early days of our friendship, defined my limits in a very precise fashion."

"Yes," I answered, laughing. "It was a singular document. Philosophy, astronomy, and politics were marked at zero. I remember. Botany variable, geology profound as regards the mud-stains from any region within fifty miles of town, chemistry eccentric, anatomy unsystematic, sensational literature and crime records unique, violin-player, boxer, swordsman, lawyer, and self-poisoner by cocaine and tobacco. Those, I think, were the main points of my analysis."

Holmes grinned at the last item. "Well," he said, "I say now, as I did then, that a man should keep his little brain-attic stocked with all the furniture that he is likely to use, and the rest he can put away in the lumber-room of his library, where he can get it if he wants it. Now, for such a case as the one which has been submitted to us to-night, we need certainly to muster all our resources. Kindly hand me down the letter K of the American Encyclopedia which stands upon the shelf beside you. Thank you. Now let us consider the situation and see what may be deduced from it. In the first place, we may start with a strong presumption that Colonel Openshaw had some very strong reason for leaving America. Men at his time of life do not change all their habits and exchange willingly the charming climate of Florida for the lonely life of an English provincial town. His extreme love of solitude in England suggests the idea that he was in fear of someone or something, so we may assume as a working hypothesis that it was fear of someone or something that drove him from America. As to what it was he feared, we can only deduce that by considering the formidable letters which were received by himself and his successors. Did you remark the postmarks of those letters?"

"The first was from Pondicherry, the second from Dundee, and the third from London."

"From East London. What do you deduce from that?"

"They are all seaports. That the writer was on board of a ship."

"Excellent. We have already a clue. There can be no doubt that the probability—the strong probability—is that the writer was on board of a ship. And now let us consider another point. In the case of Pondicherry, seven weeks elapsed between the threat and its fulfillment, in Dundee it was only some three or four days. Does that suggest anything?"

"A greater distance to travel."

"But the letter had also a greater distance to come."

"Then I do not see the point."

"There is at least a presumption that the vessel in which the man or men are is a sailing ship. It looks as if they always sent their singular warning or token before them when starting their mission. You see how quickly the deed followed the sign when it came from Dundee. If they had come from Pondicherry in a steamer they would have arrived almost as soon as their letter. But, as a matter of fact, seven weeks elapsed. I think that those seven weeks represented the difference between the mail-boat which brought the letter and the sailing vessel which brought the writer" (Conan Doyle, *Sherlock Holmes*: 347–49).

What is truly remarkable about Sherlock Holmes for a sociologist is how he takes into account social structures. Moving from one country to another (or climate to climate) is typically a response to something outside of one's control—change in work status, fear, moving closer to adult children or ailing parents, and so forth. A person also cannot control conditions such as how quickly a letter moves from one place to another. While electronic communication closes that gap, the fact that e-mails and phone calls also leave trails provides detectives opportunities to follow a person's words from place to place. It is through an understanding of how structures work, and not just the mind of a criminal, that Sherlock Holmes is able to solve crimes.

No matter how much we might enjoy reading about Sherlock Holmes or watching Robert Downey Jr. bring the character to life on the big screen, most lawyers practicing in the United States would likely argue that his thoughts on Colonel Openshaw's dilemma are circumstantial and prove nothing, no matter how strong the logic. Holmes and Watson would have to find evidence to prove their points to make a stronger case. In today's society, evidence for murders and rapes and so forth often come from labs, photographs, and eyewitnesses. Even this kind of evidence, however, can be questioned and thrown out of court if not gathered or presented properly. Former football star O. J. Simpson was accused of killing his divorced wife, Nicole Brown Simpson, and her friend Ron Goldman, and nearly every piece of evidence and testimony pointed to Simpson being guilty. His lawyers, however, were able to show that some of the evidence had been tampered with or not collected according to proper police procedures. This led to a verdict of Simpson being found not guilty.

LABELING AND *THE HUNCHBACK OF NOTRE DAME*

Three years prior to the O. J. Simpson verdict of 1995, four police officers were acquitted on charges of beating Rodney King in Los Angeles, even though their actions were caught on videotape. Three of the officers were cleared of all charges, while the fourth was acquitted after the jury could not reach a consensus on whether his behaviors constituted assault. Those two verdicts—the acquittal of the police officers and O. J. Simpson—led to numerous debates over the inner workings of the criminal justice system. While there have always been critics of police work and the courts, the debate grew even more heated, as people began thinking about societal structures and the individuals who occupied roles within those structures—police chiefs, police officers, judges, jurors, lawyers, forensic lab employees, and so forth. The Simpson verdict also shed light on the importance of having the financial resources to hire good lawyers. The trial made it clear that not all attorneys are the same, and while that had been known for years, the fact that the trial was shown on television brought these concerns into the kitchens and living rooms of the American public, places where we are supposed to feel safe.

Race is also said to have played a factor in both the Rodney King and O. J. Simpson trials. King, now deceased, was African American, as is Simpson, and when the nonblack officers involved in the Rodney King case were acquitted, riots broke out in Los Angeles that involved members of the African American community. Some say that Simpson was also targeted by white police officers because of his race. It is also true that minority groups such as blacks and Latinos continue to have higher incarceration rates than whites in the United States, though it has been shown these rates can be dependent on the racial composition of political leaders in the cities where arrests are made (Stucky, 2012).

The fact that some groups are incarcerated at higher rates than others points to what is referred to as labeling (Restivo & Lanier, 2013). Labeling is the idea that some people are thought to be problematic, simply because of a label that has been attached to them such as teenager, black, poor, gay, etc. Those without these labels are thought to be good (adult, white, rich, straight, etc.), and once a person is labeled, it affects how they think about themselves and how others view that individual. A young person from the Middle East who is walking through a U.S. airport is more likely to be feared than a young white person in the same situation because U.S. society has labeled Middle Easterners as terrorists. This is not a new phenomenon, as highlighted in Victor Hugo's *The Hunchback of Notre Dame*. Esmeralda, the lead female character, is a gypsy in Paris at a time when gypsies were considered a criminal group. In this passage, Esmeralda has been arrested for a murder she did not commit. Her goat is asked to take the stand during the trial. Like gypsies, goats were thought to be agents of the devil, and therefore labeled as such.

The goat was in fact the second prisoner. Nothing was more common in those times than a charge of sorcery brought against an animal. Among others, in the Provostry Accompts of 1455, may be seen a curious detail of the expenses of the proceedings against Gillet Soulart and his sow, executed "for their demerits" at Corbeil. Everything is there,—the cost of the pit to put the sow in; the five hundred bundles of wood from the wharf of Morsant; the three pints of wine and bread, the sufferer's last repast, shared in a brotherly manner by the executioner; and even the eleven days' custody and feed of the sow, at eight deniers parisis per day. Sometimes they went farther, even, than animals. The capitularies of Charlemagne and Louis le Debonnaire impose severe penalties on the fiery phantoms which might fit to appear in the air.

Meanwhile the king's attorney in the ecclesiastical court had exclaimed: "If the demon which possesses this goat, and which has resisted all exorcisms, persist in his sorceries, if he astound the court with them, we forewarn him that we shall be obliged to have recourse against him to the gibbet or the stake."

Gringoire was all in a cold perspiration. Charmolue took up from a table the gypsy girl's tambourine, and presenting it in a certain manner to the goat, he asked her, "What's o'clock?"

The goat looked at him with a sagacious eye, raised her gilt foot, and struck it seven times. It was indeed seven o'clock. A movement of terror ran through the crowd. Gringoire could bear it no longer.

"She'll be her own ruin," cried he aloud; "you see she does not know what she's about!"

"Silence, you people at the end of the room!" said the usher, sharply.

Jacques Charmolue, by means of the same maneuvers with the tambourine, made the goat perform several other tricks, about the day of the month, the month of the year, etc., which the reader has already witnessed. And, but an optical illusion peculiar to judicial proceedings, those same spectators who perhaps had more than once applauded in the public streets the innocent performances of Djali, were terrified at them under the roof of the Palais de Justice. The goat was indisputably the devil (Hugo, *The Hunchback of Notre Dame*: 110–11).

Notice the fact that the context of the goat's behavior influences interpretations within the audience. When Djali did his tricks in the street, his antics brought praise (and money) from the crowds. Those same tricks were seen as sorcery in a courtroom, another example of how structures impact our ways of thinking. A professor who is paid to lecture in a classroom would be considered mentally unstable if found doing the same thing in an empty hallway. The same would be said of a student who was found taking notes and raising her hand to be called upon by the winds blowing through the grass in an open field on a sunny day. If you add additional labels to these individuals—elderly professor, foreign student—you start developing ideas of why they are acting in such peculiar ways, all because you have learned that the elderly and foreigners "act differently" from the rest of us. While these activities are not criminal, it would not take much more for some people to call the police because these individuals were acting suspiciously.

Once we find a person guilty of a crime, and often even before their day in court, we reward their deviant behavior by putting them in settings that are less than ideal for the human spirit. In Paris in the 1400s, the setting for *The Hunchback of Notre Dame*, prisons were not welcoming places. Rehabilitation was not a concern, and while we have made some strides in providing prisoners with a few basic necessities (and much more in some situations), the following description of Esmeralda's prison might be synonymous with going to jail today for people like Abdulrahman Zeitoun. Zeitoun was a Syrian immigrant who lived in New Orleans during Hurricane Katrina and was arrested in the hurricane's aftermath for robbery and breaking and entering (Eggers, 2009). He was locked up in a holding area behind the New Orleans Greyhound Station before being sent to a regular jail. He was finally set free, but years later he was arrested for domestic abuse, though there was no record of violence in the household prior to his arrest. Some might argue that it was his treatment by the police that turned Zeitoun into an angry person. Though few of us want to end up in jail, Zeitoun's prison would probably be considered luxurious relative to the one where Esmeralda was taken, so you can imagine what her mind was like when she was locked away in such a place:

> At the Bastille St. Antoine, at the Palais de Justice of Paris, and at the Louvre, these subterraneous edifices were prisons. The stories of these prisons, as they went deeper into the ground, grew narrower and darker. They formed so many zones, presenting, as by a graduated scale, deeper and deeper shades of horror. Dante could find nothing better for the construction of his hell. These dungeon funnels usually terminated in a low hollow, shaped like the bottom of a tub, in which Dante has placed his Satan, and in which society placed the criminal condemned to death. When once a miserable human existence was there interred, then farewell light, air, life, *ogni speranza*—it never went out again but to the gibbet or the stake. Sometimes it rotted there; and human justice called that forgetting. Between mankind and himself, the condemned felt weighing upon his head an accumulation of stones and jailers; and the whole prison together, the massive bastille, was now but one enormous complicated lock that barred him out of the living world (Hugo, *The Hunchback of Notre Dame*: 127).

The current criminal justice system seems to work in much the same way for many people—once they are in, they stay in—*ogni speranza*—abandon all hope. Some even keep coming back after being let out. Recidivism, returning to jail after being paroled, has become a major concern for those within current criminal justice systems, as well as many of its detractors. According to the Bureau of Justice Statistics, "[d]uring 2007, a total of 1,180,469 persons on parole were at-risk of reincarceration. This includes persons under parole supervision on January 1 or those entering parole during the year. Of these parolees, about 16% were returned to incarceration in 2007" (http://www.bjs.gov/index.cfm?ty=tp&tid=17, accessed June 2013). Why would someone willingly return to jail if these are the places where the human spirit rots and is forgotten? For one thing, once a person is labeled a criminal, that label influences how others react to him, including job opportunities or the lack thereof. For others, living behind bars is better in some ways than life on the streets, as a person can count on a roof over his head and three meals a day. Finally, prison is a total institution in the sense that the longer you stay in prison, the more likely you are to accept the values and norms needed there to survive. These are not the same norms and values found in most parts of society, and some who have spent years in prison find it hard to readjust to life outside the brick walls and iron bars. As mentioned in the story about pickpockets and capital punishment at the beginning of this chapter, fear of jail—or even death—is not necessarily a deterrent when there are few other options available.

PERCEPTIONS, FASCINATION, AND *"THE MURDERS IN THE RUE MORGUE"*

I assume that many readers still think that the criminal justice system is interesting, as well they should, and that it does a decent job of catching bad people when they do bad things. Part of the reason for our fascination is that cultural producers (such as Conan Doyle and the makers of the *CSI* television series) give us a glorified and captivating perspective on crime and criminal investigations, all of which play on our notions of good people trying to find bad people, including the idea that you could do it, too. This has come to be referred to as the *CSI* Effect, with critics arguing that such shows provide the audience with unreal expectations of how crimes are solved (both in terms of time and techniques), while others have shown that watching such shows can make one more critical of questionable evidence (Schweitzer & Saks, 2006–2007). As we have seen with the popularity of Sherlock Holmes, this is not a new effect. We like to play along with fictional detectives, trying to see if we can figure out who did it before they do. The following selection from Edgar Allan Poe's "The Murders in the Rue Morgue" is another example of how we are presented with the mastermind who can solve a very difficult double murder.

"You will see," he said, "that I have shifted the question from the mode of egress to that of ingress. It was my design to suggest that both were effected in the same manner, at the same point. Let us now revert to the interior of the room. Let us survey the appearances here. The drawers of the bureau, it is said, had been rifled, although many articles of apparel still remained within them. The conclusion here is absurd. It is a mere guess—a very silly one—and no more. How are we to know that the articles found in the drawers were not all these drawers had originally contained? Madame L'Espanaye and her daughter lived an exceedingly retired life—saw no company—seldom went out—had little use for numerous changes of habiliment. Those found were at least of as good quality as any likely to be possessed by these ladies. If a thief had taken any, why did he not take the best—why did he not take all? In a word, why did he abandon four thousand francs in gold to encumber himself with a bundle of linen? The gold was abandoned. Nearly the whole sum mentioned by Monsieur Mignaud, the banker, was discovered, in bags, upon the floor. I wish you, therefore, to discard from your thoughts the blundering idea of motive, engendered in the brains of the police by that portion of the evidence which speaks of money delivered at the door of the house. Coincidences ten times as remarkable as this (the delivery of the money, and murder committed within three days upon the party receiving it), happen to all of us every hour of our lives, without attracting even momentary notice. Coincidences, in general, are great stumbling-blocks in the way of that class of thinkers who have been educated to know nothing of the theory of probabilities—that theory to which the most glorious objects of human research are indebted for the most glorious of illustration. In the present instance, had the gold been gone, the fact of its delivery three days before would have formed something more than a coincidence. It would have been corroborative of this idea of motive. But, under the real circumstances of the case, if we are to suppose gold the motive of this outrage, we must also imagine the perpetrator so vacillating an idiot as to have abandoned his gold and his motive together.

"Keeping now steadily in mind the points to which I have drawn your attention—that peculiar voice, that unusual agility, and that startling absence of motive in a murder so singularly atrocious as this—let us glance at the butchery itself. Here is a woman strangled to death by manual strength, and thrust up a chimney, head downward. Ordinary assassins employ no such modes of murder as this. Least of all, do they thus dispose of the murdered. In the manner of thrusting the corpse up the chimney, you will admit that there was something excessively outré—something altogether irreconcilable with our common notions of human action, even when we suppose the actors the most depraved of men. Think, too, how great must have been that strength which could have thrust the body up such an aperture so forcibly that the united vigor of several persons was found barely sufficient to drag it down!

"Turn, now, to other indications of the employment of a vigor most marvellous. On the hearth were thick tresses—very thick tresses—of grey human hair. These had been torn out by the roots. You are aware of the great force necessary in tearing thus from the head even twenty or thirty hairs together. You saw the locks in question as well as myself. Their roots (a hideous sight!) were clotted with fragments of the flesh of the scalp—sure token of the prodigious power which had been exerted in uprooting perhaps half a million of hairs at a time. The throat of the old lady was not merely cut, but the head absolutely severed from the body: the instrument was a mere razor. I wish you also to look at the brutal ferocity of these deeds. Of the bruises upon the body of Madame L'Espanaye I do not speak. Monsieur Dumas, and his worthy coadjutor Monsieur Etienne, have pronounced that they were inflicted by some obtuse instrument; and so far these gentlemen are very correct. The obtuse instrument was clearly the stone pavement in the yard, upon which the victim had fallen from the window which looked in upon the bed. This idea, however simple it may now seem, escaped the police for the same reason that the breadth of the shutters escaped them—because, by the affair of the nails, their perceptions had been hermetically sealed against the possibility of the windows have ever been opened at all.

If now, in addition to all these things, you have properly reflected upon the odd disorder of the chamber, we have gone so far as to combine the ideas of an agility astounding, a strength superhuman, a ferocity brutal, a butchery without motive, a grotesquerie in horror absolutely alien from humanity, and a voice foreign in tone to the ears of men of many nations, and devoid of all distinct or intelligible syllabification. What result, then, has ensued? What impression have I made upon your fancy?"

I felt a creeping of the flesh as Dupin asked me the question. "A madman," I said, "has done this deed—some raving maniac, escaped from a neighboring Maison de Santé."

"In some respects," he replied, "your idea is not irrelevant. But the voices of madmen, even in their wildest paroxysms, are never found to tally with that peculiar voice heard upon the stairs. Madmen are of some nation, and their language, however incoherent in its words, has always the coherence of syllabification. Besides, the hair of a madman is not such as I now hold in my hand. I disentangled this little tuft from the rigidly clutched fingers of Madame L'Espanaye. Tell me what you can make of it."

"Dupin!" I said, completely unnerved; "this hair is most unusual—this is no human hair."

"I have not asserted that it is," said he; "but, before we decide this point, I wish you to glance at the little sketch I have here traced upon this paper. It is a facsimile drawing of what has been described in one portion of the testimony as 'dark bruises, and deep indentations of finger nails,' upon the throat of Mademoiselle L'Espanaye, and in another, (by Messrs. Dumas and Etienne), as a 'series of livid spots, evidently the impression of fingers.'

"You will perceive," continued my friend, spreading out the paper upon the table before us, "that this drawing gives the idea of a firm and fixed hold. There is no slipping apparent. Each finger has retained—possibly until the death of the victim—the fearful grasp by which it originally imbedded itself. Attempt, now, to place all your fingers, at the same time, in the respective impressions as you see them."

I made the attempt in vain.

"We are possibly not giving this matter a fair trial," he said. "The paper is spread out upon a plane surface; but the human throat is cylindrical. Here is a billet of wood, the circumference of which is about that of the throat. Wrap the drawing around it, and try the experiment again."

I did so; but the difficulty was even more obvious than before.

"This," I said, "is the mark of no human hand."

"Read now," replied Dupin, "this passage from Cuvier." It was a minute anatomical and generally descriptive account of the large fulvous Ourang-Outang of the East Indian Islands. The gigantic stature, the prodigious strength and activity, the wild ferocity, and the imitative propensities of these mammalia are sufficiently well known to all. I understood the full horrors of the murder at once (Poe, "The Murders in the Rue Morgue," available on the Internet).

Much like Djali in *The Hunchback of Notre Dame*, we find an animal at the center of a crime. In this case, an orangutan has killed two women, though the possibility of such an occurrence had escaped the capacities of the investigating police officers, as it probably does most readers (you can test this by asking a friend to read the whole story and see when they begin to assume that something is amiss; the whole of "The Murders in the Rue Morgue" can be found at http://www.poemuseum.org/works-morgue.php, accessed June 2013). We have been trained to think that "murder" is tied to a "culprit," who is a bad person doing bad things to good people. Many of us might also be thinking that this is no longer a murder because animals are unable to premeditate such an event, though there are stories of elephants killing cruel handlers years after they have parted ways. Typically, when we hear of an animal killing or maiming a person, we immediately think of having that animal euthanized, though we would typically not refer to this as the animal facing the death penalty.

Poe's work is also similar to Conan Doyle's, in that Dupin and Sherlock Holmes are able to see where structures provide opportunities and barriers to solving a crime. Dupin understands what humans, even mad ones, can and cannot do, as well as the fact that detectives are trained to think of murders as caused by the hands of humans. It is through the understanding, twisting, and opening up of these structures that fiction guides us through our own thoughts.

Our notions of crime and punishment are controlled by the societies in which we live (Foucault, 1995). This includes the labels that we give to others and receive ourselves. Once we begin to understand that part of criminal activity is based on people's expectations of themselves and others, we can begin to change the structures that make criminal activity an easy option for some. Such thinking can also be used to expand our own ideas of what is and what is not criminal activity that pushes us beyond the psychological rut in which we often find ourselves.

REFERENCES AND RECOMMENDED READINGS

Burroughs, W. S. (2001). *Naked Lunch: The restored text*. New York: Grove Press.

Conan Doyle, A. (2012). *Sherlock Holmes, Volumes 1 and 2*. Barnes & Noble Kindle Edition.

Denzin, N. K. (1977). "Notes on the Criminogenic Hypothesis: A case study of the American liquor industry." *American Sociological Review*, 42: 905–20.

Eggers, D. (2009). *Zeitoun*. San Francisco: McSweeney's Books.

Foucault, M. (1995). *Discipline and Punish*. New York: Vintage.

Hugo, V. (1899). *The Hunchback of Notre Dame*. New York: Little, Brown, and Company.

Leonard, W. N., and Weber, M. G. (1970). "Automakers and Dealers: A study of criminogenic market forces." *Law & Society Review*, 4(3): 407–24.

Poe, E. A. *The Portable Edgar Allan Poe* (edited by J. Gerald Kennedy). New York: Penguin.

Restivo, E., and Lanier, M. M. (2013). "Measuring the Contextual Effects and Mitigating Factors of Labeling Theory." *Justice Quarterly* (available online January 2013).

Schweitzer, N. J., and Saks, M. J. "*CSI* Effect: Popular fiction about forensic science affects the public's expectations about real forensic science." *Jurimetrics*, 47: 357–64.

Stinchcombe, A. L. (1987). *Constructing Social Theories*. Chicago: University of Chicago Press.

Stucky, T. D. (2012). "The Conditional Effects of Race and Politics on Social Control: Black violent crime arrests in large cities, 1970 to 1990." *Journal of Research in Crime and Delinquency*, 40(1): 3–30.

12 WAR AND POLITICS

INTRODUCTION AND *THE ILIAD*

Around 1500, both China and the Ottoman Empire were in a position to expand their territories (Kennedy, 1987), but China experienced a religious revival, closed its borders, and let its navy rot in its ports. The Ottomans were unwilling to give up their horses for the sea. It was the European countries, all relatively small compared to China and the Ottoman Empire, that took to the water and were able to bombard their enemies from afar and set up naval blockades, all of which allowed them to become dominant powers by the 1600s. This position of power continued through the First World War, when the United States began to exert its influence on the world, as well as Japan and other Asian countries before and after the Second World War. Some European countries such as England, France, and Germany continue to be considered powerful actors in the global village.

Many students I have come across could care less about such events. To them, history and politics are for old people and have very little to do with anything they want to accomplish in terms of jobs and their own pursuit of happiness. Such attitudes often come off as apathy to professors. The position of both sides is understandable, as the structures of politics seem to be well beyond the control of the average college student, while professors remember their own youthful vigor and wanting to change the world. Is there any common ground? Can an understanding of the world between 1500 and 1600 help with navigating contemporary social structures? Can an understanding of how politics look to the average undergraduate help a professor develop lectures and lesson plans that would be of interest to her students? The answer is "yes" to each of these, and I hope to be able to provide the framework needed to begin closing the gap between these groups.

According to Shlapentokh (2007: 75), "[s]ince ancient times, there has been the view that only rich people can effectively run society. The oligarchic ideology supposes that the rich tend to be hardworking, virtuous, and talented, while most poor people are lazy and prone to drinking and committing crimes." An oligarch is a power structure comprised of a handful of people or organizations. This is in contrast to a totalitarian structure controlled by a single person or organization or a democracy that is controlled by all members. Those within the inner circles of an oligarch have a vested interest in maintaining their position, so stories of who is hardworking and who is lazy become part of the political landscape constructed by the cultural producers who are rewarded for their loyalty to the oligarchs, another example of Marx's superstructure.

Sociologists interested in politics often ask questions about how a political structure or event becomes legitimated, whether that structure or event is tied to an oligarchy, supreme leader, or a democracy. Answers range from Marx's cultural superstructure controlled by those in power to functionalist accounts that contend legitimation of power is key to social control and societal progress. Homer's *Iliad* is an example of the justification of power played out in a battle between the Greeks and Trojans, as it is only the warrior who can bring honor to one's country, as well as protect its citizens. The deaths around the heroes make their accomplishments that much greater:

The bold Antilochus the slaughter led,
The first who struck a valiant Trojan dead:
At great Echepolus the lance arrives,
Razed his high crest, and through his helmet drives;
Warm'd in the brain the brazen weapon lies,
And shades eternal settle o'er his eyes.
So sinks a tower, that long assaults had stood
Of force and fire, its walls besmear'd with blood.
Him, the bold leader of the Abantian throng,
Seized to despoil, and dragg'd the corpse along:
But while he strove to tug the inserted dart,
Agenor's javelin reach'd the hero's heart.
His flank, unguarded by his ample shield,
Admits the lance: he falls, and spurns the field;
The nerves, unbraced, support his limbs no more;
The soul comes floating in a tide of gore.
Trojans and Greeks now gather round the slain;
The war renews, the warriors bleed again:
As o'er their prey rapacious wolves engage,
Man dies on man, and all is blood and rage.

In blooming youth fair Simoisius fell,
Sent by great Ajax to the shades of hell;
Fair Simoisius, whom his mother bore
Amid the flocks on silver Simois' shore:
The nymph descending from the hills of Ide,
To seek her parents on his flowery side,
Brought forth the babe, their common care and joy,
And thence from Simois named the lovely boy.
Short was his date! by dreadful Ajax slain,
He falls, and renders all their cares in vain!
So falls a poplar, that in watery ground
Raised high the head, with stately branches crown'd,
(Fell'd by some artist with his shining steel,
To shape the circle of the bending wheel,)
Cut down it lies, tall, smooth, and largely spread,
With all its beauteous honours on its head
There, left a subject to the wind and rain,
And scorch'd by suns, it withers on the plain
Thus pierced by Ajax, Simoisius lies
Stretch'd on the shore, and thus neglected dies.

At Ajax, Antiphus his javelin threw;
The pointed lance with erring fury flew,
And Leucus, loved by wise Ulysses, slew.
He drops the corpse of Simoisius slain,
And sinks a breathless carcase on the plain.
This saw Ulysses, and with grief enraged,
Strode where the foremost of the foes engaged;
Arm'd with his spear, he meditates the wound,
In act to throw; but cautious look'd around,
Struck at his sight the Trojans backward drew,
And trembling heard the javelin as it flew.
A chief stood nigh, who from Abydos came,
Old Priam's son, Democoon was his name.
The weapon entered close above his ear,
Cold through his temples glides the whizzing spear;
With piercing shrieks the youth resigns his breath,
His eye-balls darken with the shades of death;
Ponderous he falls; his clanging arms resound,
And his broad buckler rings against the ground.

Seized with affright the boldest foes appear;
E'en godlike Hector seems himself to fear;
Slow he gave way, the rest tumultuous fled;
The Greeks with shouts press on, and spoil the dead:
But Phoebus now from Ilion's towering height
Shines forth reveal'd, and animates the fight.
"Trojans, be bold, and force with force oppose;
Your foaming steeds urge headlong on the foes!
Nor are their bodies rocks, nor ribb'd with steel;
Your weapons enter, and your strokes they feel.
Have ye forgot what seem'd your dread before?
The great, the fierce Achilles fights no more"
(Homer, *The Iliad*: Project Gutenberg).

According to historical accounts, the battle between the Greeks and Trojans lasted ten years (~1193–1183 BC). Some of you may be thinking that after a few days (or even hours) of such brutality as described by Homer, some of these soldiers would have decided enough was enough and that it was time to go back to families where they could tend their flocks and grow their crops. Wars, however, continue to be fought to determine such things as who owns a piece of land, whose religion is better, and so forth. Current military fighting has proven to be just as brutal as the Trojan War, if not more so, since it is now harder to control collateral damage among citizens, and the recognition of posttraumatic stress disorder (PTSD) among soldiers points to the toll that such fighting takes, even on survivors. Why, then—nearly 4000 years since the Trojan War ended—do we keep fighting?

The problem with this kind of question is that it assumes those doing the fighting are starting the wars, or will somehow gain fame and fortune from it. Agger (1992) instead asks us who benefits from such events. Those named in Homer's epic poem rarely benefit, except to have their names recorded as they die on the battlefield with some sort of metal or wooden implement sticking into and out of some vital body part. Those dying are usually of common birth, though at times a king or some noble knight would meet his end on the battlefield. A skeleton recently discovered under a parking lot in England has been confirmed by DNA to be that of Richard III. Richard is reported to have died in 1485 during the battle of Bosworth, and archaeologists found an arrow near the spine of this skeleton and a crushed skull, both of which would have been received during fighting. Shakespeare made Richard III into a hunchbacked monster, and the skeleton does show signs of deformity, but prior to his death Richard is said to have been a popular leader. If he had won that day, his fame and popularity would have increased, and Shakespeare might have written a very different play.

Instead, the Tudors won, and Henry VII became king of England (Henry VII was father to Henry VIII, best known for beheading a couple of his wives). Today, we find very few political leaders leading the charge into battle. Instead, modern warfare is carried out by soldiers told to fight by politicians, officers, and businessmen who will never see the battlefield. One reason for the difference is that kings could surround themselves with soldiers who would protect them during hand-to-hand fighting. There was little concern then of being killed by something like a bomb, though as Richard III found out, arrows could still reach a person who was supposed to be protected. Today's weaponry does not respect such boundaries, and rarely do we find a nation's leader in harm's way until a bomb is dropped on a bunker, or a fortress is stormed by soldiers carrying grenades and automatic weapons that extend one's ability to bring death to others.

Soldiers not of noble birth have been dying in these battles since before the Trojan War, and those who benefit the most also remain the same. While we do hear of decorated heroes who come home to cheering crowds—also true of knights and a few others who fought in past wars—politicians, military contractors, and weapon manufacturers stay in their factories and offices and are typically the ones who benefit the most from the fighting. This ranges from economic rewards to trips to exotic places to rally the troops, to favorable public opinion by being in command of a winning army.

Many readers may think I am downplaying or even degrading the sacrifices made by soldiers, and that there are things worth fighting and dying for. I agree that soldiers make incredible sacrifices, including their own lives, and that there are things worth fighting and dying for. In addition, members of my family have served in the military over the years, including an uncle who died in 2010, still carrying shrapnel from World War II. Wars, however, are typically not started by the people who are asked to make the ultimate sacrifice. Instead, their actions are controlled by others, including joining the military when there are few options available for those growing up in certain areas or under certain conditions. A political leader may tell a country that we have to fight to protect our freedoms and privileges, and to hear such a speech makes a lot of sense when threatened. However, the "we" in such speeches more often consists of the poor who are considered to be "lazy and prone to drinking and committing crimes" than the rich who tend to be hardworking. If they are deserving of leadership positions, should that include leading on the modern battlefield?

HISTORY, POLITICS, AND *1984*

If you agree with Karl Marx (1983) that humans started off as small bands with little or no authoritative structures, moved into a horticultural society characterized by classes of priests, warriors, and plebeians moved into an agricultural system led by lords and kings, who were supported by peasants; and then into capitalism, where the accumulation of economic resources became the basis for power, there might not be much point in knowing history and politics besides the fact that each of these systems has failed to this point, except capitalism, though it too has had to weather some very serious challenges such as depressions and wars. History, from such a standpoint, will continue on its mysterious path, and there is little we can do about it. It is Melville's sea that has rolled on for thousands of years, consuming everything in its wake.

Not everyone, however, is inclined to think of history as a steady march toward some specific societal structure, possibly one in which wars are a thing of the past. Shlapentokh (2007) argues for a segmented approach to history in which events are often chaotic, and political regimes are outcomes of chance events that would include a king with spinal deformities being killed by an arrow and ax on a battlefield. Foucault (2004) came to much the same conclusion, contending that historical accounts often overlook chance encounters and the stochastic nature of even the best-planned human endeavors. History, however, is written from the point of view of the victors, so much of what we read leads us to believe that the political structures—including the leaders who hold positions of power—are both natural and legitimate. How this process unfolds can be found in Henry VII's treatment of Richard III's body after the battle at Bosworth. According to some accounts, Richard III's popularity meant that Henry VII had to humiliate him by having his body stripped naked, thrown over a horse, paraded around town, and then buried in a place followers could not find. By desecrating the body in such a way, Richard III was shown to be weak (his army was thought to be stronger than Henry VII's going into the battle, so the loss was another sign of poor leadership), making his defeater strong and kinglike. Modern-day politicians use some of the same strategies against their opponents, though we rarely see a leader ordering another leader's body to be paraded naked through the streets. Instead, they have statues and other public tokens destroyed in an attempt to disgrace the leadership abilities of their rivals. Such acts continue the tradition of showing that the winning side is more right or righteous (Thompson, 2000), with little heed paid to the potential historical value of what is being destroyed.

If you are still inclined to think that your country is truly marching toward progress and ultimate human happiness, then you should be aware of Weber's typology of authority (Orum & Dale, 2009), and how it changes depending on circumstances. Weber states that authority took one of three forms—traditional, charismatic, and legal-rational. Traditional authority is based on lineage (e.g., thrones being passed down from father to son, such as Edward VI gaining the crown when he was nine years old after Henry VIII died) and narratives about divine provenance (e.g., the king is God's choice for a leader). Charismatic authority is based on an individual's ability to motivate people to follow him, such as the Reverend Sun Myung Moon of the Unification Church (his followers are known as Moonies). Legal-rational authority is based on laws that are used to designate a leader, such as voting for a president or governor. There are many leaders who combine various aspects of these hierarchies—John F. Kennedy was elected president due in part to his family's influence and his own charisma—though Weber treated each type as ideal. He argues that as bureaucracies sprang up in various parts of society, and not just in the churches and courts, there would be a tendency toward the legal-rational approach to leadership, as that is the type of authority most attuned to a society steeped in bureaucracy. If a group attached to a charismatic leader begins to develop bureaucracies, it would likely experience changes in how leadership is perceived. The pinnacle of such an approach to political power can be found in George Orwell's *1984* (first published in 1948, three years after the end of World War II), which became the rallying cry for many who feared the Communist regime that had evolved in Soviet Russia and was suspected of spying on its citizens.

Outside, even through the shut window-pane, the world looked cold. Down in the street little eddies of wind were whirling dust and torn paper into spirals, and though the sun was shining and the sky a harsh blue, there seemed to be no colour in anything, except the posters that were plastered everywhere. The black-moustachio'd face gazed down from every commanding corner. There was one on the house-front immediately opposite. BIG BROTHER IS WATCHING YOU, the caption said, while the dark eyes looked deep into Winston's own. Down at street level another poster, torn at one corner, flapped fitfully in the wind, alternately covering and uncovering the single word INGSOC. In the far distance a helicopter skimmed down between the roofs, hovered for an instant like a bluebottle, and darted away again with a curving flight. It was the police patrol, snooping into people's windows. The patrols did not matter, however. Only the Thought Police mattered.

Behind Winston's back the voice from the telescreen was still babbling away about pig-iron and the overfulfilment of the Ninth Three-Year Plan. The telescreen received and transmitted simultaneously. Any sound that Winston made, above the level of a very low whisper, would be picked up by it; moreover, so long as he remained within the field of vision which the metal plaque commanded, he could be seen as well as heard. There was of course no way of knowing whether you were being watched at any given moment. How often, or on what system, the Thought Police plugged in on any individual wire was guesswork. It was even conceivable that they watched everybody all the time. But at any rate they could plug in your wire whenever they wanted to. You had to live—did live, from habit that became instinct—in the assumption that every sound you made was overheard, and, except in darkness, every movement scrutinised (Orwell, *1984*: 21–23).

If this is the ultimate outcome of legal-rational authority, is this progress toward absolute happiness? Habermas (1989) argues that the public sphere, which is comprised of spaces where societal issues and problems are discussed, has come to look something like Orwell's society. During the Middle Ages, most social issues were dealt with in the royal courts and chambers. Citizens considered their lives directly tied to these groups, so whatever was decided within the castles' walls and churches was considered the decision of the community. The makeup of the nobility and who sat in these courts may have changed due to wars and deaths, but the common people tended to follow the decisions of whoever was in charge to the point that a "self" that was free of these structures would have been unimaginable. The rise of the mercantile class led to a wider distribution of financial independence and more stories of the workings of other societies, and with this came a change in the public sphere from the courts to the salons and teahouses, where the men of letters and business would discuss the same types of societal issues that had once been dealt with by the nobles in their royal courts. The nobility became more and more secluded from the public sphere, with their roles becoming mainly symbolic, as it was the accumulation of capital that made one an expert on an issue. If you were rich because of your backing of a sewer system in London, then you were an expert on sanitation. The workers who dug the sewers were not part of the salon crowd, and therefore not experts. Politics were played out among the elite capitalists who discussed and fought among themselves of how to create more efficient factories, compliant workers, and open new markets in foreign lands. This was the time of the industrial revolution, when many changes were taking place in industries, including the rise of the printing press. Certain members of the public sphere began using these presses to pass along their thoughts to similar gatherings in other salons, and soon the press was controlling at least a portion of the political narrative, as people began to discuss the issues that were in the pamphlets and early newspapers from other parts of the country or world, instead of what was happening in their own neighborhoods and communities. With the advent of radio and television, as well as a number of other changes to transportation and information technology, soon the public sphere was back in the hands of a relatively few individuals and institutions that controlled a great deal of the information moving from one place to another. The interests of these individuals continued to revolve around the accumulation of capital, so the stories (news) were often tied to economic concerns such as reporting stock market gains and losses, even though only a minority of the population owns stocks or controlling interests in companies.

In addition to the public sphere moving back to being controlled by a small group of individuals, it began making inroads into the private sphere of the home and other spaces we once thought to be free of politics. To understand this process, Habermas makes a distinction between the life world (where we live our lives) and the systems world (where systems function, such as the government), arguing that encroachments of the systems world onto the life world is partly to blame for the expansion of the public sphere and contraction of the private sphere. This encroachment becomes obvious in situations such as buying a new cell phone. The device itself is regulated by the government, as are the services, the contract you sign is tied to legal concerns, the purchasing is tied to certain government services (e.g., the money you use for the phone is printed by the government), the shipment of phones from the country in which it was manufactured to the one where it is purchased is under government control, and now there are concerns that our phone calls are being monitored by the government. The consumer purchasing the phone has very little—if anything—to say about any of these structures, and moving from one carrier to another does virtually nothing to alleviate this control. Marriage, the culmination of true love in the United States, is only legal if it is state approved, and many states will let you know whom you can marry in terms of their sex organs or blood relationship, what kinds of sexual practices you can engage in, and whether it is even legal to buy certain sex toys. Why does the state have the right to tell you what you can and cannot do in your own bedroom? If we return to Agger's (1992) question of who benefits from such a decision, we begin to understand why certain actions might be considered problematic, because the individual who is the ultimate target of the political decision is not the one benefiting from it. Sex toys provide an interesting example. You may think that having something to sell would be appreciated by politicians, as it generates tax dollars. Sell whatever you can as often as possible, and give the government the sales taxes. The person buying the sex toy is hoping to enjoy the experience, so it looks to be a win-win situation. If, however, a government official is in office because of a campaign promise to do away with indecency or uphold a specific religious platform, the availability of sex toys challenges those stances. Given that the sex toys typically under fire are substitutes for penises—dildos and vibrators—it may also challenge male domination over females. Since most politicians are male, such a threat is not to be tolerated, so the system world must control the life world if a certain group is to maintain its privileges. These are theories and ideas that still need to be tested.

POLITICAL ACTIONS, JUSTIFICATIONS, AND *WAR AND PEACE*

If you are still wondering why you should take an interest in politics, read what Leo Tolstoy has to say about how people act when they are facing a dangerous political upheaval. Almost every nation is rife with people debating whether the end is near, such as concerns with current immigration policy transforming the United States into a foreign country, or a rogue terrorist state developing nuclear weapons. What we do in the face of such dangers is often the opposite of what makes the most sense, because sometimes the structures that are in place lead us through difficult times by doing the least amount of work. The following is a narrative of Russian life as French troops approach Moscow in *War and Peace*:

After the Emperor had left Moscow, life flowed on there in its usual course, and its course was so very usual that it was difficult to remember the recent days of patriotic elation and ardor, hard to believe that Russia was really in danger and that members of the English Club were also sons of the Fatherland ready to sacrifice everything for it. The one thing that recalled the patriotic fervor everyone had displayed during the Emperor's stay was the call for contributions of men and money, a necessity that as soon as the promises had been made assumed a legal, official form and became unavoidable.

With the enemy's approach to Moscow, the Moscovites' view of their situation did not grow more serious but on the contrary became even more frivolous, as always happens with people who see great danger approaching. At the approach of danger there are always two voices that speak with equal power in the human soul; one very reasonably tells a man to consider the nature of the danger and the means of escaping it; the other, still more reasonably, says that it is too depressing and painful to think of the danger, and since it is not in man's power to foresee everything and avert the general course of events, and that it is therefore better to disregard what is painful until it comes, and to think about what is pleasant. In solitude a man generally listens to the first voice, but in society to the second. So it was now with the inhabitants of Moscow. It was long since people had been as gay in Moscow as that year (Tolstoy, *War and Peace*: downloaded from Google Books).

I own a button that states, "Do as You're Told, Unless Told Otherwise." While I am somewhat reluctant to give such bumper sticker advice in what I consider to be a serious treatment of the matter, Tolstoy's writing points to the notion that humans are quick to do what they are told to do, unless told otherwise, which points to the structures that shape our actions even in the face of death. When the emperor asks for resources to fight a war, he stirs up feelings of nationalism among his fellow Russians, which is why it is important in certain societies to maintain noble families, even if they are no longer an active part of daily political processes. People begin throwing balls and acting as if nothing is wrong once the emperor leaves, because to think of war is too difficult. There is always the chance that one will lose everything in such a fight, so it is best to not think about it and live like there will be no tomorrow (or that tomorrow will always come). We do, however, find ways to justify our actions, arguing that what we do is of our own making, and that there are good reasons for it. Boltanski and Thévenot (2006) find six ways that we go about doing this. We can say that we are being creative or inspired (creative order of worth); that our popularity or renown allows us to do certain things (renown order of worth); that what we are doing is the most effective and efficient way to do it (industrial order of worth); that we are just doing what has always been done (domestic order of worth); that our actions will bring people together (civic order of worth); or that we are gaining something in return for our actions (market order of worth). We often draw on more than one of these orders of worth to make sense of our actions, and often feel that once we have made the justification that everyone will be on board, as do politicians. When President Kennedy said that you should not ask what your country can do for you but what you can do for your country, he was drawing from the civic order of worth. When you are told that you should eat local food because that is what the governor of your state does, the justification is coming from the renown order of worth. As Tolstoy continues in *War and Peace*, certain justifications do not always make sense, though we continue to believe them if they come from sources of power and authority:

For reasons known or unknown to us the French began to drown and kill one another. And corresponding to the event its justification appears in people's belief that this was necessary for the welfare of France, for liberty, and for equality. People ceased to kill one another, and this event was accompanied by its justification in the necessity for a centralization of power, resistance to Europe, and so on. Men went from the west to the east killing their fellow men, and the event was accompanied by phrases about the glory of France, the baseness of England, and so on. History shows us that these justifications of the events have no common sense and are all contradictory, as in the case of killing a man as a result of recognizing his rights, and the killing of millions in Russia for the humiliation of England. But these justifications have a very necessary significance in their own day.

These justifications, as well as others, release those who produce the events from moral responsibility. These temporary aims are like the broom fixed in front of a locomotive to clear the snow from the rails in front; they clear men's moral responsibilities from their path.

Without such justifications there would be no reply to the simplest question that presents itself when examining each historical event. How is it that millions of men commit collective crimes—make war, commit murder, and so on?

With the present complex forms of political and social life in Europe can any event that is not prescribed, decreed, or ordered by monarchs, ministers, parliaments, or newspapers be imagined? Is there any collective action which cannot find its justification in political unity, in patriotism, in the balance of power, or in civilization? So that every event that occurs inevitably coincides with some expressed wish and, receiving justification, presents itself as the result of the will of one man or of several men.

In whatever direction a ship moves, the flow of the waves it cuts will always be noticeable ahead of it. To those on board the ship the movement of those waves will be the only perceptible motion.

Only by watching closely moment by moment the movement of that flow and comparing it with the movement of the ship do we convince ourselves that every bit of it is occasioned by the forward movement of the ship, and that we were led into error by the fact that we ourselves were imperceptibly moving (Tolstoy, *War and Peace*: downloaded from Google Books).

While politicians justify their actions so as to provide a moral background for their decisions, politics on a larger scale is about engagement among citizens, understanding that the ship is moving, and realizing that you are part of the crew no matter how apathetic (or seasick) you might feel. There are structures in place, including the fighting of wars, that set boundaries to what can be accomplished, but changes to regimes have been made, laws have changed, and people have left one political structure to live under another that is more to their liking. All of these actions, however, take time and commitment, but if you have any interest in determining the direction of the ship, then you have to take your turn at the wheel.

REFERENCES AND RECOMMENDED READINGS

Agger, B. (1992). *Cultural Studies as Critical Theory*. Washington, DC: Falmer Press.

Boltanski, L., and Thévenot, L. (2006). *On Justifications* (trans. Catherine Porter). Princeton, NJ: Princeton University Press.

Foucault, M. (2004). *Archaeology of Knowledge*. New York: Routledge.

Habermas, J. (1986). *The Structural Transformation of the Public Sphere* (trans. Thomas Burger). Cambridge, MA: MIT Press.

Homer. *The Iliad* (trans. Alexander Pope). Plain Label Books.

Kennedy, P. M. (1987). *The Rise and Fall of the Great Powers*. New York: Vintage.

Marx, K. (1983). *The Portable Karl Marx* (trans. Eugene Kamenka). New York: Viking.

Orum, A. M., and Dale, J. G. (2009). *Introduction to Political Sociology*. New York: Oxford University Press.

Orwell, G. (1983). *1984*. Boston: Houghton Mifflin Harcourt.

Shlapentokh, V. (2007). *Contemporary Russia as a Feudal Society*. New York: Palgrave Macmillan.

Thompson, J. B. (2000). *Political Scandal*. Malden, MA: Blackwell.

Tolstoy, L. (1956). *War and Peace* (trans. Louise Shanks Maude and Alymer Maude). BompaCrazy.com.

13 THE MEDIA

INTRODUCTION AND *THE OBITUARY WRITER*

As you read in Chapter 4, my first effort at college ended in my sophomore year, which was followed by an 18-month stint at Sea World of San Diego before returning to college in 1985. This time I was enrolled at Lane Community College (Eugene, Oregon) for the purpose of pursuing a degree in radio broadcasting. Over the next seven years, I worked at four commercial music radio stations: KZEL, Eugene, Oregon; WYBT/WPHK, Blountstown, Florida; KOWB/KCGY, Laramie, Wyoming; and KJUN, Puyallup, Washington, mostly as an on-air personality. In 1993, I was hired to teach radio broadcasting classes at Green River Community College in Auburn, Washington, as well as to oversee the student radio station, KGRG. During my time there, the station was mentioned, though very briefly, in *Rolling Stone* magazine, and it had nothing to do with my presence.

I have also spent a good portion of my academic career studying the media, and have come to think of it as being composed of four parts: the actor who creates a message (individuals or organizations); the way the message will be disseminated (face to face, social media, television, radio, newspaper, etc.); the actor who receives the message (individuals or groups); and the content of the message. Each component is worthy of a chapter, and scholars have built extensive literature on each of them, as are all the intersections. I will treat each one separately, beginning with those creating the messages before concluding with a discussion of the intersections.

An understanding of the structures in media organizations begins when one turns on the television for the evening news and notices that the different networks (ABC, NBC, CBS, MSNBC, CNN, etc.) are all covering the same story.

Gans (1979), Gitlin (1980), and Tuchman (1978) were sociologists interested in how newsrooms worked, and each studied larger organizations such as CBS and the *New York Times*, and came to the conclusion that news is about the relationships between reporters and their sources, which include government officials, police officers, hospital staff, business leaders, sports stars, and Hollywood celebrities, as well as what makes the best visuals or sound bites that generate emotional responses. These stories are not necessarily about events that have the greatest impact on the most people, but what fits the current notion of what makes a good news story. A tornado that kills a hundred people in a rural town will be the main story on most nightly news shows that evening. This is a tragic event, as people have died and the lives of those left behind will never be the same. During that same year, however, over 5000 U.S. citizens will die from sepsis (blood poisoning), which is the third leading killer across the globe, yet fewer news stories on this topic are found in a typical newscast. Instead, we are given pictures and sound bites of wrecked homes and grieving parents. These are stories that tug at our heartstrings, or so we have been conditioned to think this is what news is about.

To understand why the tornado gets more attention than someone dying from blood poisoning, we must look at how a newsroom operates. The structures in place are based on both triage and linkages to news sources. Triage is the notion that editors and reporters must decide on what is important, as they are typically given too much information to provide to their consumers. Another person dying from sepsis is not nearly as dramatic as a town being wiped out in one day. (Approximately 13 people die from blood poisoning each day in the United States; these deaths would be scattered around the country, making it hard to find a common storyline besides mode of death.) A typical nightly newscast—which lasts less than 25 minutes when you take commercials into consideration—contains less information than one page of newsprint. So, television reporters and editors look for stories that will be watched—and wanted—by the masses. Stories of people dying from blood poisoning in a rural area where there are no reporters are considered unimportant relative to the carnage left behind by a tornado.

Deciding what is important also depends on who is asking for an audience. If the president of the United States calls CBS and asks that a reporter be available for his speech that afternoon on sepsis, he is much more likely to have a reporter show up to his speech than a professor who calls CBS and asks if a reporter is available to cover her lecture on the link between sepsis and risk communication. A news organization must also be careful about whom they put in their sights when engaged in investigative reporting meant to uncover injustices. Gamson et al. (1992) tell a story of how NBC's *The Today Show* called a boycott watchdog group to get a scoop on the largest international boycott that was taking place at that time. When the group told *The Today Show* that the biggest boycott was against General Electric for its relations with the South African government during apartheid, *The Today Show* asked about the second largest boycott. Why? Because General Electric was owned by NBC, and *The Today Show* was not going to accuse its owner of being a bad global player. Human tragedy is part of the triaging of news, but so are the sources and the amount of business they do with the media outlet.

A newspaper, which typically has more room for information than a television newscast, is also inundated with requests for coverage and must decide what is important enough to print. The same kind of triage protocol is followed, as editors and reporters must determine whether they cover a rally of food irradiation opponents on the steps of the state capitol or the luncheon speech at the University Club by the national spokesperson for the Red Cross, who will say something about the current blood shortage. Both are important for the people involved as well as various members of the audience, but the newspaper might only have enough reporters to cover one of the events. If they think both are important, they may have to rely on a news agency such as the Associated Press to cover one of the events and buy the story from them.

Not only are powerful sources important, but so are advertisers. If the anti–food irradiation group mentioned above bought advertising from the local television station, reporters from that station may be asked by their editors to cover the protest (Franklin & Murphy, 1998). As with *The Today Show* and the GE boycott, newspapers, magazines, radio and television stations, and various social media outlets rely on advertisers to stay afloat. The money you spend buying a newspaper or magazine pays mainly for its distribution, not its creation. When a sales representative from the local newspaper calls you to see if you would be interested in a subscription, this is not out of concern for more money to print more news. Instead, the point of subscribers—audience members—is to show (potential) advertisers how big the newspaper's market is. Your subscription is much more likely to equal more advertisements than news.

Money is important enough in the media that it can impact interpersonal relationships between the people working for a station or media organization. David Sarnoff and Edwin Armstrong were friends in the early days of commercial radio. Sarnoff was business minded, while Armstrong was an inventor. Both made major contributions to the growth in radio broadcasting, with Sarnoff becoming the president of RCA in 1930. At this time, radio was only broadcast through AM (amplitude modulation), which made it difficult to listen to the radio in large, concrete office buildings in places like New York City.

Sarnoff asked Armstrong to work at RCA, and by 1934, Armstrong was conducting experiments with FM (frequency modulation), including listening to an FM signal while standing in Sarnoff's office. Sarnoff may have realized this was important work, but if he had bought the idea at that time, any unsold RCA radio units with AM-only capabilities would have become obsolete; RCA warehouses were filled with AM-only radios. He and Armstrong had a long fight about Armstrong's work and accumulated debt (much of the work on FM came from Armstrong's own pocket), with Armstrong committing suicide in 1954 after arguing with his wife regarding money.

Economics and power cannot be overlooked in the newsroom, but there is also agency that we need to take into account. As noted by Gitlin (1980), reporters can and do decide how to write a story (from a liberal, conservative, or middle-of-the-road standpoint), though many have been fired for swaying too far from the political leanings of the media outlet or editors for whom they work. They can also do extra work—freelancing—hoping to find a way to make more money or cover a story that no one else is willing to cover to build on their experiences, especially when their current job offers few opportunities for quick advancement. This is what happened to one of Porter Shreve's characters in *The Obituary Writer*:

> My father's first job out of the Navy was on the city desk at the *Wichita Kansan*. Back in the early sixties a midrange paper sent out maybe a dozen reporters, and the cub, my father at the time, usually got the police beat. He checked with the hospitals, kept contact with the precincts, and reported to accidents, robberies, and the occasional homicide, where he'd call his stories back to the office for rewrite. He liked the work but, according to my mother, he was restless. He wanted to make an impact on the world, and toward the end of 1963, eight months into the job, his opportunity arrived.
>
> In those days, the Associated Press put out a calendar of upcoming national events every other Thursday, and late one November afternoon my father picked off the wires the news that President Kennedy would be in Dallas the next day. He was off Friday and Saturday, so he called my mother and cut out of work early and bought a ticket on the five-fifteen Silversides Thruliner, the overnight bus to Dallas (Shreve, *The Obituary Writer*: 5).

We all know what happened next in Dallas, and Shreve's novel dovetails nicely with Zelizer's (1992) research on how reporters covered the Kennedy assassination on Friday, November 22, 1963. None of the reporters in Dallas saw Kennedy being shot as they were on a bus well behind the rest of the presidential motorcade. Reporters had to rely on the regular people who were watching the president's car drive by, but when they called in these reports, some began saying that they were eyewitnesses. To some extent, this could be said to be true, as they were in Dallas and were covering the president's visit. As other reporters heard these stories, they too began to say that they were there and saw the whole thing. There are numerous examples of reporters changing stories or reporting practices in this way. In addition to the Kennedy assassination, Zelizer (1989) shows how reporting changed after Edward R. Murrow challenged Senator Joseph McCarthy's stance on communism. Before Murrow's attack, reporters rarely challenged political leaders, even if they thought they were wrong. She also points to how reporters changed tactics after Bob Woodward and Carl Bernstein engaged in criminal acts—talking to people on the grand jury during the Watergate scandal. This is an excellent example of the sociological imagination at work, as we begin to understand reporting practices as an outcome of both personal preferences and structural aspects of the job that were put in place long before a reporter started writing news stories.

Zelizer (1989) refers to this practice of imitating others as an interpretative community. In the newsroom, this means following the lead of award-winning reporters. Since those individuals are the role models for all reporters, it becomes easy to see why stories look so similar across newscasts and media organizations. It can also mean talking to the same sources, so as to give the audience a consistent message. As Shepherd (1979) learned, once a source is willing to talk to a reporter, that individual or organization will continue to be used by reporters—even when the person is not an expert on the subject. When I asked a newspaper editor how her reporters decided on sources to talk to when covering a food irradiation story, she told me that they usually begin with old newspaper articles to see who had been willing to talk to reporters in the past (Ten Eyck, 1999).

Being labeled an expert, in fact, seems to be one of the main concerns for reporters, regardless of the topic for which one is being labeled as knowledgeable. Given their deadlines, which are very often daily, reporters need to find people who are willing to talk right now. I found this to be the case when I spoke with a person from NASA who was said to be an expert on food irradiation. When I asked this person what kind of research he had done with irradiated food, he told me he had never done any research on it. Instead, he had read about it and thought that it was the safest food to give to the astronauts aboard space shuttles. Obviously, the newspaper did some background checking to make sure this person had a PhD in food (he set the menus for the astronauts), which made him an expert on food. In addition, the newspaper's audience would likely see NASA as a legitimate organization to be discussing food safety in space, as no one wants to have an upset stomach in zero gravity. This provides the two main ingredients for a believable story—plausibility (the audience can imagine the events happening), and a credible source (the person must have the necessary background to be talking about the issue). Though what makes for a plausible story and credible spokesperson varies widely in society.

DISSEMINATION AND *AN AMERICAN DREAM*

In addition to understanding the creation of news stories, it is also important to understand how those stories will be disseminated. A picture of a star exploding in the night sky will not easily transfer to radio, while covering a band that plays behind a curtain might not be viewed as appropriate for a television audience. In my own work on graffiti (Ten Eyck & Fischer, 2012), it was found that the topic could be either an art form, the typical Internet portrayal—or vandalism, the typical newspaper portrayal. Our study consisted of looking at graffiti images from the nine largest cities in the United States, as well as news stories concerning graffiti from those same cities (and *USA Today*). We found that there was very little violence or crime tied to the Internet images, but a majority of the news stories linked graffiti to economic downturns and criminal activities. Given that the images were most likely posted by individuals interested in graffiti, including the graffiti writers themselves, and the news stories by reporters tied to local businesses, it is not surprising that the form of the information and how that information traveled was so different. If the newspapers had used the images we found on the Internet to accompany their stories about crime and violence, there would be a number of instances in which the reporter would have had to explain why a multilayered piece of graffiti that portrayed a popular video character was tied to a violent crime or economic concerns.

McLuhan and Fiore (1967) were some of the first scholars to argue that we need to understand that a story in a newspaper is interpreted differently than the same story broadcast on television (or radio, face to face, etc.). The following is from Norman Mailer in his novel, *An American Dream*, in which his main character, Stephen Rojack, who teaches and has a television show, kills his estranged wife. The following shows Rojack reading about the death in the newspapers:

I bought several newspapers, took another cab, and went back to my apartment. On the ride I did my reading. There was no need to go too thoroughly through the news stories. They splashed the front page, spoke of the death as suicide, gave details about Deborah and details about me, half of them correct, half incorrect, gave promise in their excitement that the story was good for two days more and probably a feature for the weekend round-up, they hinted—but very lightly—that police were on the scene, they announced me as unavailable for comment, Barney Oswald Kelly was unavailable for comment, and the television studio and the university as willing to give no comment. An unidentified colleague at the university was quoted as saying, "They were a splendid couple." Two of the papers had used the same picture of Deborah. It was a terrible picture and years old. "Beautiful Young Society Matron Takes Life in Plunge," said the little headline over the photograph, and beneath was Deborah looking fat and ugly and somewhat idiotic for she was getting out of a limousine at a wedding and was caught with a frozen supercilious smile as if her mind said to the news photographer, "Shall I look like this for the masses?" (Mailer, *An American Dream*: 127–28).

How would this have played out if Rojack had been at home watching this same story on television? That story may have shown Rojack hiding his head while trying to push away the reporters' cameras, a sign that he had something to do with his wife's death, even if the television reporter said that the death was being treated as a suicide. Instead, a photograph of the deceased wife and a written story about her possible suicide provides a very different feel of the event.

Not only do stories change from medium to medium within the mass media, it can also change depending on whether it is found in the mass media or coming from a friend. When I was a graduate student at Louisiana State University, I asked undergraduates if they trusted their friends more than the media. Most of them agreed that their friends were more trustworthy, a typical reaction among people when asked about the media and people they know personally and trust. I then provided these students scenarios in which they heard about either a free concert or a new restaurant from either a radio station or a friend (four possible scenarios—hearing about a concert from the radio, hearing about a concert from a friend, hearing about a restaurant from the radio, and hearing about a restaurant from a friend). What I found was that students tended to have the most trust in a story about a free concert from the radio and the least amount of trust in a story about a restaurant from the radio. In other words, the same medium—a radio station—had both the highest and lowest levels of trust, depending on the message. Sociologists would argue that there is nothing intrinsically more or less trustworthy concerning the source of information, but that we are socialized to think that friends are more trustworthy than the media. That, however, can depend on the message.

Before we move to the audience, it is important to think about how these various mediums are structures, in the sense that our agency is bounded. The nature of radio broadcasts means you will not be seeing images, newspapers cannot provide readers with images that move (though they are now providing such images on their web pages), and the bandwidth given to radio and television stations dictates who can listen to them and when. Some of these structures have been put in place by agencies—the Federal Communications Committee determines the width of frequencies, as well as the placement of stations on this bandwidth and content—and others by their nature: Radio receivers do not have the capacity to show images. These structures impact how stories are told, which means they also affect how stories are interpreted.

INTERPRETING THE STORY AND *BACK TO BLOOD*

Does the fact that producers, editors, and reporters must think about their advertisers and how their stories will be disseminated make them biased? According to Gitlin (1980), what makes a reporter biased are her political beliefs, though some reporters are better at hiding this than others. Tom Wolfe, in *Back to Blood*, wrote that most reporters have a very specific leaning, and these become clear early in life:

In the schoolyard boys immediately divide into two types. Immediately! There are those who have the will to be daring and dominate, and those who don't have it. Those who don't ... spend half their early years trying to work out a modus Vivendi with those who do ... and anything short of subservience will be okay. But there are boys from the weaker side of the divide who grow up with the same dreams as the stronger. ... They, too, dream of power, money, fame, and beautiful lovers. Boys like this ... grow up instinctively realizing that language is an artifact, like a sword or a gun. Used skillfully, it has the power to ... well, not so much *achieve* things as to tear things down—including people ... including the boys who came out on the strong side of the sheerly dividing line. ... They are weak. ... That's why so many journalists are liberals! ... You will put yourself in dangerous situations amid dangerous people ... *with relish*. You will go alone, without any form of backup ... *eagerly!* You—you with your weak manner—end up approaching the vilest of the vile with a demand. "You have some information, and I *need* it. And I *will* have it" (Wolfe, *Back to Blood*: 116–17).

Wolfe is not the only person who argues that the media are full of liberals. Glenn Beck (2012), who makes a living through mass media via the Internet, argues that the United States is failing because of the progressive stance of the media (along with mainstream Protestant churches, border patrols, Democratic politicians, etc.). Whether it is the reporters or the audience who are biased is a topic we will turn to shortly, but it is safe to say that reporters are human, with all the frailties and desires of other humans. Most reporters believe they are objective because they provide at least two sides to every story, though the "other" side—the side they might not agree with—is often couched in unfavorable terms. As one newspaper reporter told me about an activist group she was following, she was happy to print their side of the story, but those articles were written in such a way as to show that they were basically nuts.

Reporters are not the only people interpreting the stories they cover. According to Gunther (1992), those working for the media might be biased, but so are consumers. His study consisted of asking ordinary people if they thought the media were biased. Those who said they were Republican said that of course the media were biased in favor of Democrats and against Republicans. Democrats, on the other hand, said that of course the media were biased in favor of Republicans and against Democrats. Both might be right depending on where they are getting their information, which issues they are reading about, and who is paying the bills on the other end.

Political affiliations are not the only structures that influence how we interpret information from the mass media. Höijer (1992) studied how people's personal backgrounds influenced how they watched soap operas. The soap opera her subjects watched was based in a country inn, and when Höijer asked someone who grew up in such a place to watch the show, that person talked about whether or not he had done the same things being portrayed in the show. When she asked an actress to watch the same episode, the actress talked about the pros and cons of the script and talents of the actors and actresses. Morley and Brunsdon (1999) found that socioeconomic class mattered as to what shows were watched and why, while Chew and Palmer (1994) found that interest in a topic was a better predictor of people watching a show than their educational backgrounds. Trying to figure out what people watch and how they interpret the information they receive is not a simple puzzle with an easy solution.

Besides our own interpretations, we also spend time and energy wondering how other people are interpreting the same information. This is because most people believe that they are not affected by the media, or at least not as much as other people. This is known as the third-person effect (e.g., Wei, Chia, & Lo, 2011), and such a perception of how the media affects others impacts what we think should and should not be broadcast. Information we feel might cause someone else to act against our own best interests (unprotected sex, violence, politics, etc.) should be censored. If we believe that violent television is going to make someone else—never us—act violently, then we might ask stations to stop showing crime dramas. If we think that young children will lose their moral compasses if they are exposed to sex, then we ask that sexual activity be banned. We may think of this as agency—asking the government or a station to censor some material—but when so many people have the same approach, censorship becomes a structural component of society (Atkins & Mintcheva, 2006).

THE MESSAGE

If everyone interprets information differently, does it make sense to spend time thinking about what goes into a news report or daytime soap opera? In addition, with the growth of information technologies such as the Internet, there are now millions of information sources that can be used to find just about any angle on any story. To take a random example, there is currently a debate in Michigan about hunting wolves, and an Internet search on "wolf hunting in Michigan" returned over 900,000 web pages. I did not check every page to see if it was related to this specific topic, and I assume many of them were about other topics, but it shows how much information can be found searching one set of words. There seem to be too many things to take into consideration when thinking about any specific mass-mediated message, as any given message is likely to get lost in our media-saturated society.

There are two ways to think about this issue from a sociological perspective. One is to think about how any specific news article or show is written, produced, and broadcast. We may not be too concerned about a story covering a Little League baseball tournament in our town, but if we read something about a rogue terrorist cell being discovered in our backyard, we might become edgy. This is how most of us respond to risks. A Little League tournament is not a risk, so we might read the story with a smile as we remember our own time playing in such leagues. Terrorism, on the other hand, is a risk that causes death. We dread the thought of being caught in a terrorist attack, and as Woods (2012) has shown, if the news report states that the terrorists are dealing with nuclear materials and are religious radicals, we see that as much worse than a story about a kid in the neighbor caching a few small-caliber rifles. Words carry meanings; thus, how an article is written will have an impact on how we react to it.

There is also the fact that news articles can influence what issues we think about and how we think about those issues. Dearing and Rogers (1996) argue that the media do set agendas for us by focusing on certain issues, while ignoring others. Returning to the stories of tornadoes and blood poisoning, we tend to be more worried about the former than the latter, though blood poisoning kills more people. Gamson (1992) makes the same point in saying that how we think about issues is partly based on media portrayals. He points to three sources of information that we use to make sense of our world—our own experiences, public myths, and the media. To understand how powerful the media can be, take something as simple as an apple. You know whether or not you like apples based on your own experiences with them. If you tell me your favorite apples are Granny Smiths, my insistence that the best apples are Fujis will not change your mind. You know what a Granny Smith tastes like, and you know it is your favorite. Apples also come with stories, such as it being the fruit of knowledge (Adam and Eve), its place in U.S. history (Johnny Appleseed), as an icon for a very popular electronics company, and as a present given to popular teachers. Most of us would say that these experiences and stories are all we need to make sense of the apple, and anything that might be said in the media would have no effect on our thoughts. We also believe this to be true of many of the topics and issues we think about on a daily basis.

Ever heard of Alar? This is a chemical that was used by some farmers to promote growth in their apple crops. An environmental group did some tests on Alar and came to the conclusion that it was a carcinogen and could cause cancer if digested. This statement was picked up by the media and disseminated widely in the United States. Apple sales plummeted, despite the experiences and stories of apples mentioned above. A cancer threat reported by the media trumped our ideas about apples and how one a day can keep the doctor away. The same thing happened to coffee. An article published in 1981 in the *New England Journal of Medicine*, a prestigious medical journal, stated that there was a link between coffee consumption and pancreatic cancer. This was picked up by the media, and coffee sales dropped (and tea sales increased—reflexive modernity). The article was later refuted, but it took a long time for coffee sales to return to where they were before the article was published.

Finally, there are issue frames that go beyond a single article or word. Gamson and Modigliani (1989) followed the changes in how nuclear power was discussed beginning at the end of World War II until the 1970s and 1980s. What began as a clean energy source that was going to be "too cheap to meter" became a Pandora's Box and a deal-with-the-devil scenario, all of which coincided to some degree with public opinion toward nuclear power. Opinion had changed from mostly positive to mostly negative over the same time period. How an issue such as nuclear power is framed in the media will give readers a sense of how they should be thinking about it. Readers with more knowledge of the issue may be more active in interpreting what they read and hear, while others with less background will likely have little else to go on. Regardless of your experience with a topic, the media can—and often do—influence our ways of thinking.

THE MIX

The complexity of every story and the structures of the media and audiences have led a number of scholars to argue that we have moved beyond modern society in which institutions play very specific roles in society and our lives (e.g., Baudrillard, 1998). We now live in a postmodern world where the media bring us so many stories about all the things that institutions can and cannot do that we can no longer distinguish between reality and fantasy because we are constantly being told different versions of life across all communication media. Even when we take a vacation, we often talk about it in terms of what we have seen on television ("My family stayed at the same hotel as Brad Pitt and Angelina Jolie when they went to the same place."). Our lives are pieced together by the stories we hear about others—typically celebrities—and we live vicariously through these others, as well as the products they use (or at least advertise as using). In such a world, every experience becomes mediated, and that offers us an opportunity to put together some pretty interesting narratives about ourselves.

Whether we are still modern or have become postmodern, when we begin to put all these pieces together—those who are creating messages, how those messages are being disseminated, who is interpreting the messages, the messages themselves, and the sheer volume of it all—we begin to understand the complexity of the media and their impact on society and ourselves. It is not a simple decision to trust or not trust what we hear or see on television, radio, the Internet, our friends, or even a textbook like this. There are too many structural factors and opportunities for agency to say that the media and our approaches to them are one-dimensional. It is only through the sociological imagination that we can begin to pull apart, and put back together, the role the media play in contemporary society.

REFERENCES AND RECOMMENDED READINGS

Atkins, R., and Mintcheva, S. (Eds.). (2006). *Censoring Culture*. New York: New Press.

Bagdikian, B. H. (1983). *The Media Monopoly*. Boston: Beacon Press.

Baudrillard, J. (1998). *The Consumer Society*. Thousand Oaks, CA: Sage.

Beck, G. (2012). *Cowards*. New York: Threshold.

Chew, F., and Palmer, S. (1994). "Interest, the Knowledge Gap, and Television Programming." *Journal of Broadcasting & Electronic Media*, 38(3): 271–87.

Franklin, B., and Murphy, D. (1998). *Making the Local News*. London, UK: Routledge.

Gans, H. J. (1979). *Deciding What's News*. New York: Pantheon.

Gamson, W. A. (1992). *Talking Politics*. New York: Cambridge University Press.

Gamson, W. A., and Modigliani, A. (1989). "Media Discourse and Public Opinion on Nuclear Power: A constructionist approach." *American Journal of Sociology*, 95(1): 1–37.

Gamson, W. A., Croteau, D., Hoynes, W., and Sasson, S. (1992). "Media Images and the Social Construction of Reality." *Annual Review of Sociology*, 18: 373–93.

Gitlin, T. (1980). *The Whole World Is Watching*. Berkeley: University of California Press.

Gunther, A. C. (1992). "Biased Press or Biased Public?" *Public Opinion Quarterly*, 56(2): 147–67.

Höijer, B. (1992). "Reception of television narration as a socio-cognitive process: A schema-theoretical outline." *Poetics*, 21(4): 283–304.

Mailer, N. (1999). *An American Dream*. New York: Vintage.

McLuhan, M., and Fiore, Q. (1967). *The Medium Is the Massage*. New York: Random House.

Morley, D., and Brunsdon, C. (1999). *The Nationwide Television Studies*. New York: Routledge.

Shepherd, R. G. (1979). "Science News of Controversy: The case of marijuana." *Journalism Monographs*, 62.

Shreve, P. 2000. *The Obituary Writer*. New York: Houghton Mifflin Harcourt.

Ten Eyck, T. A. (1999). "Shaping a Food Safety Debate: Control efforts of newspaper reporters and sources in the food irradiation controversy." *Science Communication*, 20(4): 426–47.

Ten Eyck, T. A., and Fischer, B. E. (2012). "Is Graffiti Risky? Insights from the internet and newspapers." *Media, Culture, & Society*, 34(7): 832–46.

Tuchman, G. (1978). *Making News*. New York: Free Press.

Wei, R., Chia, S. C., and Lo, V.-H. (2011). "Third-Person Effect and Hostile Media Perceptions Influences on Voter Attitudes toward Polls in the 2008 Presidential Election." *International Journal of Public Opinion Research*, 23(2): 169–90.

Wolfe, T. (2012). *Back to Blood*. New York: Little, Brown, and Company.

Woods, J. (2012). *Freaking Out*. Washington, DC: Potomac Books.

Zelizer, B. (1992). *Covering the Body*. Chicago: University of Chicago Press.

———. (1993). "Journalists at Interpretive Communities." *Critical Studies in Mass Communication*, 10(3): 219–37.

14 SPORTS

INTRODUCTION AND *THE ART OF FIELDING*

Given the popularity of viewing sports and the fact that many people participate in some kind of organized athletic endeavor at some point in their lives, whether it be in Little League, gym classes, or yoga sessions, as well as the history of the Olympics and other sports that would provide numerous opportunities to engage the sociological imagination, you might be led to believe that sports are a central concern to sociology. In fact, this chapter could have appeared before or after the chapter on education, as many of us started to play and learn about sports by the time we started school. The study of games and sports, however, is often thought of as little more than a subfield or topic in which to look at how structural aspects of society such as gender, race, and age play out in contemporary settings. This is unfortunate, as many of us learned a great deal about ourselves and society by placing our athletic prowess up against others, such as when Henry Skrimshander and Mike Schwartz meet on a baseball diamond for the first time in Chad Harbach's *The Art of Fielding*:

Schwartz didn't notice the kid during the game. Or rather, he noticed only what everyone else did—that he was the smallest player on the field, a scrawny novelty of a shortstop, quick of foot but weak with the bat. Only after the game ended, when the kid returned to the sundrenched diamond to take extra grounders, did Schwartz see the grace that shaped Henry's every move. ...

During the game, Schwartz had figured the kid was too small to hit high heat, so he'd called for one fastball after another, up and in. Before the last, he'd told the kid what was coming and added, "Since you can't hit it anyway." The kid swung and missed, gritted his teeth, turned to make the long walk back to the dugout. Just then Schwartz said—ever so softly, so that it would seem to come from inside the kid's own skull—"*Pussy*." The kid paused, his scrawny shoulders tensed like a cat's but he didn't turn around. Nobody ever did (Harbach, *The Art of Fielding*: 3–4).

Those who have competed in sports can relate to the situation of being told we are too weak to perform or telling others the same thing, and probably both. We would also argue that whatever comes out of our mouths on the field, diamond, court, or rink is of our own accord. When so many people say the same thing, we have to dig deeper into what structures the activity to begin to understand why we tend to sound so much alike no matter what sport or at what level we are playing. Female athletes have told me that their coaches also call them "pussies" when yelling at them for lack of effort or to overcome an injury.

Fine (1987) spent time with boys on Little League teams in Massachusetts, and came to the conclusion that social structures were key to understanding the operation of the leagues, including the typical banter you hear among players. This ranged from not allowing games or practices on Sundays so families could attend church services, to brothers and sons of coaches being on the same team, to asking local businesses and government agencies for funding so the teams and leagues would be seen as legitimate. What does any of this have to do with what the kids are saying to and about each other? For one thing, these leagues rarely allowed girls to participate, which became translated into girls being weaker than boys. When a boy did poorly, he was said to act like a girl. Fathers would be embarrassed by this, and tell their sons the same thing—"don't act like a girl," or "stop being such a pussy." The other boys would hear this, or notice that people laughed when calling someone else a girl or pussy, which reinforced the behavior. Movies about baseball such as *The Bad News Bears* add to the stock of knowledge of how to talk when playing. Sports were not as important as activities like church, so one could cut up during an activity that was second rate because it really did not matter. All of these factors play into how we talk during practices and games, and this happens across the country and around the globe. Many of the jokes and lines used for teasing Fine heard among the boys in Massachusetts were the same ones I used and heard while playing Little League baseball between 1973 and 1977 in Oregon (Fine did much of his research in the late 1970s and early 1980s). Fine also talked about the roles parents played in Little League, and I experienced the same kind of engagements, including the disorganization caused by both over- and under-involvement on the part of parents and coaches. This included a sprained thumb from an overly involved parent/coach during infield practice and watching a fight break out between two parents, though it is hard to determine if fighting is a sign of over- or under-involvement—given the lack of participation in practices and games on the one hand, and being overzealous about their offspring on the other. One of the participants was the father of a female player who was good, and the other was the father of a male who was challenged on the baseball field. The fight involved pushing and shoving, yelling, the wielding of a baseball bat (though no one was hit), and two mothers stepping in to put an end to the hostilities. That I still remember this incident points to how the actions of others come to shape our own actions.

To say this happens across the globe as well comes, in part, from watching sports played in other countries and a discussion of cricket with a British colleague. Having only seen snippets of this game on television with the players in their white uniforms, I thought cricket was probably a gentleman's game. I asked my colleague if there was much trash talking during games. He told me that he heard of a professional player telling an opponent that he was getting fat, to which the opponent replied, "That's because every time I go to see your wife she gives me a biscuit." Bragging among boys of sexual conquests apparently rarely goes out of fashion, even as they get older.

If the talking that takes place on the field is consistent across settings, at least the decision to play sports is based on our own thoughts and desires. A closer look at how people decide to play sports, however, tells a different story. Many of us choose to play a sport because of what we hear from parents, friends, teachers, and coaches, as well as seeing how athletes are treated in the news. The decision to play sports at a more advanced level is also structured by scholarships and contracts, as not just anyone can play major college or professional sports, no matter how much they crave the free tuition and multimillion-dollar contracts.

Even if we are not interested in playing sports at an advanced level, many adults can no longer simply spend time playing at nothing in particular. According to Fink (1968), to play means to have no end result in mind. Kicking a pebble down the street would be considered playing until the individual begins adding rules, such as trying to place the pebble close to a line in the sidewalk or down a storm drain. Once a rule is engaged, playing becomes a game. Most adults must have boundaries to make sense of their actions because that is how we live our lives, but to play means there is no reason for the activities one is undertaking. When I asked a class to kick ping-pong balls from our classroom to another building and back, every group told me about the rules (and roles) they created during this activity, though I made no mention of having to do so. Not a single group just played by kicking the ball and not worrying about where it went or how fast they could make it back to the classroom. In fact, those groups who lost their balls down storm drains or were run over by cars or bicycles were very apologetic for their failures.

In addition to what is exchanged between players and how we play, structures also shape the intensity of sports, including violence that has taken the lives of players, coaches, and umpires at the hands of other participants and parents. If Schwartz had called some of the guys I knew in high school a pussy, there would have been a fight shortly thereafter, no matter how big Schwartz might have been. While often treated as isolated incidents, the trend toward violence among participants in sports is unmistakable, and this includes injuries that are not tied to someone trying to intentionally hurt someone else. According to Marar et al. (2012), football leads all sports in concussions among players, a sport that is geared toward physical contact, followed by women's soccer, which is not based on hitting each other, while ice hockey, another contact sport, has the highest rate of concussions among reported injuries. Rates have increased over the years, though this may be at least partly due to better on-field detection and reporting practices.

Why would a sociologist be interested in sports-related injuries? For one thing, increases in injuries have come at a time when some scholars are arguing that sports have become more civilized (Elias, 1978). This includes, among other things, providing gloves and headgear to boxers and putting on pads and helmets in American football. What has been found, however, is that these sports have become more violent as more equipment is added to the game. When a person is worried about breaking a hand in a fight, they will be more cautious about when and where they hit their opponent, but when that hand is protected by a padded glove there is no reason to hold back, unless it provides openings to your opponent, who also has padded hands. Putting helmets on football players' heads and wrapping their bodies in padding turns them into missiles as the players feel like they are invincible. A game that used to be filled with broken noses is now replete with concussions and spinal injuries. Dunning (1990), who worked with Elias on the civilization process, has argued that such thinking is too short term. A longer history of sports shows that extreme violence was much more prevalent from ancient times to the beginning of modern societies, as feeding people to lions and having gladiators fight to the death were once considered sporting events. Dunning also brings up the topic of soccer hooliganism, a subject that is receiving increased scholarly attention.

When we take a step back from any specific game or our own time in sports, we can begin to see how structure and agency intersect in sports in the topics mentioned above. Many of us have never created a game from scratch. There are plenty of games based on adapting a situation to existing games, such as the link between official baseball rules and stickball games played on the streets of New York, or softball and over-the-line tournaments played on the beaches of San Diego. We might make the decision to go outside and play a game with friends instead of sitting in the house with our video games, but that decision is a choice that is given to us; both the outdoor and indoor games are structured by forces outside our control. We make decisions on what to play and how to play (our agency) but within the rules provided by larger social forces (structure).

PLAY, GAMES, SPORTS, THE SELF, AND *CALICO JOE*

Besides the everyday decisions of what to play, a longer look at the evolution of games and sports sheds even more light on how social structures influence how and what (and even when) we play. Concerns with players' safety have led to equipment and rule changes. The professionalization of sports grew out of an expanding leisure class, as more people had time to watch games, and wanted those games played by people with more talent than themselves. We can also make sense of the development of the self through sports. Mead (1962) uses playing and games to show how the self develops between infancy and adolescence. According to Mead, we tend to only play until about eight years of age. During these years, we can mimic other people, but lack the ability to understand that these others can play roles that complement what we are doing. When young children play a team sport such as soccer, they rarely stay in an assigned position; instead, all members from both teams (including the goalies) will go wherever the ball goes. This has been referred to as beehive soccer, as the kids' actions look like a swarm of bees, in which every individual is moving in the same direction in the same place (Brady, 2004). When I was coaching my son's tee-ball league in Louisiana (six-to-seven-year-olds), I experienced the same phenomenon. Coaches were allowed to stand in the outfield to direct the kids and make sure they stayed out of harm's way. On one particular play, a ball was hit to right field, and I told the outfielders around me to go and get it. Two of them ran after it and tackled each other as they both wanted to end up with the ball. Suddenly, the second baseman ran by me and jumped into the fray. Finally, one of the kids (I will call him Josh) got the ball and began running toward the infield. I told Josh to throw the ball to another player multiple times, though he looked at me with bewilderment, probably wondering why I would want him to give up his newly attained prize. He ran the ball all the way into the infield before giving it to another coach. Meanwhile, the kid who had hit the ball ran all the way around the bases for a home run, though he had to be coaxed off each base, knowing that he was safe standing on those square pieces of plastic.

If we follow Mead's (1962) logic, we understand that, while Josh may have had the capability to throw the ball toward a teammate, he was unable to comprehend that the other players were playing roles different from his. As an outfielder (Josh may have been the second baseman that ran by me), his role is to get the ball as quickly as possible and throw it to an infielder. For someone Josh's age, every kid on the field would be playing identical roles, if they were even taken into consideration, so there was no point in throwing the ball to someone else because that would mean he would lose the thing everyone seemed to want. This is what Mead referred to as the play stage in a person's development.

Once children reach approximately eight years of age, they begin to understand that other people play roles. It is at this age that you can begin to feel more confident in telling a player to play shortstop and if a ball is hit to her, to throw it to first base, and that the player will actually attempt to throw the ball to first base instead of running it over to the base or a coach. This is what Mead refers to as the game stage, and it is at this point that children begin to understand the significance of generalized others, including the importance of rules. Anyone who has played games with other kids between the ages of eight and 15 will remember that a great deal of time is spent coming up with and arguing over rules, especially when no adults are around and there are not enough players or the proper equipment to play the game as it is shown on television or in the instructions. Learning that new rules can be created and others bent to fit the situation provides insight into how rules might work in other settings such as school.

In the summer of 1973, the country was slowly emerging from the trauma of Vietnam. Spiro Agnew was in trouble and would eventually go down. Watergate was getting hot with much more to come. I was eleven years old and slightly aware of what was happening out there in the real world, but I was wonderfully unburdened by it. Baseball was my world, and little else mattered. My father pitched for the New York Mets, and I lived and died with each game. I pitched too, for the Scrappers in the White Plains Little League, and because my father was who he was, great things were expected of me. I rarely met those expectations, but there were moments of promise (Grisham, *Calico Joe*: 5).

In addition to developing an understanding of how a game is played, children show varying levels of skill in sports. Perceived talent, or lack thereof, can lead to expectations for players, as was the case for John Grisham's main character in *Calico Joe*. This character played Little League in New York at the same time I was playing in Oregon and Gary Fine was helping with teams in Massachusetts:

Much like life in general, when you fall short of expectations, you either try harder, withdraw (or adults withdraw the children, as in places like Cheyenne, Wyoming, and Spokane, Washington, where the game of tag has been outlawed during school recesses because certain kids were getting bullied or hurt), or try to find ways to make everyone, including yourself, happy. This may involve cheating. There is, however, a caveat to cheating in sports. Suits (1966) argues that if you cheat, then you do not really play the game, even if your excuse is that the other players are also cheating. Suits uses a poker game as an example. The way to win in poker is to end up with more money than anyone else in the game (there are gradations to winning at poker, but this is an ideal situation). If, however, a player hits another player and takes his money, then he has not played the game, even if he has met the standard of having the most money at the table. While cheating negates the game, it is often a much more effective way to play than trying to stick to the rules. Suits, in fact, contends that following rules is often a very ineffective way to reach the desired goal of a game. Players, however, rarely determine the rules they have to play by. This is referred to as a disjoint constitution, as the governing bodies that make the rules do not have to play by them. In professional sports, owners are often the main actors on rules committees, though they never see the field as players. The main objective in American football is to take the ball and pass it over the line that demarcates the end zone. The most effective way to do this is to pick up the ball and walk it into the end zone—no passes, rushes, or reverses. Just pick it up, cross the end zone line, and award yourself a touchdown. Let both teams do this a few times and call it a day. A rules committee made up of owners who make money from the playing of football would see this as a problem, because no one would pay to see two groups of individuals wandering around a football field. If the point of a hitter in baseball is to have the ball fall safely into the field of play, then take the ball and place it where no one from the other team is playing and go stand on the base that has the best view of the park. Playing by the rules is much more difficult, but also more profitable for owners. At the professional level, a batter must swing a wooden bat that is round and try to make contact with a ball that is also round and traveling approximately 90 mph, with the hope that if contact is made, none of the nine players on the other team either catches it in the air or throws it to a base before he gets there. A good professional player does this three out of ten tries, a business plan that would lead to failure in most industries. We have, unfortunately, made winning so important that players (e.g., steroid use), coaches (filming other teams' practices), and even fans (throwing things at opposing players as they try to make plays) try to find ways to skirt the rules. If, however, you or your team win by cheating, have you really played the game?

We not only learn if we are good athletes (or good cheaters) in sports, we also learn about what it means to be male or female. In many communities, boys play football and baseball, while girls play volleyball and softball. While there are many sports that involve both genders—basketball, soccer—teams are often divided between boys and girls once they reach a certain age, and then we return to coed teams after a certain age. Even in a sport such as horse racing, trainers and owners see male jockeys as having an advantage over women.

Jockeys are often chosen because of their weight—a smaller rider adds less weight to a horse—yet there are very few female jockeys in the professional ranks, even though a woman will typically weigh less than a man of the same height. Besides being told that they are weaker and would not be able to handle a difficult horse in a tense situation, women aspiring to be jockeys have been told that their bottoms are the wrong shape for racing saddles. Not only do the men tell the women these stories, but many of the women tell each other the same thing (Velija & Flynn, 2010).

There are also structures in sports based on race. In football, whites are thought to be better quarterbacks and blacks better receivers and running backs. In baseball, whites are thought to be better pitches and catchers and blacks better in the outfield (Margolis & Piliavin, 1999). These attitudes toward race play out in other areas such as media coverage. According to Coogan (2012), media coverage of crimes committed by two professional quarterbacks, Ben Roethlisberger (white; rape) and Michael Vick (black; dog fighting), was very different. Roethlisberger's rape charges garnered much less attention than Vick's participation in dog fighting. Coverage of Vick contained many more references to black culture and Vick's race, while Roethlisberger's alleged rape was chalked up to either the violence of football or the accuser trying to frame Roethlisberger for money.

Other aspects of our selves are also highlighted in sports. Age determines when we can begin playing in Little League teams, as well as when we need to move from high-impact sports to walking and taking tai chi classes. Height and weight often determine both what sports and what positions we are expected, or even allowed, to play. While some athletes such as Bo Jackson, Danny Ainge, and Deion Sanders played professionally in different sports, I know of no such crossovers between horse jockeys and professional basketball players. Where we live will influence our access to certain sports. Camel races are a big event in the United Arab Emirates, where a tradition of camel racing has been recently created by national and tribal leaders (Khalaf, 2000), though this is not a sport that is available to many people in the United States. The weather will also determine when certain seasons start, as baseball teams in Wyoming experience a very short season. All of these structures impact the way we think about and play games and sports.

FANS, UMPIRES, COACHES, OWNERS, THE MEDIA, AND *MILLION DOLLAR BABY*

Games and sports involve much more than the players and rules. Unruly fans for one team are a home field advantage for another. Boyko, Boyko, and Boyko (2007) find that professional soccer games are often called differently, depending on where it is played (home teams receive more favorable calls), due partly to perceived crowd hostilities. Soccer hooliganism has gained interest in recent years (e.g., Frosdick & Marsh, 2005), though the impact of fan violence on games is not straightforward.

There is also betting on games, and while there are (in)famous cases of players throwing games to make good on bets (e.g., the 1919 Chicago "Black Sox"), coaches betting on games (e.g., Pete Rose), and even umpires (Tim Donaghy), all of whom could impact the outcome of games, there is little reason to believe that players change their games depending on the odds of winning or losing (being an underdog has been said to be motivation to play harder, but so can being a favorite, as you do not want to lose to a weaker opponent). Gambling is also a game itself with rules and structures like any other game. One of the more interesting aspects of gambling is the fact that gamblers know the odds of winning, yet many of them think they have a way to beat the system (Rabin & Vayanos, 2010).

Umpires and referees affect the games they officiate, and while any sports fan will have a favorite story of a good or bad call, studies have shown that umpires believe they are objective while showing favoritism toward teams depending on previous fouls and score (Anderson & Pierce, 2009), as well as the races of the players. Parsons, Sulaeman, Yates, and Hamermesh (working paper available at http://www.nber.org/papers/w13665, accessed June 2013), showed that umpires tend to call more strikes for pitchers of the same race, though this is dependent on a number of factors. If umpires and referees are unaware of their biases, then their calls are at least partially based on social structures that have impacted their approach to officiating.

Coaches also play a role in sports and a player's performance. Injuries can often be tied to poor training and coaching, and losing a player can impact a team. As with officiating, race is key to understanding coaching. The percentage

Today in the U.S., for the most part, the white boys of boxing are gone, though the percentage of white fighters who fight well is quite high. In fact it surprises me that more midsized white athletes don't come into the game.

White trainers, with some exceptions, are faded memories as well. Angelo Dundee, of course, still hangs with the big kids, as do a few others. My situation is unusual: 95 percent of my friends and associates are of a different color than I. I recently gave a rubdown to a 240-pound Ugandan who speaks English, Swahili, and Japanese. By the time I spread extra-virgin olive oil over him and then worked wintergreen liniment into him, he was black and shiny as a berry. He has a temperament sweet as a berry, as well. He's a polite and gentle Catholic boy—outside the ring. He lives and fights out of Japan. His regular trainer is Hawaiian Japanese (Toole, *Million Dollar Baby*: 13–14).

of minority players in college and professional basketball, baseball, and football does not match the percentage of minority coaches, as a much larger percentage of coaches are white. In *Million Dollar Baby*, F. X. Toole points to one sport that has a higher percentage of nonwhite coaches, though the pay is often much less than for coaches in the other sports just mentioned:

That the race of everyone is mentioned highlights the importance of this topic in sports, as race matters as much—if not more so—than performance in the eyes of many fans, coaches, umpires, and fellow participants.

The professionalization of sports, along with the money involved, has also brought team owners into the spotlight. George Steinbrenner (New York Yankees, deceased), Al Davis (Oakland Raiders, deceased), Jerry Jones (Dallas Cowboys), Mark Cuban (Dallas Mavericks), and Jeffrey Loria (Miami Marlins), and others who sign the paychecks of players have all made headlines for their actions regarding their teams. Owners have also been known to ask the cities where their teams play for new stadiums and fields, at times offering ultimatums that the new facilities be built or they will move the team. Given that professional teams generate revenue for the cities in which they are located, losing a team means losing business and tax dollars. Not every city has buckled under such pressure, but others have decided that teams are important enough to pay millions for a new football stadium, baseball diamond, basketball court, or hockey rink. Even teams without owners, such as the Olympics, generate and demand billions of dollars from fans and others as cities compete against each other to host the next round of games that will bring in thousands of visitors and millions of television viewers, and, of course, their money.

Finally, sports are structured by the media. Important games are played at times when there are large audiences available to watch. College conferences are based on television and media markets, and instant replay officials make decisions about overturning calls based on the video feeds supplied by the networks covering the games. Calls and plays are scrutinized ad nauseam through instant replay from numerous angles and all-day-and-all-night sports shows, adding to the pressure felt by participants to perform at a higher level, or at least not to make the same mistake again. This has led to players, coaches, and umpires refusing to talk to reporters so that sports fans are unable to hear their side of the story. Small-market professional teams (e.g., Kansas City and St. Louis) tend to receive less media coverage, leading to fewer players wanting to play for these teams and less fan merchandise being sold. Potential audience members on the East Coast may be in bed by the time a game starts at 7:00 P.M. on the West Coast. On the other hand, those on the West Coast may still be at work when a game starts in the east. Time and space have always been structural concerns for sports, but these are exacerbated by the media. This concern should not be overstated, as fans can now watch many more teams playing than before, though schedules have to be adjusted to watch a live feed instead of knowing that you will read about the game in tomorrow morning's newspaper.

While many of us enjoy sports and do not want to think about everything that goes into the making of a player, team, game, league, and so forth, to the sociological imagination sports are ripe for a deeper understanding of the link between agency and structures. Someone who is interested in how transportation and immigration patterns have affected games will have plenty of theories and data to work with, especially if they are interested in the historical aspects of their chosen sport and the current workings of modern athletics. The nationality of a player becomes important when a team representing a nation is being created, but does a person have control over the immigration of parents or grandparents, as well as the committee determining how nationality is to be determined? These and many other topics provide a great deal of opportunities for someone interested in how sports are embedded in society, and vice versa.

REFERENCES AND RECOMMENDED READINGS

Anderson, K. J., and Pierce, D. A. (2009). "Officiating Bias: The effect of foul differential on foul calls in NCAA basketball." *Journal of Sports Sciences*, 27(7): 687–94.

Boyko, R. H., Boyko, A. K., and Boyko, M. G. (2007). "Referee Bias Contributes to Home Advantage in English Premiership Football." *Journal of Sports Sciences*, 25(11): 1185–94.

Brady, F. (2004). "Children's Organized Sports: A developmental perspective." *Journal of Physical Education, Recreation & Dance*, 75(2): 35–41.

Coogan, D. (2012). "Race and Crime in Sports Media: Content analysis and the Michael Vick and Ben Roethlisberger Cases." *Journal of Sports Media*, 7(2): 129–51.

Dunning, E. (1990). "Sociological Reflections on Sport, Violence and Civilization." *International Review for the Sociology of Sport*, 25(1): 65–81.

Elias, N. (1978). *The Civilization Process* (trans. Edmund Jephcott). New York: Urizen Books.

Fine, G. A. (1987). *With the Boys*. Chicago: University of Chicago Press.

Fink, E. (1968). "The Oasis of Happiness: Toward an ontology of play." *Yale French Studies*, 41: 19–30.

Frosdick, S., and Marsh, P. (2005). *Football Hooliganism*. Portland, OR: Willan.

Grisham, J. (2012). *Calico Joe*. New York: Bantam Books.

Harbach, C. (2011). *The Art of Fielding*. New York: Hachette Digital.

Khalaf, S. (2000). "Poetics and Politics of Newly Invented Traditions in the Gulf: Camel racing in the United Arab Emirates." *Ethnology*, 39(3): 243–61.

Marar, M., McIlvain, N. M., Fields, S. K., and Comstock, R. D. (2012). "Epidemiology of Concussions Among United States High School Athletes in 20 Sports." *American Journal of Sports Medicine*, 40(4): 747–55.

Margolis, B., and Piliavin, J. A. (1999). "'Stacking' in Major League Baseball: A multivariate analysis." *Sociology of Sport Journal*, 16(1): 16–34.

Mead, G. H. (1962). *Mind, Self, and Society*. Chicago: University of Chicago Press.

Messner, M. (2002). *Taking the Field*. Minneapolis: University of Minnesota Press.

Rabin, M., and Vayanos, D. (2010). "The Gambler's and Hot-Hand Fallacies: Theory and applications." *Review of Economic Studies*, 77(2): 730–78.

Suits, B. (1966). "What is a game?" *Philosophy of Science*, 34(2): 148–56.

Toole, F. X. (2012). *Million Dollar Baby*. New York: Open Road Media.

Velija, P., and Flynn, L. (2010). "Their Bottoms Are the Wrong Shape: Female jockeys and the theory of established outsider relations." *Sociology of Sport Journal*, 27(3): 301–15.

Wacquant, L. (2004). *Body and Soul*. New York: Oxford University Press.

15 THE ARTS

INTRODUCTION AND *THE PICTURE OF DORIAN GRAY*

At last, a chapter that is all about agency. Art, after all, is a creative process, unlocked by such great masters as Rembrandt, Van Gogh, and Picasso. It is through the creative imagination of these great men that art is created. The fact that we know of these masters because their work hangs in museums has nothing to do with the art itself. Museums are organizations with structures, and the art was created elsewhere. In addition, that all of these famous painters are men points to something about agency that we just cannot quite put our fingers on.

Much of that seems reasonable until you begin to ask yourself a few questions. First, what is the difference between art and craft? Whatever your answer, do you think someone at the New York Metropolitan Museum of Art would care if you decided that your seashell sculptures from first grade were art and worthy of being shown in a world-class art museum? Why is it that many of us can easily name ten famous male artists (besides the three mentioned above, I can quickly include Dali, Klee, Van Eyck, Kandinsky, Monet, Manet, and Pollock without looking up anything online or in my bookcase), but find it difficult to name five female artists (Lempicka, O'Keeffe, Chicago, and Hesse are four that pop into my head without having to look up anything)? Why do so many of us agree on what counts for beauty in a painting or photograph? Is Marilyn Monroe that much more attractive than Minnie Pearl (1912–1996, an American country comedienne), and who decided on that standard? Are popular movies a form of art? What about the actors and actresses, or are they practicing a craft? Why did Vincent Van Gogh die poor, having sold only one or two paintings while he was alive, but now his work is worth millions? Why do we think of great artists as creative individuals, when the creation of art involves others? Few famous painters would have been able to make the canvas they painted on or the brushes they used. Creating a brush from scratch would involve raising animals for bristles, cutting and shaping the wood for the handle, and forging the metal for the ferrule. These and many other questions show that while art does involve creativity, it is also bounded by numerous structures.

Becker (1982) points out a number of these structures, referring to them as aspects of the art world. One insight into the art world is that the value of a piece of art is not intrinsic to the art itself. A Van Gogh painting, for example, cost Van Gogh just a few francs for the canvas, brushes, and paints. Van Gogh was rarely, if ever, asked to paint for money. For much of the time he stood behind an easel, he was not being paid by some rich patron, but supported by his brother, Theo, who worked for an art dealer. That his paintings are now worth millions has nothing to do with any of the materials he used, or how long he spent creating the paintings. Instead, what makes a Van Gogh painting valuable is that certain people and institutions say it is valuable, and these are people he did not know when he was alive. Vincent Van Gogh died when he was only 37 years old, having supposedly sold only one painting; this is hard to determine, however, as he gave away many of his paintings to friends and his brother, hoping the latter would be able to sell some of them. There may have been some money or food exchanged in some of these transactions, though it was known that many of the paintings were considered ugly and quickly stored in closets, basements, and attics. It was not until after Theo and he had passed away that Theo's wife, Johanna, Vincent's sister-in-law, began campaigning to have her brother-in-law's work recognized as truly genius. It was many years before anyone took her seriously. Manet painted such masterpieces as *Olympia* and *Le Déjeuner sur l'herbe* (Luncheon on the Grass) and is often credited as the forefather of Impressionism. He was ridiculed for his imprecise brushwork and extended palette (which means he used more colors than many of his contemporaries) and was asked to take his paintings out of shows, partly because one of his main models was a known prostitute. It was not until after a well-known critic took note of his work that people began to think maybe Manet was on to something (King, 2009). Up to that point, he was supported by his mother, who was well-enough off to support a son who liked to paint and throw parties.

While gaining recognition in the art world is what most artists strive for, too much of a good thing can be problematic, since becoming famous can become another structure. Not only does your audience begin to expect certain features in your work, but success can also make the network greedy, as they push for the artist to create more pieces. This is what Rudolf Bauer experienced. Bauer was born and lived in Germany prior to World War II, and his abstract paintings were collected by the Guggenheim Museum in New York, one of the most prestigious art museums in the world. Bauer left Germany for the United States when the Nazis came to power, and was told that the people at the Guggenheim would take care of him. He signed a contract with this in mind, or so he thought—he could not read the contract as it was written in English and not German—until he realized that the contract bound all the work he had completed, was completing, and would complete in the future to the Guggenheim. At this point, Bauer quit painting, having felt betrayed by the people who had promised to protect him in a new country.

Such stories and experiences lead to a volatile life and market for artists and gallery owners. The quest for stability in the art world can lead one to do desperate things, such as signing contracts or taking commissions for work that one does not enjoy. Commissioned work can also be very fulfilling if artists are allowed to work in their own style and know that someone else values their work. When one moves away from commissions and into juried shows, being rejected for a show can be traumatic, as one's art becomes a piece of oneself. To have art rejected is to have the self rejected.

The passion that artists feel toward their creative endeavors can be partly explained through the concepts of work discussed in Chapter 5. Artists often feel they are in control of their efforts, and can pour themselves into their work without consequence. Such an approach can backfire if one's masterpiece is considered garbage or the artwork takes on a life of its own, as shown in Oscar Wilde's *The Picture of Dorian Gray*:

> The studio was filled with the rich odour of roses, and when the light summer wind stirred amidst the trees of the garden, there came through the open door the heavy scent of the lilac, or the more delicate perfume of the pink-flowering thorn.
>
> From the corner of the divan of Persian saddle-bags on which he was lying, smoking, as was his custom, innumerable cigarettes, Lord Henry Wotton could just catch the gleam of the honey-sweet and honey-coloured blossoms of a laburnum, whose tremulous branches seemed hardly able to bear the burden of a beauty so flamelike as theirs; and now and then the fantastic shadows of birds in flight flitted across the long tussore-silk curtains that were stretched in front of the huge window, producing a kind of momentary Japanese effect, and making him think of those pallid, jade-faced painters of Tokyo who, through the medium of an art that is necessarily immobile, seek to convey the sense of swiftness and motion. The sullen murmur of the bees shouldering their way through the long unmown grass, or circling with monotonous insistence round the dusty gilt horns of the straggling woodbine, seemed to make the stillness more oppressive. The dim roar of London was like the bourdon note of a distant organ.

In the centre of the room, clamped to an upright easel, stood the full-length portrait of a young man of extraordinary personal beauty, and in front of it, some little distance away, was sitting the artist himself, Basil Hallward, whose sudden disappearance some years ago caused, at the time, such public excitement and gave rise to so many strange conjectures.

As the painter looked at the gracious and comely form he had so skillfully mirrored in his art, a smile of pleasure passed across his face, and seemed about to linger there. But he suddenly started up, and closing his eyes, placed his fingers upon the lids, as though he sought to imprison within his brain some curious dream from which he feared he might awake.

"It is your best work, Basil, the best thing you have ever done," said Lord Henry languidly. "You must certainly send it next year to the Grosvenor. The Academy is too large and too vulgar. Whenever I have gone there, there have been either so many people that I have not been able to see the pictures, which was dreadful, or so many pictures that I have not been able to see the people, which was worse. The Grosvenor is really the only place."

"I don't think I shall send it anywhere," he answered, tossing his head back in that odd way that used to make his friends laugh at him at Oxford. "No, I won't send it anywhere."

Lord Henry elevated his eyebrows and looked at him in amazement through the thin blue wreaths of smoke that curled up in such fanciful whorls from his heavy, opium-tainted cigarette. "Not send it anywhere? My dear fellow, why? Have you any reason? What odd chaps you painters are! You do anything in the world to gain a reputation. As soon as you have one, you seem to want to throw it away. It is silly of you, for there is only one thing in the world worse than being talked about, and that is not being talked about. A portrait like this would set you far above all the young men in England, and make the old men quite jealous, if old men are ever capable of any emotion."

"I know you will laugh at me," he replied, "but I really can't exhibit it. I have put too much of myself into it."

Lord Henry stretched himself out on the divan and laughed.

"Yes, I knew you would; but it is quite true, all the same."

"Too much of yourself in it! Upon my word, Basil, I didn't know you were so vain; and I really can't see any resemblance between you, with your rugged strong face and your coal-black hair, and this young Adonis, who looks as if he was made out of ivory and rose-leaves. Why, my dear Basil, he is a Narcissus, and you—well, of course you have an intellectual expression and all that. But beauty, real beauty, ends where an intellectual expression begins. Intellect is in itself a mode of exaggeration, and destroys the harmony of any face. The moment one sits down to think, one becomes all nose, or all forehead, or something horrid. Look at the successful men in any of the learned professions. How perfectly hideous they are! Except, of course, in the Church. But then in the Church they don't think. A bishop keeps on saying at the age of eighty what he was told to say when he was a boy of eighteen, and as a natural consequence he always looks absolutely delightful. Your mysterious young friend, whose name you have never told me, but whose picture really fascinates me, never thinks. I feel quite sure of that. He is some brainless beautiful creature who should be always here in winter when we have no flowers to look at, and always here in summer when we want something to chill our intelligence. Don't flatter yourself, Basil: you are not in the least like him."

"You don't understand me, Harry," answered the artist. "Of course I am not like him. I know that perfectly well. Indeed, I should be sorry to look like him. You shrug your shoulders? I am telling you the truth. There is a fatality about all physical and intellectual distinction, the sort of fatality that seems to dog through history the faltering steps of kings. It is better not to be different from one's fellows. The ugly and the stupid have the best of it in this world. They can sit at their ease and gape at the play. If they know nothing of victory, they are at least spared the knowledge of defeat. They live as we all should live—undisturbed, indifferent, and without disquiet. They neither bring ruin upon others, nor ever receive it from alien hands. Your rank and wealth, Harry; my brains, such as they are—my art, whatever it may be worth; Dorian Gray's good looks—we shall all suffer for what the gods have given us, suffer terribly" (Wilde, *The Picture of Dorian Gray*: downloaded from Project Gutenberg).

Later we are shown how the painting absorbs all of Gray's sins, and begins to show Gray's dark side including growing old, while Gray himself stays young. Basil sets out to destroy the painting, which is in Gray's possession, and his final suffering is to be killed at the hands of Gray, who is well aware of the power of Basil's work. Gray finally decides to destroy the painting, and the novel ends with a thump and scream in the attic where the painting is stored. Readers assume that by destroying the painting, Gray has destroyed himself.

While obviously fictitious, Wilde captures both the power of art, as well as the importance of the people involved. This would have been a much different story if the painter had attended a community college in Kansas instead of Oxford, that Lord Henry Wotton was actually Henry Wotton who ran the convenience store on the corner, Gray was bald, had a hooked nose, was married to a farmer's daughter, the couple had a young child who was always dirty, and the exhibition hall was at the county fair next to the prize pig. A piece of art moving through London in the hands of lords and Oxford-educated men is much different from one moving through a small rural village. It is also important to note the passion of the artist, whose life became forfeit in numerous ways with the completion of his greatest work. These are the stories we link to the art world, fictional or not. When the stories do not meet our expectations, the art also falls short of greatness.

ART, THE SOUL, AND *DOCTOR FAUSTUS*

Volatility in the art market is exacerbated by the fact that too many artists rely on a relatively small group of individuals and organizations to buy their works, and such buyers have a limited capacity for both buying and hanging art. Even the largest foundation housed in a spacious office suite has a finite amount of wall space to exhibit art. There are also social structures that determine what is and is not creative that are outside the control of artists. This was recognized by Nietzsche (1967: 70), who stated that, "[t]he Greek artist in particular had an obscure feeling of mutual dependence when it came to the gods," meaning that while the artist understood that he was created by the gods, he also understood that he created the gods, or at least their likeness. In such a setting, priests would have a great deal of influence concerning the construction of a piece of art dedicated to the gods. Nietzsche also argued that great Greek art was defined by both the Apollonian and Dionysian perspectives. The former is found in dreams (this is where Greek sculpture was generated) and the latter in inebria- tion (good Greek music was heavily influenced by Dionysus). While both may seem illusory to us, Nietzsche places creative logic within the Apollonian sphere and impulsive creativity within the Dionysian. Socrates spoiled the whole thing by saying that art should be thought out more logically in terms of scientific or formulaic knowledge, instead of relying on dreams and illusions brought about by alcohol. The role of science in art has waxed and waned ever since, as philosophers, sociologists, and neurologists have tried to determine how art brings pleasure to humans, an area that is often subsumed under the label of taste and aesthetics.

Whether Socratic logic or the Nietzsche formula of combining Apollonian and Dionysian is the most appropriate for understanding both the making and con- suming of art is open to interpretation. Artists such as Picasso contend that asking an artist to explain his art is like asking a bird to explain its song (Chipp, 1968). For an individual like Picasso or the surrealists who found their inspiration in dreams and hallucinations (e.g., Salvador Dali would look at photographs from different angles until he found a different picture within the original picture, such as holding a photo of people sitting in front of a round hut on its side and seeing the photo morph into a face), it was often difficult to pinpoint this inspiration with any kind of scientific accuracy. Wassily Kandinsky (Kandinsky & Marc, 1974), an artist himself, tried to figure out formulas for art. These statements were often written in ways meant to challenge other disciplines, such as coming up with the idea that 2-1>2+1 and justifying it by saying that sometimes less is more. A small red dot in a dark painting can have a greater impact on the viewer than a whole canvas covered with the same red paint. The point is not to frame one of these approaches as more sociologically relevant, but to note that each approach should be understood as part of the scripts we have regarding artists, and that they think about their work from their hearts, minds, and souls—or so we are told and like to think that is how the art world works.

One of the structures that artists come up against is basic survival. To succeed as an artist, one must find a market for one's work, whether that be through barter arrangements, painting for the royal court, or by accumulating enough money to survive in a capitalist society. The lengths artists will go to become recognized and able to sell their work can range from asking a local gallery to show their work, to asking someone much more powerful to provide them with the necessary tools to be great, as was the case for Adrian Leverkühn in Thomas Mann's *Doctor Faustus*. We might not be shocked at what takes place in Mann's novel, since these are the lengths artists—whom we often label as bohemian, reclusive, and eccentric—will go to for recognition:

"Surely you are in fundamental agreement with me that it can be termed neither sentimental nor malicious if one acknowledges the facts of one's world and time. Certain things are no longer possible. The illusion of emotions as a compositorial work of art, music's self-indulgent illusion, has itself become impossible and cannot be maintained—that which has long since consisted of inserting preexisting, formulaic, and dispirited elements as if they were the inviolable necessity of this single occurrence. Or put the other way around: The special occurrence assumes an air as if it were identical with the preexisting, familiar formula. For four hundred years all great music found contentment in pretending such unity was achieved without a breach, took pleasure in conventional universal legitimation, which it endeavours to confuse with its own concerns. My friend, it will work no more. Criticism of ornament, of convention, of abstract generality—they are all one and the same. What falls prey to criticism is the outward show of the bourgeois work of art, an illusion in which music takes part, though it produces no external image. To be sure, by producing no such image, music has the advantage of the other arts, but in the unwearying reconcilement of its specific concerns with the rule of convention, music has nevertheless taken part in this sublime chicanery with might and main. The subordination of expression to all-reconciling generality is the innermost principle of musical illusion. And that is over. The claim to presume the general as harmonically contained within the particular is a self-contradiction. It is all up with conventions once considered prerequisite and compulsory, the guarantors of the game's freedom."

I: "One could know all that and yet acknowledge freedom again beyond any criticism. One could raise the game to yet higher power by playing with forms from which, as one knows, life has vanished."

He: "I know, I know. Parody. It might be merry if in its aristocratic nihilism it were not so very woebegone. Do you think such tricks promise you much happiness and greatness?"

I (repost angrily): "No."

He: "Short and peevish! But why peevish? Because I put to you friendly questions of conscience, just between us? Because I have shown you your desperate heart and with a savant's insight set before your eyes the downright insuperable difficulties of composing now-a-days? You might hold me in esteem as a savant at least. The Devil surely knows something of music" (Mann, *Doctor Faustus*: 256–57).

Given the anger and subject matter of numerous contemporary punk songs (e.g., The Sex Pistols' "Anarchy in the U.K."), rock (e.g., the Teddybears' "Crystal Meth Christian"), and gangsta rap songs (e.g., Ice T's "Cop Killer"), some people may already believe that the devil truly is as much, if not more, a part of today's music as he was when Thomas Mann wrote *Doctor Faustus*. Thinking that music plays a part in a specific approach to life shows us that our thoughts come from larger scripts developed within society. It is hard to make it in today's music world without selling at least a part of your soul. This may be true of art as well, at least in our interpretation of successful artists in a field that is very much saturated.

For the artists reading this, it may seem that the point is to become more and more shocking, to sell a larger piece of one's soul to the devil, and so forth if one is to be recognized. Robert Mapplethorpe's homosexual photographs, Andres Serrano's *Piss Christ*, and Madonna scheduling a concert in Poland on the same day that the country celebrated the Church's true Madonna all seem to point in this direction. There are too many people to count who have gained notoriety by being scandalous. It seems that few people notice a painting or photograph of a field of flowers unless it contains nudes or a corpse. For those unfamiliar with the contemporary art world, the envelope has been pushed even further. Artists have started to use blood and feces in their paintings, or a woman strips and pulls poems out of her vagina before reading them to the audience (Freeland, 2001). While possibly shocking to some, these works are simply following specific social scripts concerning art and are found at highly respected museums and galleries. We might not be able to predict the next form of art, but we can predict that it will be something that is meant to make us stand up and take notice. Such art movements are an excellent example of the intersection of structure and agency, as well as how we can use the sociological imagination to make sense of things that might seem nonsensical at first glance. The recent history of art points to the desire to make people uncomfortable. Couple this with the idea that artists are supposed to draw inspiration from dark moments in their lives (e.g., Kowit, 2003), make deals with the devil—who is always on the lookout for lost souls—and you have a new contemporary art movement.

INTERPRETING ART AND *CAT'S EYE*

Some readers may understand that the choice of what to hang in a gallery or museum is based on structures, including allowing a person to read poems pulled from her own private parts. After all, there are not enough museums or galleries in the world to exhibit every piece of art that has ever been created, so someone or some group has to make a determination of what is good enough to be shown. When you walk into a museum or gallery, however, what you like or find repulsive is all about your own taste. This is pure agency, and no one can tell you what to like or not like. Your tastes are your own, developed over the years by looking at art (or trying to ignore it). No one can take that away from you or tell you otherwise. I will show you that this might not be the case, as even our tastes in art are influenced by society.

One of the first places to start is the distinction between high and low culture. The former consists of cultural products such as million-dollar paintings, opera, professional symphonies, ballet, and polo. The latter consists of velvet Elvis posters, grunge concerts, tractor pulls, dirty dancing, and NASCAR. According to Bourdieu (1984), people from the different classes are exposed to these different types of cultural products (e.g., the upper classes are more likely to purchase opera and symphony tickets, while those of the lower classes are more likely to attend country music concerts and monster truck rallies), and tastes are shaped by exposure (how can you know if you like opera if you have never been to one or heard a recording?). Some people will even say they like or dislike something because of how they think a piece of art is tied to larger social structures ("only snooty people like opera, so I hate it," or "only rednecks listen to country music, and I'm no redneck"). Even the idea of what it means to be a cultural consumer is shifting. For centuries, it was enough if someone could talk about one of the finer arts that people would consider them to be from the upper classes, but social media has changed that. Many people can now watch a clip of an opera or polo match on YouTube and talk to their friends about it. Knowing a few bits of information regarding these leisure activities has pushed the true leisure class to begin adding quantity to the supposed quality of consumption. Peterson and Kern (1996) find that individuals from the leisure class are more likely to express interest in many types of culture (cultural omnivores), while those from the middle and lower classes are more likely to say they really enjoy one or two types of cultural products (cultural univores). It seems that in modern society, being from the upper classes means having enough leisure time to know who is performing at the Met, which team is leading the American League Central division in Major League Baseball, and which singers and groups are at the top of the country music charts. Those of us who have to go to work every day have a hard time keeping up with all the fads and fickleness of cultural production and consumption, so we just pick one or two that seem interesting and fun. These are typically the same ones we enjoyed as kids because our parents or friends exposed us to them.

Another aspect of our upbringing that influences how we consume and interpret art is what Bourdieu (1984) refers to as the disinterested gaze. This is the notion that when we look at something from the standpoint of an expert or as someone who is well-versed in that specific cultural product, we can look at it without being overly excited. This is easy to understand if you think about something you really like, such as a genre of music. For example, if you have been listening to rap music all your life, you might have a good idea of who is in or out in that scene at any given time. You have your favorite groups and songs, but for the most part you simply like listening to that type of music and learning as much about it as possible. One day you are sitting in your dorm room with the stereo on, and a new roommate comes in and asks what you are doing. When you tell him that you are listening to some of your favorite songs, your roommate becomes overly excited about finally being able to hear what you like to listen to, since you are always talking about your music. Your roommate starts asking lots of questions and trying to sing the lyrics, but gets most of it wrong. Do not be surprised to find yourself annoyed if this ever happens. A true connoisseur likes to consume in peace, or with others who share the same level of knowledge, appreciation, and understanding of the art. Think of the person who has grown up visiting art museums and studying art history listening to a tourist in their favorite museum who is pointing at paintings and exclaiming that they have never seen such a large collection of Van Gogh paintings, when the work is Monet's.

This disinterest is especially profound among some artists, as is captured by Margaret Atwood in *Cat's Eye*. Put yourself in this artist's shoes, and think about how difficult it would be to entertain a friend while in this situation:

I open the gallery door, walk in with that sinking feeling I always have in galleries. It's the carpets that do it to me, the hush, the sanctimoniousness of it all: galleries are too much like churches, there's too much reverence, you feel there should be some genuflecting going on. Also, I don't like it that this is where paintings end up, on these neutral-toned walls with the track lighting, sterilized, rendered safe and acceptable. It's as if somebody's been around spraying the paintings with air freshener, to kill the smell. The smell of blood on the wall.

> This gallery is not totally sterilized, there are touches of cutting edge: a heating pipe shows, one wall is black. I don't give a glance to what's on the walls, I hate those neo-expressionist dirty greens and putrid oranges, post this, post that. Everything is post these days, as if we're all just a footnote to something earlier that was real enough to have a name of its own.
>
> Several of my own paintings have been uncrated and are leaning against the wall. They've been tracked down, requested, gathered in from whoever owns them. Whoever owns them is not me; worse luck, I'd get a better price now. The owners' names will be on little white cards beside the paintings, along with mine, as if mere ownership is on a par with creation. Which they think it is.
>
> If I cut off my ear, would the market value go up? Better still, stick my head in the oven, blow out my brains. What rich art collectors like to buy, among other things, is a little vicarious craziness (Atwood, *Cat's Eye*: 92).

Atwood's character is not excited about seeing the work she created. The paintings are just objects in the room. The whole place is viewed like a church, a place of reverence where one is to be quiet and just let the ambience seep in. It is a place of quiet reflection. Now, add a couple of noisy kids and a distracted parent, and the scene takes on a whole new meaning that could make it unbearable for the true art connoisseur.

There is another aspect of this passage that should be mentioned, which are the links to other artists and events. The part about cutting off the ear is about Van Gogh, who did exactly that and sent the ear piece to a prostitute in an attempt to prove his love for her. Sylvia Plath stuck her head in an oven and died from carbon monoxide poisoning, while numerous artists, such as Ernest Hemingway, Robert Malaval, and Kurt Cobain, have shot themselves in the head. Others have jumped out of studio windows or hanged themselves near their easels. This ability to list the accomplishments and demise of artists is another aspect of interpreting art that is tied to social structures. In some of my own work (e.g., Ten Eyck & Christensen, 2012), I found that information sources like the *New York Times* will use names of artists and rich patrons in news articles about the avant-garde art world without ever giving the reader much in the way of background. How many readers, you may ask, would understand that Kara Walker or Ellsworth Kelly, two artists on exhibit at the Whitney Museum of American Art in New York, are extending the work of Bill Viola and Kazimir Severinovich Malevich, respectively? While this is my own interpretation of Walker's and Kelly's work and is based solely on shared mediums, even if it were a famous art critic's interpretation of their approaches, it would tell you very little about Walker and Kelly, unless you knew something about Viola and Malevich. If I asked you whether you agreed with this interpretation, and you told me you had no idea what I was talking about, that would tell me that you had very little leisure time to study American art, and that you probably did not attend a school in which it was important for you to learn such facts. You most likely attended a public school, as I did (I have only come to know something about the art world since becoming a professor at Michigan State University, as well as a practicing artist). Interpreting art is not just about looking at a piece of work quietly, but understanding the history of the artist and art, and being able to tell others about it so that you can distinguish yourself from those who are (supposedly) less cultured.

Geography can also play into how we think about art. When asking students about graffiti, I have found that if they think about graffiti in their hometowns, they tend not to like it. If they think of graffiti in another city, such as a student who grew up in East Lansing, Michigan, but is thinking of graffiti she has seen in Chicago, they are more likely to say it is cool. This is a NIMBY effect—Not In My Back Yard—as we tend to think of graffiti as part of a larger crime scene, and we want to protect our homes and neighborhoods from such degradation. At the same time, seeing graffiti somewhere else is interesting, because much of it is very colorful and creative and provides more information about a place we are visiting, including that it might be dangerous. These are narratives that shape our understanding of art forms.

While class background, teaching art, and geography are typically thought of as larger social structures, micro processes are also at work when looking at art. How a friend or respected colleague looks at an artwork may impact your own feelings of what to think. This happens during art juries, as jurors can influence each other. Some of my students and I were allowed to watch a jury decide on pieces that would be shown during an exhibit on socially engaged art. There were approximately 300 pieces entered for the show, and the gallery could exhibit approximately 90 of them. A jury of five practicing artists was asked to judge the pieces, and we were allowed to watch this process, though we were not allowed to give any input. Photos of the artworks were randomly placed in a slideshow and projected onto a large screen at the front of the gallery, and all pieces were shown to the jurors before they began the process of deciding what would be part of the show. Jurors were also told the title of the pieces, but nothing else, including who the artist was or why they thought their pieces were socially engaged. One particular entry showed a pen-and-ink drawing of some men who were naked above the waist and looked to be lined up against a wall. On their backs were words such as "black," "gay," "poor," that looked to have been spelled with a whip. When I first saw this picture, I thought of it as socially engaged, though I had no idea if it was good enough to be juried into the show.

After all entries had been shown without judgment, the manager of the gallery began the show again and the jurors began talking about what did and did not belong in the show. At times they would discuss what was meant by social engagement, though this was not always inspired by a piece of art, but would be a somewhat spontaneous side conversation between photos. This led to some pieces being accepted or rejected quickly, and much of it made sense to me and the students. When we came to the piece showing the men with those words lashed into their backs, there was a short pause before one of the jurors said, "Nope, doesn't fit." All the other jurors agreed and there was no conversation about whether or not it was socially engaged art, or what it meant to have said that it did not fit into the show. A couple of the students looked at me with either surprised or pained expressions, though I just shrugged my shoulders as it was not our place to make comments. I was thinking that peer pressure had some role in the process, even though these were professional artists. The jurors did choose to put a large ceramic penis into the show, though there was little discussion of how it was socially engaged (sexuality is an important component of society that we often ignore, until it is takes the form of pornography or a five-foot tall penis with many smaller penises sticking out of it, and we are forced to try to make sense of it). After the jury process was completed, I asked one of the jurors about the pen-and-ink piece and was told, "Yeah, I remember that piece. I didn't think it was any good." I responded by saying that I thought it captured social engagement pretty well, and was rebuffed by saying that it was not very good art. To disqualify a piece might or might not have anything to do with the quality of the art, though it was easy to see that when one respected person said it was out, it was easy for the others to follow along. Art is about connections as much, if not more, than what has been created.

The art world is fun and interesting, but also full of individuals who believe it should be protected from the prying eyes of the uneducated. There are structures in place that are difficult to overcome, but without them, we might not be able to distinguish between a gang tag on the back of a street sign and one of Monet's water lily paintings. Should such a distinction even exist? Next time you find yourself saying that you like or hate a piece of art, look to your sociological imagination to understand why.

REFERENCES AND RECOMMENDED READINGS

Atwood, M. (1988). *Cat's Eye*. New York: Doubleday.

Banksy. (2007). *Wall and Piece*. London, UK: Random House.

Bayles, D., and Orland, T. (1993). *Fear and Art*. Santa Barbara, CA: Capra.

Becker, H. S. (1982). *Art Worlds*. Berkeley: University of California Press.

Bourdieu, P. (1984). *Distinctions* (trans. Richard Nice). Cambridge, MA: Harvard University Press.

Chipp, H. B. (1968). *Theories of Modern Art*. Berkeley: University of California Press.

Freeland, C. A. (2001). *But Is It Art?* Oxford, UK: Oxford University Press.

Kandinsky, W., and Marc, F. (Eds.). (1974). *The Blaue Reiter Almanac*. London: Thames and Hudson.

King, R. (2009). *The Judgment of Paris*. New York: Walker.

Kowit, S. (2003). *In the Palm of Your Hand*. Gardiner, ME: Tilbury House.

Mann, T. (1999). *Doctor Faustus*. New York: Vintage.

Nietzsche, F. (1967). *The Birth of Tragedy and the Case of Wagner*. New York: Vintage.

Peterson, R. A., and Kern, R. M. (1996). "Changing Highbrow Taste: From snob to omnivore." *American Sociological Review*, 61: 900–907.

Ten Eyck, T. A., and Christensen, E. (2012). "Speaking of Art: Class code or historical residue?" *Social Science Journal*, 49: 330–38.

Wilde, O. (2011). *The Picture of Dorian Gray*. Indo-European Publishing.

16 SOCIAL MOVEMENTS AND CHANGE

INTRODUCTION AND *THE DHARMA BUMS*

Given all the structures discussed to this point, it may seem somewhat silly and useless to discuss social change. No matter which way you turn, there is another structure that you have to make sense of and navigate. If you happen to be a pessimist, then the answer is that you should just sit back and let those structures have their way with you. If you are an optimist, you realize that with a sociological imagination you can make those structures work in your favor, and possibly even change the ones that seem problematic for yourself and others.

People have had success in this area, and most of us are familiar with organized efforts such as the civil rights movement, women's rights, and the anti–Vietnam War student protests. All of these movements have brought change to society by being willing to take chances and looking at structures from a different perspective. They have forced politicians, big businesses, and even the general public to rethink their beliefs about certain groups and events, which led to changes in laws and foreign policies. Such movements take place in many cities and countries. One of my favorite such groups is the art movement Dada, which is often overlooked in introductory sociology textbooks.

Dada consisted of a group of avant-garde artists, mainly writers and a few others, who met in Zurich, Switzerland, during the First World War. When they began comparing notes, they realized that many of the patrons of the arts—rich businessmen, political figures, high-ranking military officials, etc.—were the people who had started and continued the war. These people were not dying in the trenches—those were the soldiers, whose age and lot in life were much like the artists'—but instead were getting rich from war profiteering. This led the Dadaists to begin creating anti-art, including nonsensical plays in which the actors would speak gibberish throughout the performance. These plays would lead to riots among the audience who had paid for tickets, which the Dadaists found to be gratifying (Ades, 2006). Their work provided insights into how art was connected to class, and how class was connected to war. While their efforts did not stop the war, nor did it defuse future wars (Hitler applied to art school twice and was denied both times), it shed light on the connections between economics and societal violence.

Another group that formed along similar lines was the Beats (Allen Ginsberg, who penned "Howl," was part of this group). This was a group of writers who spent time with jazz musicians, the latter often saying they were beat after a music gig, an attitude that was the outcome of a combination of a hard life and alcohol and marijuana use. The writers felt much the same way as they tried to make a living from their writing during the 1950s, a time when America was thought to be prosperous for everyone who wanted a good job and was willing to work hard (Charters, 2003). Jack Kerouac was a Beat writer who had dropped out of Columbia University before traveling around the United States and taking jobs that ranged from farm laborer to railroad work. This selection from his book, *The Dharma Bums*, is about his life on the road with various other characters he knew. (Kerouac changes the names, but you can figure out who is who if you know this group.)

"And who am I?"
  "I dunno, maybe you're Goat."
  "Goat?"
  "Maybe you're Mudface."
  Who's Mudface?"
  "Mudface is the mud in your goatface. What would you say if someone was asked the question, 'Does a dog have the Buddha nature?' and said 'Woof!'"
  "I'd say that was a lot of silly Zen Buddhism." This took Japhy back a bit. "Lissen Japhy," I said, "I'm not a Zen Buddhist, I'm a serious Buddhist, I'm an oldfashioned dreamy Hinayana coward of later Mahayanism," and so forth into the night, my contention being that Zen Buddhism didn't concentrate on kindness so much as on confusing the intellect to make it perceive the illusion of all sources of things. "It's *mean*," I complained. "All those Zen Masters throwing young kids in the mud because they can't answer their silly word questions."
  "That's because they want them to realize mud is better than words, boy." But I can't recreate the exact (will try) brilliance of all Japhy's answers and

come-backs and come-ons with which he had me on pins and needles all the time and did eventually stick something in my crystal head that made me change my plans in life.

Anyway I followed the whole gang of howling poets to the reading at Gallery Six that night, which was, among other important things, the night of the birth of the San Francisco Poetry Renaissance. Everyone was there. It was a mad night. And I was the one who got things jumping by going around collecting dimes and quarters from the rather stiff audience standing around in the gallery and coming back with three huge gallon jugs of California Burgundy and getting them all piffed so that by eleven o'clock when Alvah Goldbrook was reading his, wailing his poem "Wail" drunk with arms outspread everybody was yelling "Go! Go! Go!" (like a jam session) and old Rheinhold Cacoethes the father of the Frisco poetry scene was wiping his tears of gladness. Japhy himself read his fine poems about Coyote the God of the North American Plateau Indians (I think), at least the God of the Northwest Indians, Kwakiutl and what all. "Fuck you! sang Coyote, and ran away!" read Japhy to the distinguished audience, making them all howl with joy, it was so pure, fuck being a dirty word that comes out clean. And he had his tender lyrical lines, like the ones about bears eating berries, showing his love of animals, and great mystery lines about oxen on the Mongolian road showing his knowledge of Oriental literature even on to Hsuan Tsung the great Chinese monk who walked from China to Tibet, Lanchow to Kashgar and Mongolia carrying a stick of incense in his hand. Then Japhy showed his sudden barroom humor with lines about Coyote bringing goodies. And his anarchistic ideas about how Americans don't know how to live, with lines about commuters being trapped in living rooms that come from poor trees felled by chainsaws (showing here, also, his background as a logger up north). His voice was deep and resonant and somehow brave, like the voice of oldtime American heroes and orators. Something earnest and strong and humanly hopeful I liked about him, while the other poets were either too dainty in their aestheticism, or too hysterically cynical to hope for anything, or too abstract and indoorsy, or too political, or like Coughlin too incomprehensible to understand (big Coughlin saying things about "unclarified processes" though where Coughlin did say that revelation was a personal thing I noticed the strong Buddhist and idealistic feeling of Japhy, which he'd shared with goodhearted Coughlin in their buddy days at college, as I had shared mine with Alvah in the Eastern scene and with others less apocalyptical and straighter but in no sense more sympathetic and tearful) (Kerouac, *The Dharma Bums*: 13–15).

This was not the America of *Leave It to Beaver*, which began airing in 1957. Kerouac and the Beats, much like the Dadaists, saw society as a struggle, where many people were losing in their efforts to find a way to some unattainable utopia promised by national leaders and advertisers. Both the Beats and Dada looked to change society through their art, while others have sought change in other social systems.

The trajectory of both the Dadaists and Beats also points to the stochastic nature of social change. If Kerouac had not riled up the "stiff" crowd at the poetry reading, Goldbrook's "Wail" (Ginsberg's "Howl") may have fallen flat that evening, and we never would have had the obscenity trial that made it possible for other poets to use the words and imagery of sex and sexuality to provide readers with what it was like to be queer and living underground. Social movements, even the successful ones, suffer from growing pains, make progress in fits and starts, and often find themselves the targets of backlash from groups who feel threatened. Threats range from shaming to violence and even death. Change is rarely a linear process, and those seeking change must keep that in mind.

MAKING A DIFFERENCE AND *UNCLE TOM'S CABIN*

One of the better-known social movements in contemporary American society is the civil rights movement led by such individuals as Malcolm X and Martin Luther King Jr. Their fight was based on disparities regarding how different racial groups were treated, and while the efforts brought about numerous changes, both men (and many others) paid with their lives (Malcolm X was assassinated in 1965, and Martin Luther King Jr. was assassinated in 1968). These killings, along with those working in the Deep South to help register blacks to vote, show the volatility of challenging social structures that are thought to be beneficial to a portion of the population. Telling a group that they will need to give up some of their privileges is not an easy message to get across. Harriet Beecher Stowe wrote about these very structures in *Uncle Tom's Cabin* more than a century before Malcolm X and Martin Luther King Jr. were murdered for trying to change them.

Justice, too, obliges the author to state that the fairness of mind and generosity attributed to St. Clare are not without a parallel, as the following anecdote will show. A few years since, a young southern gentleman was in Cincinnati, with a favorite servant, who had been his personal attendant from a boy. The young man took advantage of this opportunity to secure his own freedom, and fled to the protection of a Quaker, who was quite noted in affairs of this kind. The owner was exceedingly indignant. He had always treated the slave with such indulgence, and his confidence in his affection was such, that he believed he must have been practised upon to induce him to revolt from him.

He visited the Quaker, in high anger; but, being possessed of uncommon candor and fairness, was soon quieted by his arguments and representations. It was a side of the subject which he never had heard,—never had thought on; and he immediately told the Quaker that, if his slave would, to his own face, say that it was his desire to be free, he would liberate him. An interview was forthwith procured, and Nathan was asked by his young master whether he had ever had any reason to complain of his treatment, in any respect.

"No, Mas'r," said Nathan; "you've always been good to me."

"Well, then, why do you want to leave me?"

"Mas'r may die, and then who get me?—I'd rather be a free man."

After some deliberation, the young master replied, "Nathan, in your place, I think I should feel very much so, myself. You are free."

He immediately made him out free papers; deposited a sum of money in the hands of the Quaker, to be judiciously used in assisting him to start in life, and left a very sensible and kind letter of advice to the young man. That letter was for some time in the writer's hands.

The author hopes she has done justice to that nobility, generosity, and humanity, which in many cases characterize individuals at the South. Such instances save us from utter despair of our kind. But, she asks any person, who knows the world, are such characters *common*, anywhere? (Stowe, *Uncle Tom's Cabin*: downloaded from Project Gutenberg).

How many people would be so willing to give up both a piece of property (slaves were property) and something that serves them? How many of us can truly see the other side of someone else's life? How truly common is the master who willingly gives up the slave? Even if the slave did not wait hand and foot on a master, he was still economically important on the plantation. Many of us might think that we never would have owned slaves as we are good people, but did every slave owner think of himself as a bad person? Many of them went to church, said prayers before meals, and believed they followed the Golden Rule of treating others as they would like to be treated themselves. Slaves, however, were not considered people but part of the plantation, and it was not until a person had intimate knowledge of a slave that he could see this piece of property as an individual. Even if they did happen to reach that point, to set their slaves free would have meant taking a huge financial hit and knowing that the freed slaves might end up with an even crueler master.

The civil rights movement is only the tip of the iceberg when it comes to groups who have tried to make changes to social structures, as well as the life experiences that would motivate someone or a group to seek change. Gamson (1990) collected data on over 50 protest groups to study which strategies, if any, helped these groups reach their goals. The goals of these groups range from birth control to working conditions, showing that many, many people live under oppressive conditions. Gamson's work also shows that the outcomes of a movement are not always total success or utter failure. Most of these groups want two things—to be considered a legitimate spokesperson for their cause and to gain the desired benefits. Some groups were unable to obtain either goal, which Gamson refers to as a full collapse. Numerous groups that have tried to set up Socialist communities have failed to gain legitimacy or benefits. Groups that were able to reach a level of being considered a legitimate spokesperson but did not gain any benefits are considered to be co-opted. Theodore Roosevelt's Bull Moose Party was able to get a few of its members elected into office, but the group's demands were never met. Those that gained benefits but were never given much legitimacy are said to be preempted. Many of us think of the workday as eight hours long, but few of us have heard of the Eight Hour League. Finally, those that gained both legitimacy and benefits are said to enjoy a full response. One group that fits this category is labor unions.

While the groups Gamson studied varied widely in their abilities to bring about change, his work does point to the efficacy of various strategies that can be thought of as social structures. He found, for example, that groups with a centralized command structure tended to have more success than those in which leadership was dispersed. Those asking for reforms to the system were more likely to be successful than groups seeking radical changes through revolutionary tactics. Groups backing one or just a few causes tended to enjoy more success than those that tried to make many changes, and those that made demands during times of war tended to do better than those active between wars. Media coverage is another interesting variable to take into account. According to Gamson, being a victim of violence prior to 1950 typically meant that a group would fail, as violence had a tendency to make protestors fearful of continuing their actions and demands. When television newscasts started showing police forces using fire hoses and police dogs on seemingly peaceful protestors, audience members began feeling sympathy for the victims. This, in turn, led to changes in opinion toward groups such as those behind the civil rights movement.

Each of these strategies basically echoes larger societal structures. Governments are typically centralized and bureaucratic. Each agency is focused on specific issues (the Internal Revenue Service does not worry about food safety, and the Food and Drug Administration does not worry about tax returns), and there are more resources available to the government during times of war (if it is not a long war), compared to times of peace. Gamson's argument is that governments tend to give more concessions to groups during wartime because they want to stay focused on the war, so those groups that can mobilize during a war will likely be given an audience—though if the group is challenging the war effort it can find itself under suspicion of sedition. Groups that can mimic larger social structures, even when they want to make changes to those structures, tend to do better than those that go about trying to do things differently.

In addition to looking and acting like other structures, groups interested in making changes must be able to generate commitment among their members, reach a consensus on what should be done and how to go about doing it, gaining and mobilizing resources to make their efforts possible, and developing distance between themselves and other groups that are fighting for the same causes (Rochon, 1998). Anyone can think of issues to challenge, but without commitment from members, there will be little energy to engage the structures that the group finds problematic. Once the group is committed, there must be a consensus on leadership, tactics, targets, and so forth. This does not have to be a unanimous consensus, but what is referred to as a working consensus, in that either enough members agree on how to move forward, or that those with power have reached an agreement (Goffman, 1959).

Once a group is committed and a consensus has been reached, they are ready to move ahead. To sustain their energies, appropriate resources need to be acquired. This includes economic, cultural, and social capital. A group that is committed to change and has agreed upon what needs to happen will accomplish little if their strategy is to hand out flyers on the steps of the Capitol building, but they have no access to a printer, no money to have the flyers made at a local printing shop, and no one in the group has a form of transportation to get them to the building. Finally, groups need to understand the landscape of social change. Many groups may be trying to bring about similar changes, so a group must be able to distance itself from others. Greenpeace and PETA are both interested in animal welfare issues, but we would rarely mistake one for the other. I also remembering hearing a story of two student groups working for changes regarding sexual harassment on a college campus who did very little to differentiate one from the other, and the resources needed to make one group successful were split between them; both groups failed.

Social change does not happen just because someone is upset or thinks that things would be better if done differently. Successful social change is a long process that involves patience, timing, and an understanding of the larger structures in place that may act as barriers if used one way and opportunities if approached differently. Part of the difficulty is recruiting members at a time when most of us have too many obligations to think about joining yet another group. Finding members has always been a major challenge for social movement groups, but this problem continues to grow.

MEMBERSHIP, IDENTITY, AND *THE GRAPES OF WRATH*

Most of us dream about changing something about our lives—a new job, new places to visit, new foods to try, and so forth. We may also dream about political or economic changes. If the country is too liberal, we want it more conservative.

If more conservative, then we want it more liberal, and, of course, few can agree on which way it should go. John Steinbeck highlighted the challenges facing those who seek change in *The Grapes of Wrath*. He discusses the good, the bad, and the ugly of social change, though labeling which is which will depend on your point of view.

The western land, nervous under the beginning change. The Western States, nervous as horses before a thunderstorm. The great owners, nervous, sensing a change, knowing nothing of the nature of the change. The great owners, striking at the immediate thing, the widening government, the growing labor unity; striking at new taxes, at plans; not knowing these things are results, not causes. Results, not causes; results, not causes. The causes lie deep and simply—the causes are a hunger in a stomach, multiplied a million times; a hunger in a single soul, hunger for joy and some security, multiplied a million times; muscles and mind aching to grow, to work, to create, multiplied a million times. The last clear definite function of man—muscles aching to work, minds aching to create beyond the single need—this is man. To build a wall, to build a house, a dam, and in the wall and house and dam to put something of Manself, and to Manself take back something of the wall, the house, the dam; to take hard muscles from the lifting, to take the clear lines and form from conceiving. For man, unlike any other thing organic or inorganic in the universe, grows beyond his work, walks up the stairs of his concepts, emerges ahead of his accomplishments. This you may say of man—when theories change and crash, when school, philosophies, when narrow dark alleys of thought, national, religious, economic, grow and disintegrate, man reaches, stumbles forward, painfully, mistakenly sometimes. Having stepped forward, he may slip back, but only half a step, never the full step back. This you may say and know it and know it.

This you may know when the bombs plummet out of the black planes on the market place, when prisoners are stuck like pigs, when the crushed bodies drain filthily in the dust. You may know it in this way. If the steps were not being taken, if the stumbling-forward ache were not alive, the bombs would not fall, the throats would not be cut. Fear the time when the bombs stop falling while the bombers live—for every bomb is proof that the spirit has not died. And fear the time when the strikes stop while the great owners live—for every little beaten strike is proof that the step has been taken. And this you can know—fear the time when Manself will not suffer and die for a concept, for this one quality is the foundation of Manself, and this one quality is man, distinctive in the universe.

The Western States nervous under the beginning change. Texas and Oklahoma, Kansas and Arkansas, New Mexico, Arizona, California. A single family moved from the land. Pa borrowed money from the bank, and now the bank wants the land. The land company—that's the bank when it has land—wants tractors, not families on the land. Is a tractor bad? Is the power that turns the long furrows wrong? If this tractor were ours it would be good—not mine, but ours. If our tractor turned the long furrows of our land, it would be good. Not my land, but ours. We could love the tractor then as we have loved this land when it was ours. But this tractor does two things—it turns the land and turns us off the land. There is little difference between this tractor and a tank. The people are driven, intimidated, hurt by both. We must think about this.

One man, one family driven from the land; this rusty car creaking along the highway to the west. I lost my land, a single tractor took my land. I am alone and I am bewildered. And in the night one family camps in a ditch and another family pulls in and the tents come out. The two men squat on their hams and the women and children listen. Here is the node, you who hate change and fear revolution. Keep these two squatting men apart; make them hate, fear, suspect each other. Here is the anlage of the things you fear. This is the zygote. For here "I lost my land" is changed; a cell is split and from its splitting grows the things you hate—"We lost *our* land." The danger is here, for two men are not as lonely and perplexed as one. And from this first "we" there grows a still more dangerous thing: "I have a little food" plus "I have none." If from this problem the sum is "We have little food," the thing is on its way, the movement has direction. Only a little multiplication now, and this land, this tractor are ours. The two men squatting in a ditch, the little fire, the side-meat stewing in a single pot, the silent, stone-eyed women; behind, the children listening with their souls to words their minds do not understand. The night draws down. The baby has a cold. Here, take this blanket. It's wool. It was my mother's blanket—take it for the baby. This is the thing to bomb. This is the beginning—from "I" to "we" (Steinbeck, *The Grapes of Wrath*: 150–52).

Old social movements relied on this kind of organic growth of people coming together to discuss their problems and seeing those problems from a collective perspective. Today, many people come together via computers, fracturing the bonds that used to bring us together and hold us there. Bennett (2012) contends that in such a world, politics move from the group level to the individual, as each of us sees our lives and the world around us as constructed by our own decisions. The structures that we used to fight are fading into the background of computer noise, though they are no less formidable today than a year, decade, or century ago.

The fracturing of the social world means that people must be recruited through identity politics (Aronowitz, 1992). This encompasses two strategies. First, a movement must find causes that motivate people. Greenpeace and PETA have been exemplary at this by showing us tortured and abused animals, and saying that they need our help to bring such violence to an end. The second strategy is to make messages in such a way that potential members think that if they do join the group their efforts will be rewarded. This is the approach used by groups that tell you that for only pennies you can make a difference for a hungry child in a poor country. The message is accompanied by a picture of a child looking forlorn into the camera. Your small contribution, especially if it is multiplied by the contributions of thousands, if not millions, of other audience members, will be used to save this poor creature. This is not to say that such groups are scamming its audience, and that the pennies you send in are funneled into someone else's pocket (I used to "Trick-or-Treat for UNICEF" in North Bend, Oregon), but that these groups understand identity politics. They have to make you feel for their cause, and make you think that your efforts count. Old social movements were focused on gathering large crowds to strike fear into their targets, while new social movements want you to think that it is through your efforts that the world will be changed for the better, and you can do this while sitting in front of your computer in pajamas. Let me reiterate that I am a firm believer in social change, and if it takes such strategies to get people to engage with the world beyond their computers, then these are the appropriate strategies to use. The point is that your feelings of agency are structured in such a way that you are expected to think that your actions will benefit a group and its causes.

There is one more piece in understanding the recruitment of members. Early work on social movements and collective behavior often describes the actions of these groups as mobs. It was thought that the individual is peaceful, but as a group they are easily led into violent action by charismatic leaders. McPhail (1991) argues that if you took the time to watch a protest march or even a riot at a sporting event, you would quickly notice that in most groups only a small percentage of the participants are ever violent. Others might chant slogans, sing songs, and hold hands en masse, but they will quickly become spectators if things turn violent. This is not true of every group, but most are character-ized by a small group of extremely active members and many, many so-called tourists who just show up and participate because they think it might be fun or interesting until they feel threatened. Instead of a model in which people become absolute followers in a group, McPhail puts forth a cybernetic model, in which a person's needs must be taken into account. A person who is hungry will not have the strength or desire to be part of a group. This was found to be true during the student protests against the Vietnam War. Protests would often start in the middle of the afternoon, end around 5:00 o'clock, and pick up again around 7:00 P.M. The late afternoon start was due to the students having classes and eating lunch, and the two-hour reprieve in the evening gave students time to eat dinner. Even someone who is very interested in a movement may find it difficult to participate if they need to eat, find transportation, have no money, etc. Even if one does have the resources to join a group, becoming violent during a protest only takes place if all other needs are met, such as not fearing physical pain or being arrested. As with reporters who triage stories, protestors triage their own lives while in the middle of a demonstration. Violence is one possible outcome in such a setting, and the likelihood of that outcome is not equal across members. It is also important that friends are involved, as individuals are much more likely to join a group because of a friend being a member than showing up at a meeting without any social connections.

Social change can be difficult, as it puts our agency to the test. This is especially true when those seeking change are treated like Steinbeck's participants—leave the individual alone but attack the gathering, or be more concerned with the end of bombing and labor strife than with actual bombs and strikes. Few of us want to get beat over the head or jailed, even for a cause we believe in. Instead, we will talk about it with anyone who is willing to listen, as that is much easier and safer. Do, however, take chances. It can be exciting and rewarding to see your efforts become a change in the actions of others or the making of a new policy. Being a part of a group is also important for potential employers, as many of their interviewees are better at communicating with a computer than a real person. Find a group on campus or in the community that is fighting for something you believe in, take a friend who feels the same way to a meeting, find a way to be committed, search for a consensus on messages and tactics, provide needed resources when you can, look for ways to make your group and its causes different from others, and then give change your best shot. Find out how much your agency can be used to challenge the social structures that impact your life.

REFERENCES AND RECOMMENDED READINGS

Ades, D. (Ed.). (2006). *The Dada Reader*. Chicago: University of Chicago Press.

Aronowitz, S. (1992). *The Politics of Identity*. New York: Routledge.

Bennett, W. L. (2012). "The Personalization of Politics: Political identity, social media, and changing patterns of participation." *Annals of the American Academy of Political and Social Science*, 644(1): 20–39.

Charters, A. (Ed.). (2003). *The Portable Beat Reader*. New York: Penguin.

Gamson, W. A. (1990). *The Strategy of Social Protest*. Belmont, CA: Wadsworth.

Goffman, E. (1959). *Presentation of the Self in Everyday Life*. Garden City, NY: Doubleday.

Kerouac, J. (1976). *The Dharma Bums*. New York: Penguin.

Larana, E., Johnston, H., and Gusfield, J. R. (Eds.). (1994). *New Social Movements*. Philadelphia: Temple University Press.

McPhail, C. (1991). *The Myth of the Madding Crowd*. New York: Aldine de Gruyter.

Rochon, T. R. (1998). *Culture Moves*. Princeton, NJ: Princeton University Press.

Steinbeck, J. (1939/1967). *The Grapes of Wrath*. New York: Penguin.

Stowe, H. B. (1879). *Uncle Tom's Cabin*. New York: Oxford University Press.

17 GLOBALIZATION

INTRODUCTION AND *GULLIVER'S TRAVELS*

In the last chapter, I mentioned that most people dream about change in their lives. You may have pictured yourself touring the Colosseum in Rome, or standing on the Great Wall in Beijing, or diving on the Great Barrier Reef in Australia on a sun-soaked day. Traveling to these destinations has become easier with improvements in transportation. This has also made it easier to move things and ideas from place to place in our global village. Sociologists typically think of this as globalization—a set of processes that lead to the movement of people, things, and ideas. A group of people may leave an area because of a drought or war; a new food item and how to cook it may travel from one place to another through a business franchise; and an idea may move from one place to another by sharing thoughts over the Internet with someone in another country. At times, these are very structured transactions, while others are chaotic and spur-of-the-moment situations.

The desire to see new things and travel the world—even beyond our planet—is an old one, as we learn from the lives of Marco Polo, Christopher Columbus, Francis Drake, Neil Armstrong, and other travelers. In 1726, Jonathan Swift published *Gulliver's Travels*, which many of us grew up thinking was a children's book. Swift, however, was satirizing the outlandish stories being told by European businessmen who were trying to coax people into traveling to foreign lands. His descriptions of places like Lilliput, Laputa, and others, however, became legend and continue to inspire dreams of travel to faraway lands and fantastic adventures. The following passage from Swift's book highlights both the excitement and difficulties of embarking on such a journey, capturing difficulties we still face today:

I had not been at home above ten days, when Captain William Robinson, a Cornish man, commander of the Hopewell, a stout ship of three hundred tons, came to my house. I had formerly been surgeon of another ship where he was master, and a fourth part owner, in a voyage to the Levant. He had always treated me more like a brother, than an inferior officer; and, hearing of my arrival, made me a visit, as I apprehended only out of friendship, for nothing passed more than what is usual after long absences. But repeating his visits often, expressing his joy to find me in good health, asking, "whether I were now settled for life?" adding, "that he intended a voyage to the East Indies in two months," at last he plainly invited me, though with some apologies, to be surgeon of the ship; "that I should have another surgeon under me, beside our two mates; that my salary should be double to the usual pay; and that having experienced my knowledge in sea-affairs to be at least equal to his, he would enter into any engagement to follow my advice, as much as if I had shared in the command."

He said so many other obliging things, and I knew him to be so honest a man, that I could not reject this proposal; the thirst I had of seeing the world, notwithstanding my past misfortunes, continuing as violent as ever. The only difficulty that remained, was to persuade my wife, whose consent however I at last obtained, by the prospect of advantage she proposed to her children.

We set out the 5th day of August, 1706, and arrived at Fort St. George the 11th of April, 1707. We staid there three weeks to refresh our crew, many of whom were sick. From thence we went to Tonquin, where the captain resolved to continue some time, because many of the goods he intended to buy were not ready, nor could he expect to be dispatched in several months. Therefore, in hopes to defray some of the charges he must be at, he bought a sloop, loaded it with several sorts of goods, wherewith the Tonquinese usually trade to the neighbouring islands, and putting fourteen men on board, whereof three were of the country, he appointed me master of the sloop, and gave me power to traffic, while he transacted his affairs at Tonquin.

We had not sailed above three days, when a great storm arising, we were driven five days to the north-north-east, and then to the east: after which we had fair weather, but still with a pretty strong gale from the west. Upon the tenth day we were chased by two pirates, who soon overtook us; for my sloop was so deep laden, that she sailed very slow, neither were we in a condition to defend ourselves.

We were boarded about the same time by both the pirates, who entered furiously at the head of their men; but finding us all prostrate upon our faces (for so I gave order), they pinioned us with strong ropes, and setting guard upon us, went to search the sloop.

I observed among them a Dutchman, who seemed to be of some authority, though he was not commander of either ship. He knew us by our countenances to be Englishmen, and jabbering to us in his own language, swore we should be tied back to back and thrown into the sea. I spoken Dutch tolerably well; I told him who we were, and begged him, in consideration of our being Christians and Protestants, of neighbouring countries in strict alliance, that he would move the captains to take some pity on us. This inflamed his rage; he repeated his threatenings, and turning to his companions, spoke with great vehemence in the Japanese language, as I suppose, often using the word *Christianos*.

The largest of the two pirate ships was commanded by a Japanese captain, who spoke a little Dutch, but very imperfectly. He came up to me, and after several questions, which I answered in great humility, he said, "we should not die." I made the captain a very low bow, and then, turning to the Dutchman, said, "I was sorry to find more mercy in a heathen, than in a brother christian." But I had soon reason to repent those foolish words: for that malicious reprobate, having often endeavoured in vain to persuade both the captains that I might be thrown into the sea (which they would not yield to, after the promise made me that I should not die), however, prevailed so far, as to have a punishment inflicted on me, worse, in all human appearance, than death itself. My men were sent by an equal division into both the pirate ships, and my sloop new manned. As to myself, it was determined that I should be set adrift in a small canoe, with paddles and a sail, and four days' provisions; which last, the Japanese captain was so kind to double out of his own stores, and would permit no man to search me. I got down into the canoe, while the Dutchman, standing upon the deck, loaded me with all the curses and injurious terms his language could afford (Swift, *Gulliver's Travels*: downloaded from Project Gutenberg).

This movement of people and things from one place to another is part of globalization, though at a much slower pace than we are used to today. Much like Swift's Gulliver, I have had the opportunity to travel to other countries, including Mexico, Denmark, Costa Rica, Italy, France, Portugal, and Greece, all places where English is not the native language. While I am happy to report that I have never been taken captive by pirates, it is disconcerting to be in a country where your language skills are of little use, much like Gulliver saying that the pirates were speaking in Japanese because of the term Christianos. We compensate by talking louder or gesticulating more emphatically toward anyone who seems to be paying attention to us. I have heard Americans complain that no one speaks English in these countries, though we are often quick to complain about non–English speaking tourists and immigrants who come to the United States. This treatment of others, as well as expectations of ourselves, often reflects larger structures that shape international relations.

The structure of travel has also changed our opinions about the world. Today, we complain about how many hours it takes to travel from the United States to Australia or Sri Lanka, while Swift makes mention of the nearly nine months Gulliver spent on his ship as they traversed the globe. Quicker forms of transportation offer more possibilities to see new things and have different experiences. Many of us would not have the patience to take a year out of our lives to sail to a new land, or even 80 days to float around the world in a hot air balloon.

GLOBAL SYSTEMS AND *AROUND THE WORLD IN EIGHTY DAYS*

Sociologists think of global systems in various ways, and theories and models come in and out of favor, depending on what issues are being studied. All agree that like any village, the global village is stratified with some wealthy citizens, some middle-class citizens, and many poor citizens. Wallerstein (1979) argues that global stratification is based on a zero-sum system, as there is only so much room at the top for rich countries (first world countries), though plenty of room at the bottom for poor ones (third world countries). Within this system, any time a country expands its economy another one experiences a contraction. Wallerstein points to countries such as Spain and Portugal, which were once superpowers, but had lost their positions, while countries like the United States and Germany gained in status. The rise of Japan meant the fall of Spain, and so forth.

Others have argued that nations cannot be easily grouped into an overarching system. Dependency theorists (e.g., Firebaugh, 1992) contend that rich nations find ways to extract resources (natural products, labor, ideas) from poorer countries, leaving the poor countries to depend on the rich countries for exports to fund their economies. Numerous natural resource industries—e.g., copper and diamonds—have been built on such relationships. But when the market crashes, the dependent nation suffers disproportionately, as there are few other structures in place to help with unemployment and generating money for the population to use for food, clothing, and shelter.

A third perspective is referred to as modernization (e.g., Bernstein, 1971). This approach states that all nations have the ability to modernize—that is to say, they can become wealthy in the same way as the United States, Canada, and Germany, but that some are just further behind in getting to that point. These poorer countries may need help from wealthier countries, and doing so will provide more advantages to everyone through stronger trading partners and fewer handouts. This relatively optimistic viewpoint has been criticized on numerous accounts ranging from ecological concerns (if more countries become industrialized, then we will experience more global pollution), to unattainable goals (how can we expect a small, poor third world country to have the resources, even with help, to create and sustain a strong enough economy to compete on the global level?).

Whether the global village is a system, a conglomeration of dependent relationships, or a large family that is just waiting for some of the kids to grow up, it is a complex place. To make sense of the complexity, we decide that our way of doing things is best, and look at other places and their customs as strange. This is part of the process of defining the exotic other, as discussed in Chapter 7; this is called ethnocentrism. This is the idea that our culture is best, and that all other cultures should be judged based on our own standards. Jules Verne provides us with stories in *Around the World in Eighty Days* that highlight how we often think about other cultures and the people who live within them, even when we have numerous faults of our own:

Passepartout might have cudgelled his brain for a century without hitting upon the real object which the detective had in view. He never could have imagined that Phileas Fogg was being tracked as a robber around the globe. But, as it is in human nature to attempt the solution of every mystery, Passepartout suddenly discovered an explanation of Fix's movements, which was in truth far from unreasonable. Fix, he thought, could only be an agent of Mr. Fogg's friends at the Reform Club, sent to follow him up, and to ascertain that he really went round the world as had been agreed upon.

"It's clear!" repeated the worthy servant to himself, proud of his shrewdness. "He's a spy sent to keep us in view! That isn't quite the thing, either, to be spying Mr. Fogg, who is so honourable a man! Ah, gentlemen of the Reform, this shall cost you dear!"

Passepartout, enchanted with his discovery, resolved to say nothing to his master, lest he should be justly offended at this mistrust on the part of his adversaries. But he determined to chaff Fix, when he had the chance, with mysterious allusions, which, however, need not betray his real suspicions.

During the afternoon of Wednesday, 30th October, the Rangoon entered the Strait of Malacca, which separates the peninsula of that name from Sumatra. The mountainous and craggy islets intercepted the beauties of this noble island from the view of the travellers. The Rangoon weighed anchor at Singapore the next day at four a.m., to receive coal, having gained half a day on the prescribed time of her arrival. Phileas Fogg noted this gain in his journal, and then, accompanied by Aouda, who betrayed a desire for a walk on shore, disembarked.

Fix, who suspected Mr. Fogg's every movement, followed them cautiously, without being himself perceived; while Passepartout, laughing in his sleeve at Fix's manoeuvres, went about his usual errands.

The island of Singapore is not imposing in aspect, for there are no mountains; yet its appearance is not without attractions. It is a park checkered by pleasant highways and avenues. A handsome carriage, drawn by a sleek pair of New Holland horses, carried Phileas Fogg and Aouda into the midst of rows of palms with brilliant foliage, and of clove-trees, whereof the cloves form the heart of a half-open flower. Pepper plants replaced the prickly hedges of European fields; sago-bushes, large ferns with gorgeous branches, varied the aspect of this tropical clime; while nutmeg-trees in full foliage filled the air with a penetrating perfume. Agile and grinning bands of monkeys skipped about in the trees, nor were tigers wanting in the jungles.

After a drive of two hours through the country, Aouda and Mr. Fogg returned to the town, which is a vast collection of heavy-looking, irregular houses, surrounded by charming gardens rich in tropical fruits and plants; and at ten o'clock they re-embarked, closely followed by the detective, who had kept them constantly in sight.

Passepartout, who had been purchasing several dozen mangoes—a fruit as large as good-sized apples, of a dark-brown colour outside and a bright red within, and whose white pulp, melting in the mouth, affords gourmands a delicious sensation—was waiting for them on deck. He was only too glad to offer some mangoes to Aouda, who thanked him very gracefully for them.

At eleven o'clock the Rangoon rode out of Singapore harbour, and in a few hours the high mountains of Malacca, with their forests, inhabited by the most beautifully-furred tigers in the world, were lost to view. Singapore is distant some thirteen hundred miles from the island of Hong Kong, which is a little English colony near the Chinese coast. Phileas Fogg hoped to accomplish the journey in six days, so as to be in time for the steamer which would leave on the 6th of November for Yokohama, the principal Japanese port.

The Rangoon had a large quota of passengers, many of whom disembarked at Singapore, among them a number of Indians, Ceylonese, Chinamen, Malays, and Portuguese, mostly second-class travellers.

The weather, which had hitherto been fine, changed with the last quarter of the moon. The sea rolled heavily, and the wind at intervals rose almost to a storm, but happily blew from the south-west, and thus aided the steamer's progress. The captain as often as possible put up his sails, and under the double action of steam and sail the vessel made rapid progress along the coasts of Anam and Cochin China. Owing to the defective construction of the Rangoon, however, unusual precautions became necessary in unfavourable weather; but the loss of time which resulted from this cause, while it nearly drove Passepartout out of his senses, did not seem to affect his master in the least. Passepartout blamed the captain, the engineer, and the crew, and consigned all who were connected with the ship to the land where the pepper grows. Perhaps the thought of the gas, which was remorselessly burning at his expense in Saville Row, had something to do with his hot impatience.

"You are in a great hurry, then," said Fix to him one day, "to reach Hong Kong?"

"A very great hurry!"

"Mr. Fogg, I suppose, is anxious to catch the steamer for Yokohama?"

"Terribly anxious."

"You believe in this journey around the world, then?"

"Absolutely. Don't you, Mr. Fix?"

"I? I don't believe a word of it."

"You're a sly dog!" said Passepartout, winking at him.

This expression rather disturbed Fix, without his knowing why. Had the Frenchman guessed his real purpose? He knew not what to think. But how could Passepartout have discovered that he was a detective? Yet, in speaking as he did, the man evidently meant more than he expressed.

Passepartout went still further the next day; he could not hold his tongue.

"Mr. Fix," said he, in a bantering tone, "shall we be so unfortunate as to lose you when we get to Hong Kong?"

"Why," responded Fix, a little embarrassed, "I don't know; perhaps—"

"Ah, if you would only go on with us! An agent of the Peninsular Company, you know, can't stop on the way! You were only going to Bombay, and here you are in China. America is not far off, and from America to Europe is only a step" (Verne, *Around the World in Eighty Days*: downloaded from Project Gutenberg).

One gets the sense from reading this passage that places like Singapore, Hong Kong, and China are filled with second-class citizens, which we might assume encompasses more than what they can afford for a ticket, in relation to America and Europe (*Around the World in Eighty Days* was first published in 1873), and that the real purpose of these foreign countries was to provide exotic fruit and adventures to the likes of Phileas Fogg, who was accused of being a thief but never a second-class citizen. Foreign lands become exotic lands, as the cultures and environmental systems are different, and therefore lacking in some way relative to more developed cultures of the West.

This passage also brings up the problem with theories such as world systems, dependency, and modernization. The ability to move around the world—remember, this includes people, things, and ideas—makes it difficult for large theories to predict specific patterns of behavior. These theories often try to provide a roadmap for action based on rational choices, but an understanding of the prisoner's dilemma proves that rationality is context specific. The prisoner's dilemma is based on a scenario that involves two people who have been arrested for robbing a store. A gun is involved, but the police are not sure who had the gun during the robbery. The two suspects are put in separate rooms and told that there is enough evidence to put them both away for three years, but if they cooperate there might be a better deal. If one suspect cooperates and the other does not, then the one that cooperates will be let go with no time served, while the uncooperative suspect will be given ten years. If they both say that it was the other one who had the gun, then both will be given five years. What is the most rational choice here? If you are one of the suspects and you know that the other person will follow the code of honor among thieves, it might be best to say that it was your partner who held the gun during the robbery. If you cannot trust the other person, it would still be best to say she had the gun. A rational choice theorist, however, would say that the option with the highest benefits at the lowest cost would be the uncooperative option. This is because the total amount of time served is lower than all the other options (three years each versus ten years for one and none for the other versus five years each). This is known as the minimax, the minimum punishment for the maximum reward. If, in the next few years, you find yourself in jail for robbing a store with a person who also read this book, do you think they will keep to the rational choice theorist's concept of the minimax and not cooperate? Finally, if you decide not to cooperate and learn that the other person did cooperate, leaving you sitting in jail for ten years while she walks free, what would happen if you met that person after getting out, and she says there is an opportunity for you? Reiterations of the prisoner's dilemma can complicate the minimax to a point where it is difficult to comprehend what is and what is not a rational choice.

Baldwin (1993) collected a number of essays that can be tied to the prisoner's dilemma and its applications at the global level. Contemporary writers on global economics and politics talk about the concepts of neoliberalism and neorealism. The neoliberals argue that prisoners' dilemmas played out between countries can be understood through government and business policies. The neoliberal model is based on the idea that markets will determine winners and losers among businesses, and that winning businesses have become so powerful that they can determine when and if government intervention is needed. Take, for example, the case of copper mining in Zaire and Zambia (Shafer, 1983). These countries nationalized their copper mines in the 1960s after seeing companies headquartered in other countries profiting from the sale of copper taken from their lands. It was assumed that the copper market was open to all players, and the political leaders of Zaire and Zambia saw this as an opportunity to get back some of the money that was being funneled to other countries through the transnational mining companies. When this happened, those transnational companies found copper elsewhere, including recycling programs of copper originally taken out of Zaire and Zambia, and they were able to make it more difficult for those two countries to trade in the world copper markets through tariffs and other policies. The leaders of Zaire and Zambia learned that they did not have the capital to weather downturns in the copper market and were not able to capitalize on their copper mines. This is the working of neoliberalism, as the transnational companies were willing to work in a country with few or no government regulations. They found ways to protect themselves through government interventions, among other tactics, in their home countries when these mines were nationalized.

Other scholars argue that the power of any specific government changes over time, that allies change when power shifts, and the lack of any substantive international governing body is evidence that the world is characterized by neo-realism or anarchy. These writers contend that no one is truly loyal to anyone else, especially at the global level. Axelrod and Keohane (1993: 87) state, "the greater the conflict of interest between the players, the greater the likelihood that the players would in fact choose to defect." Axelrod conducted a number of experiments based on the prisoner's dilemma, and found that players in the game were willing to use any strategy to benefit themselves, even at the risk of losing allies. Axelrod and Keohane found that international relations, especially around issues of security, were more often based on the same concept of benefiting one's own interests than with concerns about political and economic relationships with other governments. They argue that this would not change, and allies and markets are only tools used to maintain power.

While *Gulliver's Travels* and *Around the World in Eighty Days* are fictional accounts of traveling and dealing with people in foreign countries, they show why both the neoliberals and neorealists might think they are right. Both argue that individuals, businesses, and governments are seeking benefits while minimizing risks. The point of departure is just how many and how stable are the links between these players. A sociologist would try to understand these linkages and level of stability by looking through historical records and contemporary narratives of how the actors are working with and against each other. At the time of this writing, for example, there is a debate over whether or not the Russian government should be supplying military weapons to the Syrian government in their fight against rebels who are trying to oust President Bashar al-Assad. The United States believes that the rebels may have a point in fighting al-Assad, so both countries risk alienating each other over their stance on Syria. Given that the United States and Russia are more equal in terms of trade and military power than either country or Syria, what role should each country's government play? If the rebels win, does that make the United States stronger, because we now have a stronger tie to Syria, or weaker, because Russia may decide to sanction the United States for its actions. The same can be said for Russia. If al-Assad's forces can quell the rebels, Russia will possibly have stronger ties with that country, but at what cost? Can Russia afford to alienate America? Winning a war or political debate is rarely a one-to-one victory, with the balance of power always going to the winners. A sociologist would take into consideration all the ramifications of backing an actor in an international conflict, and not just who wins or loses. The Treaty of Versailles, put together by the French and English at the end of the First World War, has been blamed for collapsing the German economy, which led to the collapse of the world economy and the Second World War. While the French and English were also the victors in World War II, many would argue that it was a Pyrrhic victory, in the sense that so much was lost in trying to prove an earlier point that did not need to be made.

THE MOVEMENT OF PEOPLE AND *RISING SUN*

Globalization involves more than international business and wars between countries. Migration (which includes both immigration and emigration) has been part of international narratives since at least the exodus of the Israelites out of Egypt under the guidance of Moses. Historical accounts contend that Native Americans are descendants of groups that lived in northeast Asia and eastern Russia when that continent was linked to modern-day Alaska by a land bridge (approximately 12,000 years ago) (Hoffecker, Powers, & Goebel, 1993). Immigration into the United States continues to expand, as Homeland Security notes that in 1820, 8,385 individuals obtained legal permanent status here, and by 2012, that number was 1,031,631 (http://www.dhs. gov/yearbook-immigration-statistics-2012-legal-permanent-residents, Table 1, accessed June 2013). This does not include undocumented immigrants, those on student visas, and so forth. At the world level, it was estimated that 215,764,000 people moved from one nation to another in 2010. If all these people moved to one place, it would be one of the most populated countries in the world (behind only China, India, the United States, and Indonesia, and ahead of Brazil and Pakistan) (http://www.migrationinformation.org/data-hub/charts/worldstats_1.cfm, accessed June 2013). The reasons for moving can be as diverse as the people who are traveling, and these can influence the attitudes of both the travelers and those who live in the host countries where these migrants settle. We may feel sympathetic and look to help a group displaced by war, yet are suspicious of a group that comes to our country looking for work.

As with all human actions, migration is structured by social institutions. People migrate from one place to another based on job opportunities, political asylum, social fears such as wars, climate, natural disasters, and family members who have migrated at an earlier time. Rarely does a person decide to just get up and leave one country for another (there are nomadic tribes that cross international borders on a regular basis, though these are rare), as the process of changing citizenship is difficult and complex (Gold & Nawyn, 2012); this is typically undertaken only when needed, as with Conan Doyle's Colonel Openshaw, who felt threatened. We cannot change our nationality just because we want to. Once a group or individual migrates to a new country, they are often expected to find ways to assimilate into that new culture so that they can shed the label of foreigner as quickly as possible. Work on migrant families has shown that this often happens more quickly with children than adults (Portes & Rivas, 2011).

When people move, so do their customs and practices. Voodoo, as was mentioned in Chapter 3, is practiced in places like New Orleans because of the movement of people from Africa to America. Fugu, or puffer fish, is a Japanese delicacy that can be deadly if improperly prepared, so people in the United States had to try it, as more Japanese moved here and practiced this custom. The first recorded fugu poisoning in the United States was in Los Angeles in 1996 and involved non-Japanese consumers. The Japanese have been eating fugu for centuries, with occasional deaths leading to attempts to try to stop the practice by the nation's leaders. The way business is conducted from one country to another can be very different as well, which is captured in a stereotypical manner by Michael Crichton in *Rising Sun*. In the novel, a woman is found dead and believed to have died from erotic asphyxiation administered by a white businessman, though the real culprit is discovered later.

"Ah. You remember we talked about bribery. One of Eddie's bribes was to a low-level security officer named Tanaka. I believe Eddie supplied him with drugs. Anyway, Eddie had known him for a couple of years. And when Ishiguro ordered Tanaka to pull the tapes, Tanaka told Eddie."

"And Eddie went down and got the tapes himself."

"Yes. Together with Tanaka."

"But Phillips said Eddie was alone."

"Phillips lied, because he knew Tanaka. That's also why he didn't make more of a fuss—Tanaka said it was all right. But when Phillips told us the story, he left Tanaka out."

"And then?"

"Ishiguro sent a couple of guys to clean out Cheryl's apartment. Tanaka took the tapes someplace to get them copied. Eddie went to the party in the hills."

"But Eddie kept one."

"Yes."

I thought it was over. "But when we talked to Eddie at the party, he told a completely different story."

Connor nodded. "He lied."

"Even to you, his friend?"

Connor shrugged. "He thought he could get away with it."

"What about Ishiguro? Why did he kill the girl?"

"To get Morton in his pocket. And it worked—they got Morton to change his position on MicroCon. For a while there, Morton was going to allow the sale to go forward."

"Ishiguro would kill her for that? For some corporate sale?"

"No, I don't think it was calculated at all. Ishiguro was high-strung, under great pressure. He felt he had to prove himself to his superiors. He had much at stake—so much, that he behaved differently from an ordinary Japanese under these circumstances. And in a moment of extreme pressure, he killed the girl, yes. As he said, she was a woman of no importance" (Crichton, *Rising Sun*: 355–56).

That the story is fictional matters little, as such presentations often inform us of how people from a certain culture or place act when we have little else to go on. When we read stories like this and hear about how companies such as Sony or Toyota are leading firms in their respective industries, we come to think that all Japanese businessmen must be ruthless. That is how the Carnegies and Mellons made it in America, and so Ishiguro would have had few qualms about killing "a woman of no importance," though Crichton did have Connor say that Ishiguro did not act like an ordinary Japanese person. Instead, the pressure of needing to prove his worth, or to save face, overrode any compassion for another human being.

Such fear of the other has led to numerous immigration acts in the United States (other countries have had their fair share of immigration policies as well), dating back to the 1790s, when it was decided that only white men could be residents of this country. Later acts targeted British immigrants, Chinese immigrants, eastern European immigrants, Mexican and South American immigrants, and Middle Eastern immigrants. Proposals have ranged from an outright ban on certain groups to quotas of how many people from any specific country would be allowed to immigrate. One regular exception to immigration policies involves the movement of highly educated and skilled people, as most countries are happy to admit doctors and rocket scientists. When this happens between a poor country and a rich country, it is called "brain drain," as the poorer country may find it difficult to meet the wages and benefits offered to someone like a doctor in a rich country. If this happens with some regularity, the poor country may find that it is losing yet another resource to those countries with stronger economies, leaving the poor country even further behind in terms of development.

This chapter has barely touched on the many issues of globalization that are studied by sociologists. If such a topic seems to be outside your ability to control, remember that individuals such as Gandhi and Nelson Mandela challenged global structures and forced change in their own countries, as well as attitudes around the globe. They both enjoyed huge networks of supporters, but it would have been much easier for them to maintain the status quo of the Raj, British rule (Gandhi in India), or apartheid (Mandela in South Africa). It would have kept them out of jail and from being targeted for political assassination. The global village, however, would have been a less interesting place without their efforts. While global change will have to take into account many large social structures, nothing will happen without people taking an interest in their surroundings.

REFERENCES AND RECOMMENDED READINGS

Axelrod, R., and Keohane, R. O. (1993). "Achieving Cooperation Under Anarchy: Strategies and institutions," pp. 85–115. In *Neorealism and Neoliberalism*, David A. Baldwin (Ed.). New York: Columbia University Press.

Baldwin, D. A. (Ed.). (1993). *Neorealism and Neoliberalism*. New York: Columbia University Press.

Bernstein, H. (1971). "Modernization Theory and the Sociological Study of Development." *Journal of Development Studies*, 7(2): 141–60.

Crichton, M. (2012). *Rising Sun*. New York: Random House Digital.

Firebaugh, G. (1992). "Growth Effects of Foreign and Domestic Investment." *American Journal of Sociology*, 98(1): 105–30.

Gold, S. J., and Nawyn, S. J. (2013). *Handbook of Migration Studies*. New York: Routledge.

Hoffecker, J. F., Powers, W. R., and Goebel, T. (1993). "The Colonization of Beringia and the Peopling of the New World." *Science*, 259(5091): 46–53.

Portes, A., and Rivas, A. (2011). "The Adaptation of Migrant Children." *Future of Children*, 21(1): 219–46.

Shafer, M. (1983). "Capturing the Mineral Multinationals: Advantage or disadvantage?" *International Organization*, 37(1): 93–119.

Swift, J. (2010). *Gulliver's Travels*. pubOneInfo.

Verne, J. (1876). *Around the World in Eighty Days* (trans. Geo M. Trowle). New York: James R. Osgood.

Wallerstein, I. (1979). *The Capitalism World-Economy*. New York: Cambridge University Press.

18 SCIENCE AND TECHNOLOGY

INTRODUCTION AND *FRANKENSTEIN*

I assume that many students reading through this book will have reached two conclusions by now: Sociology is basically about common sense (nothing has surprised you to this point), and that sociologists overstate the amount of control social structures have in our lives. If that is so, please do something for me. Promise to give up any social networking (Facebook, LinkedIn, etc.) or texting for one week. If you need to get in touch with someone who is outside your general vicinity, call them. If they are close (in a dorm room down the hall), then go and talk to them. If you think there is no way that you can function without a computer or cell phone, then your life is controlled by structures. Remember, humans beings were able to survive before computers and cell phones, and to say this is no longer possible means that you rely on something outside your control.

Of course you made the choice of which phone to buy, which profile picture to post, which television shows to watch, and so forth. As with most choices we make, however, these were the choices given to us. We did not make the phones or their software platforms. We did not develop the codes needed to make Facebook possible, nor did we write and produce the televisions shows we watch. These are structured by others, which in turn structure our lives.

Since the Industrial Revolution, science and technology have grown rapidly, and I have left this topic for the last chapter because these subjects have impacted so many aspects of our lives, as well as the topics covered in this book. While science and technology are overlapping concepts in many cases, there are some differences. Science consists of the thinking and efforts put into making discoveries and inventions, and technology is the use of science in practice.

Science makes it possible to conceptualize the internal combustion engine, and technology makes it real. Science makes it possible to conceptualize landing on the moon, and technology makes it possible. Technology is used in science and vice versa, which is why it is often difficult to separate the two.

Much like the links between you and your technology, science and technology are structured by existing capabilities. We can imagine traveling at the speed of light or even faster, such as the speed of imagination (I can think about traveling to the sun much faster than it would happen at the speed of light), yet we have not been able to achieve these ends due to natural structures. Latour (1987) studied how scientists work within these structures, and argues for a theory in which all actors, including nonhuman ones, are taken into account. This has come to be known as actor-network theory, and we can see how this can be applied in everyday life. When you left home for college, assuming you are reading this while taking a college course, your ties to family members changed from close proximity to being physically removed from that environment. In years past, students would have to write letters or take horse-drawn carriages back home to have conversations with parents. Telephones and cars made it possible to close these gaps, and now cell phones and computers with imaging technology make it possible to both speak and look at your family in real time, even if you are separated by oceans. This does not necessarily make contemporary family ties more closely knit than in the past, but it can impact feelings of isolation and lessen the desire to meet new people so you have someone to talk to. The technologies that make it possible to communicate are actors that are part of these networks, as their capabilities make certain actions possible (and others impossible).

Making a cell phone is also done within a network. The company that makes the phone has to have connections to suppliers of components or raw materials that work in such a way that makes a phone possible. You cannot make a working phone out of graham crackers found in the dorm cafeteria and the sand tracked into your room. The company must also have connections to downstream retailers who have connections to customers, who have the means of transportation to get to the store and the money to pay for the phone and its services. Regulations make it possible for transmission towers to be built and not overlap or interfere with other towers and providers. In other words, the making and using of a cell phone involves numerous networks that are coordinated to bring about something as simple as a phone call home to ask your dad what he is cooking for dinner, and after that asking if he can send you more money.

In addition to thinking about nonhuman actors in a network, Latour's actor-network theory shows us that the practices of science and technology involve much more than some great thinker sitting alone in a laboratory discovering and inventing such things as light bulbs, telephones, and the diesel engine (named after Rudolf Diesel, who employed many people in his labs). Any great invention or discovery is made possible by a network, which is true even in fictional accounts such as Mary Shelley's *Frankenstein*:

Although I possessed the capacity of bestowing animation, yet to prepare a frame for the reception of it, with all its intricacies of fibers, muscles, and veins, still remained a work of inconceivable difficulty and labor. I doubted at first whether I should attempt the creation of a being like myself or one of simpler organization; but my imagination was too much exalted by my first success to permit me to doubt of my ability to give life to an animal as complex and wonderful as man. The materials at present within my command hardly appeared adequate to so arduous an undertaking; but I doubted not that I should ultimately succeed. I prepared myself for a multitude of reverses; my operations might be incessantly baffled, and at last my work be imperfect; yet, when I considered the improvement which every day takes place in science and mechanics, I was encouraged to hope my present attempts would at least lay the foundations for future success (Shelley, *Frankenstein*: 35).

Dr. Frankenstein was able to develop his capacity for "bestowing animation" by attending school and being taught the intricacies of biology and mechanics. The apparatus and tools in his lab were furnished by others, though he may have used them in ways that were not part of the original intent (Peterson & Anand, 2004). In short, Frankenstein's monster never would have come to life without others helping the doctor learn about life and setting up his lab.

One of the messages from *Frankenstein*, whether intended or not, is that advances in science and technology are not always in our best interests. Nuclear weapons and chemicals used in the growing of our food are thought to be even scarier than Frankenstein's monster. This is one of the downsides of science and technology networks, as responsibilities for end results are diffused, much like the situation with the My Lai massacre. President Harry Truman may have given the order to drop atomic bombs on Hiroshima and Nagasaki, but he could not have given that order if scientists and engineers had been unable to find a way to harness atomic reactions or build aircraft to carry and drop the bombs—or if the country had not been at war, which involves even more networks.

Frankenstein's work highlights another double-edged sword of science and technology—medicalization. Death and disease have been a natural part of existence for all of human history. The ancient Greeks and Romans began working more closely in this area, including building aqueducts and other basic sanitation devices and procedures. Galen, a physician who lived in the Roman Empire in the second century, spent much of his adult life practicing medicine on gladiators and nobles. He argued that we need to keep pushing our understanding of human anatomy, though his work was so revered that little else took place until the late Middle Ages (Boorstin, 1983). Advances in science and technology during the Renaissance led to advances in medicine, as people became aware of how the natural environment worked, and how to treat certain ailments besides the use of blood-sucking leeches or trying to coax bad spirits out of the body through other means. Frankenstein thought he could cure death through science and technology. We have followed those same thoughts to the point that we have become a medicalized society, which means that many behaviors that were once considered deviant—alcoholism, gambling addiction, drug usage—are now thought of as medical conditions just like a cold, the flu, or the plague. We have yet to label death as a disease, but much effort is put into finding a cure for it. The positive side of this is that many diseases are now rare. More people are living longer; however, preventable diseases, including diarrhea, malaria, and tuberculosis, are still some of the leading killers in poorer countries, where poverty negates medical advancements or the distribution of readily available drugs. The negative side of medicalization is that we believe anything we find distasteful or deviant can be cured, leading to a rise in unneeded medical visits and greater authority being given to the medical profession over various aspects of our lives. In a June 8, 2013, editorial in the *New York Times* regarding the variable costs of colonoscopies (a range of between $740 and $8500), it was stated that, "[i]nsurers, big employers and state and federal governments can all bring pressure to bear. Possible remedies proposed by experts include having private insurers and Medicare pay the same amount for a service or procedure regardless of where it is performed ..." (http://www.nytimes.com/2013/06/09/opinion/sunday/the-weird-world-of-colonoscopy-costs.html?_r=0, accessed June 2013). These efforts are aimed at controlling the costs of medical procedures, one of the few services in the United States that are not controlled by market forces, as consumers are often told who their physicians will be and where they will be receiving their medical treatments. Insurers do not allow us to shop for doctors and medical procedures outside their specified lists of practitioners and what procedures they will cover.

WAS THERE EVER A GOLDEN AGE? AND *2001: A SPACE ODYSSEY*

Having no one to blame for technological disasters does not absolve humans from making mistakes. The Luddites of the 1800s sabotaged the machines that were outperforming them, some paying with their lives for taking a stand. The neo-Luddites of today see the rapid growth in technology eroding our social skills and expanding the system world. Mathiesen (1997), drawing on and expanding Foucault, points to how the panopticon—the few watching the many, as in Orwell's *1984*—has been combined with the synoptical process of the mass media bringing stories of the few (e.g., Tim Tebow, Barack Obama, Osama bin Laden, Lindsay Lohan, and Kim Jong-un) to millions. These processes have led numerous scholars to argue that we have become a voyeuristic society, enjoying vicarious living by watching others (e.g., reality TV, YouTube videos), while also knowing that we are being constantly watched, with cameras in most cell phones and security cameras in public places. This is all possible through the science of miniaturization and the technology that has made it possible to put these devices in our hands.

The jury is still out, however, on whether all the cameras and mirrors are a positive or negative influence on how we behave. On the one hand, studies have shown lower crime rates in areas with cameras, while on the other, lives have been ruined because someone filmed them at an inopportune moment. This is true, however, of most technologies. Fluoridation of water has been tied to a drop in cavities, though fluoride is a heavy metal and has been tied to various cancers. Medical breakthroughs have increased life expectancy, but has our quality of life improved when we are kept alive by a feeding tube? In addition, there have always been people who lived into their 80s, 90s, and 100s, and while there are more people reaching those numbers today, we have seen very little progress in making the body last longer. Hybrid cars promise to lower emissions, but how is society to generate the additional energy to power those cars? Crops created through genetic engineering have proven to increase yields, but we are beginning to find weeds and bugs that are resistant to the chemicals that are used in conjunction with these plants (Adler, 2011)—and so we create new chemicals to kill the things that were created by chemicals in the first place. The consolidation of food manufacturing has cut prices for consumers, yet if anything goes wrong in a factory that processes millions of pounds of food that is shipped across the country, that problem is spread throughout the distribution channels. We do make mistakes that have cost countless lives, but would it be a bigger mistake to stop all scientific and technological endeavors, as these have also saved lives?

Given all the concerns with new technologies, we might ask whether there has ever been a time when there was a perfect balance between humans, their thoughts, and the tools they used to survive. Some people do believe in a golden age when we were balanced and understood that our actions would affect the environment, but that it always bounced back. Maybe that is what Arthur C. Clarke had in mind in the following passage from *2001: A Space Odyssey*:

> The tools they had been programmed to use were simple enough, yet they could change this world and make the man-apes its masters. The most primitive was the hand-held stone, that multiplied manyfold the power of the blow. Then there was the bone club, that lengthened the reach and could provide a buffer against the fangs or claws of angry animals. With these weapons, the limitless food that roamed the savannas was theirs to take.
>
> But they needed other aids, for their teeth and nails could not readily dismember anything larger than a rabbit. Luckily, Nature had provided the perfect tools, requiring only the wit to pick them up.

First there was a crude but very efficient knife or saw, of a model that would serve well for the next three million years. It was simply the lower jawbones of an antelope, with the teeth still in place; there would be no substantial improvement until the coming of steel. Then there was an awl or dagger in the form of a gazelle horn, and finally a scraping tool made from the complete jaw of almost any small animal.

The stone club, the toothed saw, the horn dagger, the bone scraper—these were the marvelous inventions which the man-apes needed in order to survive. Soon they would recognize them for the symbols of power that they were, but many months must pass before their clumsy fingers had acquired the skill—or the will—to use them.

Perhaps, given time, they might by their own efforts have come to the awesome and brilliant concept of using natural weapons as artificial tools. But the odds were against them, and even now there were endless opportunities for failure in the ages that lay ahead.

The man-apes had been given their first chance. There would be no second one; the future was, very literally, in their own hands (Clarke, *2001: A Space Odyssey*, 20–21).

How many of us could survive off the things that literally fell into our laps from the land? Our ancestors did this at one point, but would this be a better life? How about the simple life of a farmer who plows the land and eats what can be grown? For those living in a cold climate, the picking becomes pretty scarce when the ground begins to freeze. Are you willing to spend your late summer and early fall months canning enough food to make it through winter? Do you want to cut enough firewood to make sure the house is warm during a hard freeze? Some people would say that we would save the earth from further destruction if we were willing to go back to those days, but those days also included large families (more childbirths), little travel (a large majority of people lived their whole lives within 20 miles of where they were born before the invention of the automobile), and entertainment options that did not include going to the movies or playing video games. Such a lifestyle is not necessarily characterized by fewer social and natural structures, but different ones that we have forgotten about.

Another era that is thought of as a golden age for humans, as well as science and technology, is the Renaissance, which took place between the 15th to the 17th centuries, when individuals such as Michelangelo, Copernicus, Martin Luther, and Isaac Newton were alive. Wuthnow (1987) contends that the institutionalization of science was well underway by the 1600s, and throughout the next two centuries science became the institution people looked to for understanding the workings of the natural and social worlds, bolstered by such discoveries as evolution (Charles Darwin) and radical economic philosophy (Karl Marx). These were exciting times, until you realize that most individuals had little or no access to formal education, and that those who did were typically rich, white males. These individuals rarely thought about poverty or hunger, but were interested in how the natural world worked, such as the laws of gravity and the structure of the universe. While some philosophers thought about the human condition, it was the natural sciences that truly came into being at this time. Disciplines such as sociology that are concerned with the human condition within group settings grew out of philosophy and economics in the late 1800s and early 1900s. Even at this late date, the new social sciences were dominated by rich, white males who saw the world differently from women, the poor, and men from minority groups.

That the sciences were dominated by rich, white men does not mean that all were in agreement as to how things worked. Science was often as much about politics as about laboratory experiments or fieldwork. Louis Pasteur, for whom the process of pasteurization is named, went head to head with other scientists in the 1800s over whether or not life could be spontaneously generated. Today, we tend to think that this is impossible, though we also tend to believe that life somehow spontaneously appeared on earth somewhere down the line. This was difficult to prove when Pasteur was alive, and his victory over his opponents was made possible by his connections to leaders in various industries (medicine, agriculture, brewing, etc.), as they had the resources to back Pasteur (Collins & Pinch, 1998). Being rich and famous tends to help even in scientific circles, as lifestyles and connections are used to back arguments, even where objectivity is deemed to be of utmost importance.

Instead of determining how to live or which culture is best, Barnes, Bloor, and Henry (1996) argue that we need to understand how science and technology are suited for the contexts in which they are found, a perspective known as the Strong Programme. This is not to say that all things are relative and criticism of a system is to be kept to a minimum, but that value judgments should be left out of sociological analyses, especially if you believe that sociology is a science. We may read Clarke's passage and think how primitive those man-apes were with their stones and sticks, and much the same will most likely be said about contemporary humans in another 10,000 years (if we are still around). Is it fair, however, to judge another group by standards of which they were not aware? Harris (1974), for example, explains that the current geographic landscape of the Middle East makes it a difficult place to raise pigs, so both Jews and Muslims have a taboo on eating pork. In many Pacific Islands, pigs are easy to raise, and are often left to run wild in the jungles, so groups there eat pork on a regular basis, even gorging on it to the point of becoming sick during certain ceremonies. There are religious rites concerning pork in both places, but religion does not necessarily determine what is and what is not practiced. In other words, if a religious edict exists regarding the consumption of pork, it is not necessarily for or against this practice. In fact, Harris points to archaeological digs that have unearthed pork bones in the Middle East. He argues that pigs were raised and consumed when the Middle East was much more temperate and covered in trees. Through continued human intervention in the area, including the herding of goats that ate tree bark which eventually killed the trees, the area became drier and hotter. Pigs need a good deal of water to survive, so more resources were needed to maintain a sounder of swine. Those same resources were needed for humans; thus, pork became problematic, and soon there were religious edicts forbidding its consumption. Prior to that, there may have been religious rituals that included pork. Religion, in this sense, becomes science and technology when we cannot explain something through natural processes, but know that there are connections between our actions and the environment. Science and technology, in turn, are also said to be faith based, much like religion, both of which are built on a metaphorical swamp with no solid basis if you are willing to dig deep enough (Popper, 1959).

All of this points to the fact that knowledge and practices are often well suited for the environment in which they are used. As the environment changes—or as knowledge is acquired from other groups—what people do and think of as best practices will likely change. It is important to understand that power needs to be part of the equation, as knowledge and technology have been used to challenge authority on the one hand, and maintain it on the other.

POWER, SCIENCE, TECHNOLOGY, AND *DUNE*

While you might think that onions would have little to do with power, Star (2001) points out that being allergic to onions in contemporary society puts you at a disadvantage. Prepared foods and formulaic fast-food restaurants are difficult to navigate when you need to make a special order to stay alive. The convenience of these products for a vast majority of the population becomes a problem for those who do not fit the mold. Anyone with food allergies knows the difficulties of going out to eat.

Star argues that the same technological approaches to food have taken place throughout society, giving power to those who understand and control it. Automatic door openers put doormen out of work, a group of individuals who were unlikely to have the skills to land a decent job in a technologically advanced society. Internet shopping has brought about the end of many small—and even large—retailers. Those who can capitalize on the technologies used in these arenas are able to move ahead, leaving behind those who are unable to upgrade. This is true in battle as well as retail, as highlighted in many science fiction novels such as Frank Herbert's *Dune*:

"What a dolt my father sends me for weaponry," Paul intoned. "This doltish Gurney Halleck has forgotten the first lesson for a fighting man armed and shielded." Paul snapped the force button at his waist, felt the crinkled-skin tingling of the defensive field at his forehead and down his back, heard external sounds take on characteristic shield-filtered flatness. "In shield fighting, one moves fast on defense, slow on attack," Paul said. "Attack has the sole purpose of tricking the opponent into a misstep, setting him up for the attack sinister. The shield turns the fast blow, admits the slow kindjal!" Paul snapped up the rapier, feinted fast and whipped it back for a slow thrust timed to enter a shield's mindless defenses.

Halleck watched the action, turned at the last minute to let the blunted blade pass his chest. "Speed, excellent," he said. "But you were wide open for an underhanded counter with a slip-tip."

Paul stepped back, chagrined.

"I should whap your backside for such carelessness," Halleck said. He lifted a naked kindjal from the table and held it up. "This in the hand of an enemy can let out your life's blood! You're an apt pupil, none better, but I've warned you that not even in play do you let a man inside your guard with death in his hand."

"I guess I'm not in the mood for it today," Paul said.

"Mood?" Halleck's voice betrayed his outrage even through the shield's filtering. "What has *mood* to do with it? You fight when the necessity arises— no matter the mood! Mood's a thing for cattle or making love or playing the baliset. It's not for fighting."

"I'm sorry, Gurney."

"You're not sorry enough!"

Halleck activated his own shield, crouched with kindjal outthrust in left hand, the rapier poised high in his right. "Now I say guard yourself for true!" He leaped high to one side, then forward, pressing a furious attack.

Paul fell back, parrying. He felt the field crackling as shield edges touched and repelled each other, sensed the electric tingling of the contact along his skin. *What's gotten into Gurney?* he asked himself. *He's not faking this!* Paul moved his left hand, dropped his bodkin into his palm from its wrist sheath.

"You see a need for an extra blade, eh?" Halleck grunted.

Is this betrayal? Paul wondered. *Surely not Gurney!*

Around the room they fought – thrust and parry, feint and counter-feint. The air within their shield bubbles grew stale from the demands on it that the slow interchange along with barrier edges could not replenish. With each new shield contact, the smell of ozone grew stronger (Herbert, *Dune*: 33–34).

If you were to engage in battle with someone who had an electronic shield to block your attacks while you stood relatively naked with only a sword, you might be wishing you had something to give you an edge, maybe the next iteration of the shield worn by your opponent. That edge over your opponent is a source of power. It fuels the envy I see among students when their friends or classmates purchase a newer computer, tablet, gaming system, or cell phone. Technology companies bank on consumers wanting to be the first to buy their newest gadgets, and, much like their customers, they are constantly trying to develop new products with more capabilities. This is what is referred to as a technological treadmill, with early adopters typically benefiting more from a new technology, so everyone is trying to be the first producer or user (Mascarenhas & Busch, 2006). To get off the treadmill risks losing that advantage and losing power, though staying on the treadmill risks adopting a problematic new technology that burns up resources that will be difficult to recoup.

Science in the form of knowledge and technology in the form of practice structure our lives. This includes both the use of science and technology and its attainment. This not only takes place at the individual level, as your classmate has a computer that works more quickly than yours, or with the disabled person who needs a special computer to maintain the same level of input and output as able-bodied students, but also at the global level. The digital divide between developed countries like the United States and Canada and developing countries like Burkina Faso and Malaysia points to the continued problem of poorer countries in gaining a strong foothold in the global village. The digital divide captures the disparities between information and communication technologies between countries, and while this gap is closing in some areas, it is getting larger in others (Sajda, 2012). Africa, for example, is one of the fastest-growing cell phone markets, though access to towers, download speeds, and understanding capabilities among users are not at the same level as in developed countries. These are some of the same problems that were encountered in many of the same countries during the green revolution, when their countries were flooded with tractors and other farming implements and aids from developed countries. This all sounds great until you realize that there was not enough knowledge, funds, or support to provide the needed infrastructure to use these technologies, or to fix them when they failed. You can experience this yourself by letting your cell phone battery completely drain and then move to a place with no electrical outlets. You have the equipment and the knowledge to know how to use and recharge your phone, but without the proper technological infrastructure, you cannot put that knowledge to use. The phone will become a doorstop or coaster, much like the tractors that became windbreaks or simply rusted flowerpots, as farmers returned to their horses and oxen to plow the fields.

As a last word, all scientific knowledge and technologies come with risks. This can be catastrophic as with nuclear weapons or relatively minor, such as coming up with a better microphone for radio broadcasting. Some of the most controversial technologies have brought hope to some (nuclear power plants have lowered the cost of electricity in some places), and the most benign can become deadly (people have burned down homes with turkey fryers). As with all social institutions, our agency within these structures will determine, to some extent, the level of costs and benefits we will pay for understanding—as well as misunderstanding—how things work.

REFERENCES AND RECOMMENDED READINGS

Adler, J. (2011). "The Growing Menace from Superweeds." *Scientific American*, 304 (April): 74–79.

Barnes, B., Bloor, D., and Henry, J. (1996). *Scientific Knowledge*. London, UK: Athlone.

Boorstin, D. J. (1983). *The Discoverers*. New York: Random House.

Clarke, A. C. (2000). *2001: A Space Odyssey*. New York: Roc.

Collins, H. M., and Pinch, T. (1998). *The Golem*. New York: Cambridge University Press.

Harris, M. (1974). *Cows, Pigs, Wars, and Witches*. New York: Random House.

Herbert, F. (2005). *Dune*. New York: Penguin.

Latour, B. (1987). *Science in Action*. Cambridge, MA: Harvard University Press.

Mascarenhas, M., and Busch, L. (2006). "Seeds of Change: Intellectual property rights, genetically modified soybeans, and seed saving in the United States." *Sociologia Ruralis*, 46(2): 122–38.

Mathiesen, T. (1997). "The Viewer Society: Michel Foucault's 'panopticon' revisited." *Theoretical Society*, 1(2): 215–34.

Peterson, R. A., and Anand, N. (2004). "The Production of Culture Perspective." *Annual Review of Sociology*, 30: 311–34.

Popper, K. (1959). *The Logic of Scientific Discovery*. London, UK: Hutchinson.

Sajda, Q. (2012). "As the Global Digital Divide Narrows, Who Is Left Behind?" *Information Technology for Development*, 18(4): 277–80.

Shelley, M. (1922). *Frankenstein*. Boston: Cornhill.

Star, S. L. (1991). "Power, Technologies and the Phenomenology of Conventions: On being allergic to onions," pp. 26–56. In *A Sociology of Monsters*, edited by John Law. New York: Routledge.

Wuthnow, R. (1987). *Meaning and Moral Order*. Berkeley: University of California Press.

AUTHOR INFORMATION

Toby A. Ten Eyck is an associate professor in the Department of Sociology and Michigan State University Extension at Michigan State University. His current research focuses on the intersections of art and social issues. He has also published on topics ranging from media coverage of food safety to public opinion of nanotechnology.

CREDITS

1. Miguel de Cervantes Saavedra; trans. John Rutherford, "Selections," *Don Quixote*, pp. 63–65. Copyright © 2000 by Penguin Group (USA) Inc.
2. Herman Melville, "Selections," *Moby Dick*, pp. 428–429. Copyright in the Public Domain.
3. Mark Twain, "Selections," *The Adventures of Huckleberry Finn*, pp. 331–332. Copyright in the Public Domain.
4. Johann David Wyss; trans. William H. G. Kingston, "Selections," *The Swiss Family Robinson*, pp. 125, 130. Copyright in the Public Domain.
5. Charles Dickens, "Selections," *Oliver Twist*, pp. 1–2. Copyright in the Public Domain.
6. Jane Austen, "Selections," *Pride and Prejudice*, pp. 3, 6, 323. Copyright in the Public Domain.
7. Johann David Wyss; trans. William H. G. Kingston, "Selections," *The Swiss Family Robinson*, pp. 125, 130. Copyright in the Public Domain.
8. Mark Twain, "Selections," *Letters from the Earth*, pp. 13. Copyright © 1962 by HarperCollins Publishers.
9. Kurt Vonnegut, "Selections," *Cat's Cradle*, pp. 127, 212–213. Copyright © 1963 by Henry Holt & Company.
10. Dante Alghieri; trans. Henry Francis Cary, "Selections," *The Divine Comedy*, pp. 134–136, 352–353. Copyright in the Public Domain.
11. Kurt Vonnegut, "Selections," *Hocus Pocus*, pp. 17–18. Copyright © 1990 by Penguin Group (USA) Inc..
12. Tom Wolfe, "Selections," *I Am Charlotte Simmons*, pp. 66–67. Copyright © 2004 by Farrar, Straus and Giroux.
13. Charlotte Bronte, "Selections," *Jane Eyre*, pp. 19. Copyright in the Public Domain.
14. Upton Sinclair, "Selections," *The Jungle*, pp. 151–152. Copyright in the Public Domain.
15. Ayn Rand, "Selections," *The Fountainhead*, pp. 14. Copyright © 1943 by Penguin Group (USA) Inc.

16. Ayn Rand, "Selections," *The Fountainhead*, pp. 14. Copyright © 1943 by Penguin Group (USA) Inc.

17. William Faulkner, "Selections," *As I Lay Dying*, pp. 43–44. Copyright © 1930 by Random House, Inc.

18. Erich Maria Remarque, "Selections," *All Quiet on the Western Front*, pp. 106. Copyright © 1929 by Little, Brown, & Co.

19. Wilson Rawls, "Selections," *Where the Red Fern Grows*, pp. 202–203, 209–210. Copyright © 1961 by Random House, Inc. Reprinted with permission.

20. Daniel Defoe, "Selections," *Life and Adventures of Robinson Crusoe*, pp. 233. Copyright in the Public Domain.

21. Harper Lee, "Selections," *To Kill a Mockingbird*, pp. 93. Copyright © 1960 by HarperCollins Publishers.

22. Kathryn Stockett, "Selections," *The Help*. Copyright © 2009 by Penguin Group (USA) Inc.

23. Gustave Flaubert; trans. Henry Blanchamp, "Selections," *Madame Bovary*, pp. 28. Copyright in the Public Domain.

24. Louisa May Alcott, "Selections," *Little Women*, pp. 84. Copyright in the Public Domain.

25. Stieg Larsson, trans. Reg Keeland, "Selections," *The Girl with the Dragon Tattoo*, pp. 196–197, 203. Copyright © 2011 by Random House, Inc. Reprinted with permission.

26. Tom Wolfe, "Selections," *The Bonfire of Vanities*, pp. 9. Copyright © 1987 by Farrar, Straus and Giroux.

27. Victor Hugo; trans. Charles Edwin Wilbour, "Selections," *Les Miserables*, pp. 1, 54. Copyright in the Public Domain.

28. William Golding, "Selections," *Lord of the Flies*, pp. 18–21. Copyright © 2011 by Penguin Group (USA) Inc. Reprinted with permission.

29. D. H. Lawrence, "Selections," *Lady Chatterley's Lover*, pp. 3–4, 27–28. Copyright © 1928 by Random House, Inc. Reprinted with permission.

30. Allen Ginsberg, "Selections," *Howl and Other Poems*, pp. 9, 13–14. Copyright © 1956 by HarperCollins Publishers.

31. Steven Fry, "Selections," *The Liar*, pp. 139–141. Copyright © 1991 by Soho Press. Reprinted with permission.

32. Arthur Conan Doyle, "Selections from 'The Five Orange Pips,'" The Adventures of Sherlock Holmes. Copyright in the Public Domain.

33. Victor Hugo, "Selections," *Hunchback of Notre Dame*, pp. 110–111, 127. Copyright in the Public Domain.

34. Edgar Allan Poe, "Selections," *The Murders in the Rue Morgue*. Copyright in the Public Domain.

35. Homer; trans. Alexander Pope, "Selections," *The Iliad*. Copyright in the Public Domain.

36. George Orwell, "Selections," 1984, pp. 21–23. Copyright © 1949 by Houghton Mifflin Harcourt Publishing Company.

37. Leo Tolstoy; trans. Louise Shanks Maude and Alymer Maude, "Selections," *War and Peace*. Copyright in the Public Domain.

38. Porter Shreve, "Selections," *The Obituary Writer*, pp. 5. Copyright © 2000 by Houghton Mifflin Harcourt Publishing Company.

39. Norman Mailer, "Selections," *An American Dream*, pp. 127–128. Copyright © 1965 by Random House, Inc.

40. Tom Wolfe, "Selections," *Back to Blood*, pp. 116–117. Copyright © 2012 by Hachette Book Group USA.

41. Chad Harbach, "Selections," *The Art of Fielding*, pp. 3–4. Copyright © 2012 by Hachette Book Group USA.

42. John Grisham, "Selections," *Calico Joe*, pp. 5. Copyright © 2012 by Random House, Inc.

43. F. X. Toole, "Selections," *Million Dollar Baby Stories from the Corner*, pp. 13–14. Copyright © 2000 by HarperCollins Publishers.

44. Oscar Wilde, "Selections," *The Picture of Dorian Gray*. Copyright in the Public Domain.

45. Thomas Mann; trans. John E. Woods, "Selections," *Doctor Faustus*, pp. 256–257. Copyright © 1999 by Random House, Inc. Reprinted with permission.

46. Margaret Atwood, "Selections," *Cat's Eye*, pp. 92. Copyright © 1988 by Random House, Inc.

47. Jack Kerouac, "Selections," *The Dharma Bums*, pp. 13–15. Copyright © 1958 by Charlotte Sheedy Literary Agency, Inc. Reprinted with permission.

48. Harriet Beecher Stowe, "Selections," *Uncle Tom's Cabin*. Copyright in the Public Domain.

49. John Steinbeck, "Selections," *The Grapes of Wrath*, pp. 150–152. Copyright © 1939 by Penguin Group (USA) Inc. Reprinted with permission.

50. Jonathan Swift, "Selections," *Gulliver's Travels*. Copyright in the Public Domain.

51. Jules Verne; trans. Geo M. Trowle, "Selections," *Around the World in Eighty Days*. Copyright in the Public Domain.

52. Michael Crichton, "Selections," *Rising Sun: A Novel*, pp. 355–356. Copyright © 1992 by Random House, Inc.

53. Mary Shelley, "Selections," *Frankenstein*, pp. 35. Copyright in the Public Domain.

54. Arthur C. Clarke, "Selections," *2001: A Space Odyssey*, pp. 20–21. Copyright © 1968 by Penguin Group (USA) Inc.

55. Frank Herbert, "Selections," *Dune*, pp. 33–34. Copyright © 1965 by Penguin Group (USA) Inc. Reprinted with permission.

40

Gao Xing

CPSIA information can be obtained at www.ICGtesting.com
Printed in the USA
BVOW01s2301051213

338291BV00003B/7/P